# TABLE OF CONTENTS

# EXECUTIVE SUMMARY

Pursuant to the requirements of Section 707 of the Office of National Drug Control Policy (ONDCP) Reauthorization Act of 1998, as amended by Section 301 of the ONDCP Reauthorization Act of 2006, P.L. 109-469, ONDCP is providing Congress with this report on the High Intensity Drug Trafficking Areas (HIDTAs). In order to present a national overview and individual HIDTA focus, this report provides background information and addresses three Congressional reporting requirements in one cohesive and coordinated document. This document is divided into an Executive Summary, Strategic Objectives, and five primary sections:

## 1.    HIDTA Program Background Information

The HIDTA program provides assistance to Federal, state, local, and tribal law enforcement agencies operating in areas determined to be critical drug trafficking regions of the Nation. There are currently 28 regional HIDTAs which include approximately 16 percent of all counties in the United States and 60 percent of the population. HIDTA-designated counties are located in 45 states plus Puerto Rico, the U.S. Virgin Islands, and the District of Columbia. Through the HIDTA program, representatives of Federal, state, local, and tribal agencies in each HIDTA region coordinate and collaborate to address the specific drug threats of that region.

## 2.    National HIDTA Program Evaluation

This report provides Congress with an evaluation of HIDTA performance. ONDCP has established two goals for the HIDTA program which address program effectiveness, program efficiency, and program management. These goals also reflect the continued refinement of the process ONDCP has developed to manage and measure HIDTA performance. The first goal is to reduce drug availability by assisting Federal, state, local, and tribal law enforcement agencies participating in HIDTAs to dismantle and disrupt drug trafficking organizations. The second goal is to improve the efficiency and effectiveness of HIDTA initiatives. In order to report on their achievement of these goals, each HIDTA is required to provide the following four documents pertaining to its geographical area, on which its performance evaluation is based: 1) Threat Assessment; 2) Strategy; 3) Initiative Budget Proposals; and 4) Annual Report.

## 3.    Assessment of Law Enforcement Intelligence Sharing in the HIDTA Program

This report outlines the formal processes of the HIDTA program to assess law enforcement intelligence and information sharing, and highlights the formal evaluation and review process of the HIDTA program, including policy and budget guidance; FY 2009 funding levels for intelligence; processes for sharing Federal, state, local, and tribal law enforcement information; and the measures needed to achieve effective sharing of information. The HIDTA program has 57 operational intelligence and information sharing initiatives. Each HIDTA capitalizes on the combined resources of the Federal, state, local, and tribal law enforcement communities. The HIDTAs prepare and review threat assessments and apply the appropriate law enforcement response to combat illegal drug activity in our Nation.

1

## 4. Assessment of Drug Enforcement Task Forces in HIDTAs

Regardless of the method of funding task forces (e.g., HIDTA, Justice Action Grant (JAG)/Byrne-sponsored), the 28 HIDTAs provide a coordination umbrella for Federal, state, local, and tribal drug law enforcement efforts; foster a strategy-driven systemic approach to integrate and synchronize efforts; facilitate efficiency, effectiveness, and cooperation among and between various agencies; and focus on outcomes and impacts. Using both formal and informal methods of coordination among drug enforcement task forces, the HIDTAs act as neutral centers to manage, deconflict, analyze, and report on drug enforcement activities in their respective regions.

## 5. Individual HIDTA Reports

To address the specific reporting requirements, an analysis of each HIDTA is included in this report. These reports are succinct descriptions of the individual HIDTAs and their responses to the Congressional report requirements. For more comprehensive information on an individual HIDTA's performance in addressing specific drug threats, ONDCP can provide, upon request, that HIDTA's Annual Report, Strategy, or Threat Assessment.

## STRATEGIC OBJECTIVES

This report demonstrates how the HIDTA program works to achieve the long-term goal of reducing drug trafficking and drug production in the United States by:

(A) facilitating cooperation among Federal, state, local, and tribal law enforcement agencies to share information and implement coordinated enforcement activities;
(B) enhancing law enforcement intelligence sharing among Federal, state, local, and tribal law enforcement agencies;
(C) providing reliable law enforcement intelligence to law enforcement agencies needed to design effective enforcement strategies and operations; and,
(D) supporting coordinated law enforcement strategies which maximize the use of available resources to reduce the supply of illegal drugs in designated areas and in the United States as a whole.

ONDCP developed three specific strategic objectives in response to an analysis of the various components of this report. These strategic objectives, to be accomplished in FY 2011, include processes ONDCP either is currently undertaking or will soon undertake to achieve a more effective and efficient HIDTA program.

### Increase the Level of Participation in HIDTA Intelligence and Investigative Support Centers (IISCs)[1] by Federal Agencies.

- Surveying every HIDTA annually to determine the percentage of full-time agency participation in HIDTA IISCs.
- Creating a headquarters-level interagency working group to assess Federal efforts to provide resources to HIDTA IISCs, and identify obstacles, and needed resources.
- Encouraging increased participation and active engagement in IISCs by Federal agencies (DEA, FBI, ICE) through a series of focused meetings outlining the benefits of pooling resources and continuing to enhance the effectiveness of IISCs through integration with federal intelligence and investigative centers.

### Improve Information Flow and Collaboration Among HIDTAs and Non-HIDTA Task Forces.

- Receive and disseminate recommendations and best practices from HIDTAs regarding the improvement of information flow and collaboration among HIDTA and non-HIDTA task forces.
- Survey the HIDTAs to:
  - identify barriers
  - determine resource requirements to connect to the National Virtual Pointer System (NVPS).[2]

---

[1] The Intelligence and Investigative Support Centers (IISCs) were previously known as Intelligence Support Centers (ISC) or Investigative Support Centers (ISC).

[2] The NVPS was developed by the DEA, in partnership with the HIDTA program and the Regional Information Sharing Systems (RISS), to connect databases of participating Federal, state and local law enforcement agencies into a single automated system. Through NVPS, participating agencies have the capability to exchange target information through a single point of entry using a sensitive but unclassified secure network. It allows participating agencies to determine if any other law enforcement agency is investigating the same subject.

- Host strategy coordination meetings with HIDTAs on improving information flow among all drug enforcement task forces in their regions.

**Ensure HIDTA Investigative and Interdiction Initiatives Focus on Primary Drug Threats and are in Alignment with the *National Drug Control Strategy* and National goals.**

- Require all HIDTAs to establish and submit operational priorities in their annual Strategies, to include the identification of primary drug threats and their corresponding task forces; and
- The HIDTA program is in the process of exploring more effective ways to conduct threat assessments using a "variables" approach. Four HIDTAs (Atlanta, Chicago, New York/New Jersey, and Washington/Baltimore) have agreed to participate in a pilot project, during which they will use a series of data sets, including overdose statistics, property crime data, and the number of substance abuse treatment admissions, for a more comprehensive and realistic approach in analyzing the nature and scope of the drug threat in HIDTA areas.

# I. HIDTA PROGRAM BACKGROUND INFORMATION

## Purpose

The purpose of the High Intensity Drug Trafficking Areas (HIDTA) program, as defined by its authorizing statute, Section 707 of the Office of National Drug Control Policy Reauthorization Act of 1998, as amended, is to reduce drug trafficking and drug production in the United States by:

(A) Facilitating cooperation among Federal, state, local, and tribal law enforcement agencies to share information and implement coordinated enforcement activities;

(B) Enhancing law enforcement intelligence sharing among Federal, state, local, and tribal law enforcement agencies;

(C) Providing reliable law enforcement intelligence to law enforcement agencies needed to design effective enforcement strategies and operations; and

(D) Supporting coordinated law enforcement strategies which maximize the use of available resources to reduce the supply of illegal drugs in designated areas and in the United States as a whole.

## Program Description

The HIDTA program provides assistance to Federal, state, local, and tribal law enforcement agencies operating in areas determined to be critical drug trafficking regions of the United States.

The statute authorizing the HIDTA program requires the ONDCP Director, when determining whether to designate an area as a high intensity drug trafficking area, to consider the extent to which: 1) the area is a significant center of illegal drug production, manufacturing, importation, or distribution; 2) state, local, and tribal law enforcement agencies have committed resources to respond to the drug trafficking problem in the area, thereby indicating a determination to respond aggressively to the problem; 3) drug-related activities in the area are having a significant harmful impact in the area and in other areas of the country; and 4) a significant increase in allocation of Federal resources is necessary to respond adequately to drug-related activities in the area.

There are currently 28 regional HIDTAs which include approximately 16 percent of all counties in the United States and 60 percent of the population. In addition, the Southwest Border HIDTA is divided into five regions (Arizona, California, New Mexico, South Texas, and West Texas), each of which operates in many respects as a separate HIDTA in a coordinated fashion with the four other regions. HIDTA-designated counties are located in 45 states, Puerto Rico, the U.S. Virgin Islands, and the District of Columbia.

The HIDTA program provides resources to Federal, state, local, and tribal agencies in each HIDTA region to carry out activities that address the specific drug threats of that region. At the local level, the HIDTAs are directed and guided by Executive Boards[3] composed of an equal

---

[3] Each HIDTA is governed by an Executive Board. Only those agencies with a staff member assigned full-time in a HIDTA initiative may be a voting member of the Board. The Board must apportion an equal number of votes between representatives of participating Federal agencies and representatives of participating State, local, and tribal agencies. The representatives are the local heads of the participating agencies and are unpaid positions.

number of regional Federal and non-Federal (state, local, and tribal) law enforcement leaders.

A central feature of the HIDTA program is the discretion granted to the Executive Boards to design and implement initiatives that confront the specific drug trafficking threats in each HIDTA region. This flexibility ensures that each HIDTA Executive Board can tailor its strategy and initiatives to local conditions and can respond more quickly to changes in conditions than if a single central office controlled the 28 HIDTAs. Each HIDTA assesses the drug trafficking threat in its defined area for the upcoming year; develops a strategy to address that threat; designs initiatives to implement the strategy; and proposes funding needed to carry out the initiatives. Each HIDTA's annual strategy contains its overall performance objectives to be attained through various initiatives. After the end of the program year, each HIDTA prepares an annual report describing its performance against the overall objectives outlined in its Strategy for the preceding year.

In addition to management and coordination initiatives that fund the basic HIDTA administrative costs (e.g., salaries, rent, facilities, and other charges for the local HIDTA Director and the HIDTA administrative staff), the types of activities funded by the HIDTA program are:

1) enforcement initiatives comprised of multi-agency investigative, interdiction, and prosecution activities targeting drug trafficking and money laundering organizations, drug production organizations, drug gangs, drug fugitives, and other serious crimes with a drug nexus;

2) intelligence and information-sharing initiatives that furnish intelligence (tactical, operational, and strategic), deconfliction services (event and case/subject)[4], information collection and dissemination, and other analytical support for HIDTA initiatives and participating agencies;

3) drug use prevention and drug treatment initiatives; and

4) initiatives that provide assistance beyond the core enforcement and intelligence and information-sharing initiatives, e.g., training, crime and forensic labs, and information technology initiatives.

*Discretionary Enforcement Projects*

Through discretionary funds, the HIDTA program supports two major projects that provide resources to HIDTAs throughout the Nation to address specific drug trafficking concerns: the Domestic Marijuana Eradication and Investigation Project (DMEIP) and the Domestic Highway Enforcement Program (DHE).

The DMEIP coordinates multi-agency efforts to investigate marijuana production with an emphasis on public lands controlled by Federal and state governments. Because of their remote locations and the limited presence of law enforcement, these public lands have become sites for the cultivation of marijuana, particularly in California, Hawaii, Oregon, Washington, Tennessee,

---

[4] Event deconfliction ensures law enforcement agencies working in close proximity of each other are immediately notified when enforcement actions are planned in a manner that threatens effective coordination or that compromises enforcement operations. Notification of such conflicts enhances officer safety and promotes the coordination of operations in a multi-agency environment. Similarly, target deconfliction alerts investigators when there is an investigatory cross-over by enforcement agencies. Notification of duplicate targets encourages investigators to share information and resources.

Kentucky, and West Virginia (the "M7 States").

The Domestic Highway Enforcement (DHE) initiative was initiated in 2006 by ONDCP to assist the HIDTAs with market disruption through a coordinated nationwide highway enforcement strategy. The DHE strategy is based on collaborative, intelligence-led policing to enhance coordinated, multi-jurisdictional operational law enforcement efforts on interstate highways specifically identified by the National Drug Intelligence Center (NDIC) as drug trafficking corridors. It increases public safety and reduces criminal utilization of the Nation's highway system. The 48 contiguous states participate in the sharing of plans and intelligence and in coordinating operations. The El Paso Intelligence Center (EPIC) supports the DHE initiative through its National Seizure System (NSS), an online DHE community website, the Tactical Incident Notification System (TINS), and Predictive Intelligence Unit. In 2010, DHE discretionary funds ($4.4M) were allocated to all but seven HIDTAs. As of the writing of this report, the initiatives funded by these dollars report seizures of drugs and related assets valued at $377 million removed from our Nation's highways in 2010.

*Administrative Support Program*

The National HIDTA Assistance Center (NHAC) is located in Miami, Florida. The NHAC provides financial services to assist ONDCP in the administration of the HIDTA program, including hosting the HIDTA financial management system, a database used for budgeting and grants administration. The center also provides training and multi-media support (e.g., website development, video recording and production, brochures) to the HIDTAs. The NHAC funds a national coordinator for HIDTA.net, a national system for HIDTA connectivity and information sharing based on the RISS.net system sponsored by the Department of Justice. HIDTA.net is not duplicative of RISS.net; rather, it is a system that utilizes RISS.net for connectivity.

The National Methamphetamine Pharmaceuticals Initiative (NMPI) assists the HIDTAs with coordination, information sharing, and training to prosecutors, investigators, intelligence analysts, and chemists to enhance the identification of criminal targets; to increase the number of chemical/pharmaceutical drug crime-related investigations and prosecutions; and to curtail foreign chemical and precursor sources that are utilized by domestic illicit drug manufacturers. The NMPI is funded through the Southwest Border HIDTA (California Region) and ONDCP discretionary funding. Most recently, NMPI has supported the Administration's *National Drug Control Strategy* efforts related to prescription drugs and precursor regulation. (*See "Program Accomplishments"* in Section II below.)

*Prevention and Treatment Initiatives*

The 2010 *National Drug Control Strategy* emphasized a balanced approach to drug control, based upon prevention, early intervention, treatment, enforcement, and international partnerships. Law enforcement can play a critical part in preventing young people from using drugs. There are now 20 HIDTAs involved in prevention initiatives across the country. The HIDTA members work with locally based community coalitions and adhere to evidence-based prevention practices, such as community mobilization and organizational change. In 2010, ONDCP funded two prevention initiatives that require HIDTAs to work together across regions of the country. One prevention initiative covers the five regions of the Southwest border, while another initiative provides funding for the four California HIDTAs to work together. These two initiatives incorporate a balanced approach to reducing drug use and its consequences. Member agencies participate in drug awareness and education in order to strengthen their prevention efforts.

In April 2010, the Milwaukee HIDTA received the Outstanding HIDTA Prevention Effort award for its Safe & Sound program. Safe & Sound is a partnership of law enforcement, prosecutors, youth-serving organizations, elected and civic leaders, businesses, city services, and clergy aimed at reducing illegal drug use and crime and rebuilding neighborhoods. The project mobilizes and partners with residents, youth serving organizations, the Milwaukee Police Department, the District Attorney's Community Prosecution Unit, and other city services to identify and report criminal activity and to prevent youth gang affiliation, crime, and substance use. Safe & Sound supports the Safe Places program that engages youth in evidence-based programming to prevent negative behaviors such as illegal substance use, gang involvement, and violent behavior. Last year, over 20,000 youths participated, with many developing their own youth-led crime reduction projects that teach leadership and decision-making skills.

*Tribal Affairs Initiatives*

Drug trafficking is a significant problem in Indian country, and ONDCP has made it a priority to collaborate with tribal leadership to coordinate and enhance law enforcement and prevention responses. There are currently six HIDTA programs collaborating in enforcement operations and training with Tribal Nations located in the states of Arizona, New Mexico, Oregon, Texas, Oklahoma, and Washington.

On October 18, 2010, nine residents of McKinley County, New Mexico, were arrested on Federal drug trafficking charges as a result of a five-month, joint DEA and Bureau of Indian Affairs (BIA) investigation code-named "Operation Yé'iitsoh" (Big Giant). The investigation leading to the arrests began in May 2010 at the request of the Navajo Nation Department of Public Safety (NNDPS) to combat the growing drug trafficking problem in and around the Navajo Reservation. This operation combined NNDPS's direct knowledge of the trafficking networks and tribal community with the investigative expertise of Federal law enforcement. The success of this operation demonstrates the unique capabilities of joint Federal and tribal efforts in disrupting drug trafficking and distribution in Indian country.

In 2010, the Warm Springs Indian Reservation was designated as a HIDTA and is now a partner in the Oregon HIDTA. Warms Springs is the first Indian Reservation to be designated as a HIDTA Reservation. Many HIDTA-designated counties include portions of Tribal Lands, but Warm Springs is the first, in the history of the HIDTA Program, to be designated regardless of county lines.

Also in 2010, Navajo County, Arizona, home to the Hopi, Navajo, and White Mountain Apache tribes, was designated as a HIDTA county. These designations are in response to growing threats within Indian country and serve as a model for future Federal drug investigation and enforcement support in tribal communities.

## II. NATIONAL HIDTA PROGRAM EVALUATION

Section 707(k)(2) of the HIDTA program's authorizing legislation, as amended by Section 301 of the ONDCP Reauthorization Act of 2006, P.L. 109-469, requires ONDCP to provide Congress with an evaluation of HIDTA performance. The specific requirements of this section are contained below. To meet this requirement, this report includes, for each HIDTA, a description of its purposes and objectives and an evaluation of its performance.

### Reporting Requirement

The text of the reporting requirement states:

"(k) EVALUATION.—

"(2) EVALUATION OF HIDTA PROGRAM AS PART OF NATIONAL DRUG CONTROL STRATEGY.—For each designated high intensity drug trafficking area, the Director shall submit, as part of the annual National Drug Control Strategy report, a report that—

"(A) describes—
"(i) the specific purposes for the high intensity drug trafficking area; and
"(ii) the specific long-term and short-term goals and objectives for the high intensity drug trafficking area; and

"(B) includes an evaluation of the performance of the high intensity drug trafficking area in accomplishing the specific long-term and short-term goals and objectives identified under paragraph (1)(B).

### Measurements Used to Evaluate the Performance of Each HIDTA

ONDCP has established two goals for the HIDTA program which address program effectiveness, efficiency, and management. These goals also reflect the continued refinement of the process ONDCP has developed to manage and measure HIDTA performance. The first goal is: to reduce drug availability by assisting Federal, state, local, and tribal law enforcement agencies participating in HIDTAs to dismantle and disrupt drug trafficking organizations. The second goal is: to improve the efficiency and effectiveness of HIDTA initiatives.

To demonstrate its efforts to accomplish the first goal, each HIDTA must collect and enter information into the HIDTA Performance Management Process (PMP) database regarding drug trafficking organizations (DTOs), money laundering organizations (MLOs), and Consolidated Priority Organization Target List (CPOT)-related DTOs and MLOs known to operate in its region. At least quarterly, each HIDTA is also required to update the PMP database with information regarding seizures of drugs and drug-related assets, as well as changes in the status of a DTO/MLO, including when a DTO/MLO has been disrupted or dismantled.

The second HIDTA goal recognizes that it is not enough for a HIDTA to simply achieve its outputs; it must do so efficiently. This more comprehensive accomplishment is measured as the average HIDTA cost per DTO disrupted or dismantled. As part of the second goal, each HIDTA must also address information sharing and training in its ongoing activities.

Regional threats determine investigatory responses. Factors include the nature of threats and the complexity of targeted organizations, which can range from large, multinational organizations, to more regional or local targets. Variances in expenditures reflect the resources required to disrupt and dismantle particular DTOs based on their size and sophistication. This approach allows HIDTAs to address DTO threats as necessary.

## Reporting Requirements Needed to Evaluate Performance

Each HIDTA is required to provide the following four reports pertaining to the geographical area it serves:

**(1) Threat Assessment.** A Threat Assessment is an annual analysis of drug trafficking and related activities taking place in a HIDTA. Its primary purpose is to provide a basis for the development of a HIDTA's Strategy by identifying and describing the organizations that manufacture, cultivate, import, transport, or distribute illegal drugs in the region. The Threat Assessment must also specifically identify and describe those drug trafficking activities that affect other parts of the United States.

**(2) HIDTA Strategy.** Using the two HIDTA program goals as starting points, the HIDTA designs a Strategy that reflects the drug threats identified in its Threat Assessment and the HIDTA's capacity to address these threats.

**(3) Initiative Budget Proposals.** HIDTAs must submit annual Initiative Budget Proposals identifying the activities that will be undertaken to implement their Strategies. These proposals must provide: (1) realistic annual funding needs for each initiative; (2) specific quantitative performance targets; and (3) sufficient detail for ONDCP to assess whether the proposed initiatives are consistent with the HIDTA's Strategy and are likely to achieve the performance targets stated therein. Individual HIDTA Strategies are available upon request.

**(4) Annual Report.** HIDTAs must produce an Annual Report that describes their activities and progress in implementing their Strategy. The Annual Reports must document how they met their performance targets for the preceding calendar year.

The HIDTA Annual Report, Threat Assessment, and Strategy must be based on DTOs and MLOs identified in the PMP database.

ONDCP uses data drawn from the PMP database to assess the performance of each HIDTA.

## Program Accomplishments

FY 2010 achievements will be shared with Congress in summer 2011, once data has been fully collected and analyzed. For FY 2009, the most recent year for which complete data is available, annual reports indicate there were 670 HIDTA initiatives[5] in the 28 HIDTAs and the 5 Southwest Border HIDTA regions. These initiatives were staffed by more than 8,700 Federal agents and analysts and nearly 16,900 state, local, and tribal officers, analysts, and other representatives.

In FY 2010, ONDCP provided $3,100,000 in HIDTA discretionary funding to the

---

[5] Initiatives are activities that implement portions of a HIDTA's Strategy as opposed to an organization of activities/investigative efforts.

DMEIP. These resources are used for officer overtime, aviation flying hours, special equipment purchases, and other investigative costs, and to help coordinate eradication efforts by the DEA, the Department of the Interior, the Department of Agriculture, the Department of Defense (National Guard), and the M7 States. Based on information provided by the DEA, ONDCP does not expect a dramatic change in the number of marijuana plants eradicated in 2010 compared to 2009. In 2009, ONDCP contributed to the eradication of nearly 10 million plants throughout the United States; 9.2 million plants were eradicated in the M7 States alone.

In FY 2010, the NMPI continued to sponsor and manage conferences among Federal, state, local, and tribal law enforcement and international partners such as China and Canada. As a result of an added focus on pharmaceuticals, the NMPI now monitors programs that impact diversion control of legal substances. In addition, the NMPI is working at the national level with state and local leaders to explore policy, regulatory, and enforcement options to reduce domestic methamphetamine production. The action taken in 2006 by the State of Oregon to return pseudoephedrine, a precursor to methamphetamine, to a prescription-only drug is a promising tool in decreasing methamphetamine labs. The results have shown dramatic decreases in the number of labs operating within the state, and a significant reduction in the public safety threat posed by labs. This approach is being replicated in Mississippi and several cities and counties in Missouri. Early indications from these two states show decreases in methamphetamine labs from 2009 to 2010. Other state legislatures, such as Indiana's, also plan to take up the issue of returning pseudoephedrine to prescription-only status in 2011. Further, DEA, in conjunction with the U.S. Attorney's Office for the Central District of California, concluded a settlement agreement with one of the country's largest chain of retail pharmacies, which admitted to criminal violations and paid the U.S. Government $75 million in civil fines and $2.6 million in civil forfeiture as a result of its failure to adhere to the requirements under the Federal Combat Methamphetamine Epidemic Act.

In 2010 the HIDTA program, and specifically the SWB HIDTA, continued to support the National Southwest Border Counternarcotics Strategy. Law enforcement leaders from Federal, state, local, and tribal entities associated with the five regions of the SWB HIDTA participated in consultation meetings held by ONDCP to gather input for the 2011 update to this strategy. The prevention community was among the parties consulted in New Mexico. The SWB HIDTA is one of the most diverse HIDTAs, and each of the five regions faces unique challenges. For example, in 2010, the Arizona Region conducted 1,199 DHE operations resulting in the seizure of 19,882 kilograms of marijuana, 140 kilograms of cocaine, 31 kilograms of methamphetamine, 8 kilograms of heroin, and more than 9 million dollars in currency. South Texas Region task forces seized 228,766 kilograms of marijuana, 2,782 kilograms of cocaine, 134 kilograms of methamphetamine, 44 kilograms of methamphetamine "ice",[6] and 86 kilograms of heroin.

As evidenced in the individual HIDTA reports below, performance information continues to show the HIDTA program is meeting performance targets and is devoted to effective and efficient performance.

Finally, in accordance with the Office of Management and Budget assessment guidance, ONDCP has developed a strategy to assess the effectiveness of the HIDTA program. Using an independent contractor, ONDCP conducts seven HIDTA region audits annually to provide

---

[6] Methamphetamine hydrochloride, clear chunky crystals resembling ice, which can be inhaled by smoking, is referred to as "ice."

assurance of the accuracy and integrity of performance information provided by the HIDTAs. All of the HIDTAs will be part of the audit cycle by September 2012. Audit results to date have provided important information that has been employed to refine the HIDTA PMP system and to improve a range of HIDTA activities, including setting appropriate performance targets, better identifying training needs, and clarifying PMP definitions. ONDCP also works with the HIDTAs to ensure findings and recommendations in audit reports are addressed accordingly. The audits will serve as another tool to assess the performance of the HIDTA program as a whole and to modify and enhance HIDTA operations where needed.

## III. ASSESSMENT OF LAW ENFORCEMENT INTELLIGENCE SHARING IN THE HIDTA PROGRAM

Section 707(m) of the HIDTA program's authorizing legislation, as amended by Section 301 of the ONDCP Reauthorization Act of 2006, requires ONDCP to provide Congress with an assessment of law enforcement intelligence sharing in the HIDTA program.

### Reporting Requirement

The text of the reporting requirement states:

"(m) ASSESSMENT OF LAW ENFORCEMENT INTELLIGENCE SHARING IN HIGH INTENSITY DRUG TRAFFICKING AREAS PROGRAM.— Not later than 180 days after the date of the enactment of this section, and as part of each subsequent annual National Drug Control Strategy report, the Director, in consultation with the Director of National Intelligence, shall submit to Congress a report—

"(1) evaluating existing and planned law enforcement intelligence systems supported by each high intensity drug trafficking area, or utilized by task forces receiving any funding under the Program, including the extent to which such systems ensure access and availability of law enforcement intelligence to Federal, state, local, and tribal law enforcement agencies within the high intensity drug trafficking area and outside of it;

"(2) the extent to which Federal, state, local, and tribal law enforcement agencies participating in each high intensity drug trafficking area are sharing law enforcement intelligence information to assess current drug trafficking threats and design appropriate enforcement strategies; and

"(3) the measures needed to improve effective sharing of information and law enforcement intelligence regarding drug trafficking and drug production among Federal, state, local, and tribal law enforcement participating in a high intensity drug trafficking area, and between such agencies and similar agencies outside the high intensity drug trafficking area."

### Introduction to the Intelligence Sharing Report

The HIDTA program has 57 operational intelligence and information sharing initiatives, including 32 primary IISCs and 25 satellite centers. Each HIDTA capitalizes on the combined resources of the Federal, state, local, and tribal law enforcement communities. The HIDTAs prepare and review Threat Assessments and apply the appropriate law enforcement response to combat illegal drug activity in our Nation.

This report constitutes an evaluation of law enforcement intelligence systems providing support to, and participating in, the various HIDTAs. It includes information on the existing and planned law enforcement intelligence systems supported by each HIDTA, or utilized by task forces receiving funding under the program. This report further describes the extent to which Federal, state, local, and tribal law enforcement agencies participating in each HIDTA are sharing law enforcement intelligence information to assess current drug trafficking threats and design appropriate enforcement strategies. Finally, it articulates the measures needed to improve effective sharing of information and law enforcement intelligence regarding drug trafficking and drug production among Federal, state, local, and tribal law enforcement agencies participating in a HIDTA, and between such agencies and similar agencies outside the HIDTA.

**Evaluation of Existing and Planned Law Enforcement Intelligence Systems**

Section 11 of the HIDTA program Policy and Budget Guidance provides specific guidance and requirements for the program review of all HIDTAs, including the intelligence and information sharing-initiatives. ONDCP reviews of individual HIDTAs are conducted in two phases:

Phase 1: Annual reviews by ONDCP of each HIDTA's budget request, including its Threat Assessment, Strategy, Initiative Budget Proposals, and Annual Report; and

Phase 2: Annual internal program reviews that each individual HIDTA is required to conduct.

*Basic Requirements of Intelligence and Information Sharing*

Section 5 of the HIDTA program Policy and Budget Guidance provides specific guidance and requirements for intelligence and information sharing among HIDTAs. Each HIDTA must develop and implement at least one intelligence and information sharing initiative that focuses on collecting, evaluating, collating, analyzing, and disseminating law enforcement information and intelligence for the entire HIDTA. The initiative must include co-located participants from Federal and state, local, or tribal agencies. Participating agencies provide direct access, on-site, to pertinent databases at the primary intelligence center, in accordance with individual agency's requirements.

HIDTA intelligence and information sharing initiatives must comply with applicable Federal, state, and local regulations, including 28 CFR Part 23, "Criminal Intelligence Systems Operating Policies." HIDTAs provide intelligence and information-sharing services from a single primary intelligence center. HIDTA Executive Boards have discretion to establish additional intelligence and information-sharing components to suit the specific circumstances of their HIDTA region. Further information regarding each HIDTA's intelligence and information-sharing initiatives is provided in the Individual HIDTA reports section, Section V below.

*Objectives of Intelligence and Information Initiatives*

Each HIDTA IISC provides actionable intelligence, information, and analytical support to HIDTA enforcement initiatives and participating agencies.

**Key Components of the Intelligence and Information-Sharing Initiatives**

Each intelligence and information-sharing initiative is comprised of the following components:

14

*Threat Assessment Documentation*

Each HIDTA prepares an annual Threat Assessment documenting the drug trafficking activities within its region, an overview of which is included in the description of each individual HIDTA in Section V of this report. The full Threat Assessment includes:

- Demographics of the region
- An overview of the drug threat, including:
  - Drug Trafficking Organizations and their impact on the region;
  - Production and/or growing of illegal drugs to include cocaine, methamphetamine, associated methamphetamine chemicals, heroin, marijuana, ecstasy, and other illegal drugs;
  - Transportation of illegal drugs, to include air, land, and sea threats; drug transportation activity; organizations; highway corridors; quantities and methods of transportation; and emerging transportation trends;
  - Distribution methods and trends;
  - Illicit finance activities; and
  - Crime rates and trends.

*Event and Case/Subject Deconfliction*

A critical component of intelligence and information sharing is ensuring safety among law enforcement agencies participating in the HIDTA program. Individual HIDTAs are required to provide a mechanism to deconflict targets and events within their respective regions.

*Analytical Support*

HIDTA initiatives support drug enforcement operations, track potential threats to officer safety, and manage and analyze case information and drug trafficking activities to prepare cases for prosecution. They provide support through telephone toll analysis, analytical case support, operational intelligence programs, officer safety bulletins, and post-seizure analysis. Additionally, some HIDTAs have the capability to provide case-specific analytical support. Drug intelligence information provided by investigators is processed and returned for appropriate action to the initial investigators.

*Information Sharing*

HIDTAs have access to systems that enable them to securely share information with intelligence components in their regions and with other HIDTAs. These systems include, but are not limited to: RISS.net, HIDTA.net, LEO, ADNET-U and Secret Internet Protocol Router Network (SIPRNet), DEA-MERLIN, Narcotics and Dangerous Drug Indexing System, Central Index System, U.S. Postal Inspector Warrant Information Network, Federal Bureau of Prisons-Sentry, Financial Crimes Enforcement Network, National Law Enforcement Telecommunications System, Homeland Security Information Network, National Drug Pointer Index, National Seizure System, commercial databases such as Autotrack, Choicepoint, Lexis Nexis, as well as numerous databases from departments of motor vehicles, county prosecution offices, sheriff offices, city police departments, and parole offices. ONDCP will continue to encourage increased intelligence sharing through DEA's Special Operations Division and DEA's deconfliction database (DICE). In addition, ONDCP will work to ensure all HIDTAs be given access to DICE accounts.  In order to ensure information integrity and security, HIDTAs maintain and enforce security rules and practices required by the agencies providing the information.  In addition, HIDTAs make use of firewalls which conform to industry standards for encryption and security.

*Core Functions of Intelligence and Information Initiatives*

Core functions of the intelligence and information-sharing initiatives within the HIDTAs include: obtaining access to, and using, law enforcement, proprietary, and public databases; establishing and maintaining electronic connectivity to other HIDTAs through the HIDTA.Net/RISS.Net; and sharing drug-related information with other HIDTA intelligence centers and national intelligence centers.

Other core features include:

- Investigative Databases:  Each participating agency is required to provide co-located access to its investigative databases at the HIDTA's primary intelligence center.
- Electronic Connectivity:  HIDTAs are responsible for establishing and maintaining the capacity (e.g., hardware, software, policies, and procedures) to continuously and securely share information with other HIDTAs and law enforcement/intelligence components.
- Sharing:  HIDTAs must ensure all participating agencies receive relevant information and intelligence products in a timely fashion.  HIDTAs also establish guidelines for disseminating information directly to other HIDTAs and law enforcement agencies that may benefit from the information.

*Staffing Requirements of Intelligence and Information-Sharing Initiatives*

Each intelligence and information-sharing initiative in a HIDTA is sponsored by at least one participating law enforcement agency.  Each HIDTA's Executive Board ensures there is joint Federal and state/local management over intelligence and information-sharing initiatives. Supervisors of such initiatives are sworn Federal, state, local, or tribal law enforcement officers or law enforcement intelligence analysts designated by a participating agency.  Each intelligence and information-sharing initiative has at least two supervisors, representing a Federal and a state or local agency.

*Coordination and Information Sharing Requirements*

HIDTA task forces rely on intelligence and information-sharing initiatives for event, case, and subject deconfliction of all enforcement and operational activities.  HIDTA intelligence components maintain working relationships with intelligence components of the participating agencies and other law enforcement agencies within their region.

Applicable Federal, state, or local laws, regulations, or policies regarding the collection, storage, and dissemination of investigative information govern the operation of a HIDTA intelligence and information-sharing initiative.  Components of intelligence and information-sharing initiatives disseminate intelligence to participating agencies, subject to appropriate legal requirements.

Event deconfliction ensures law enforcement agencies working in close proximity of each other are immediately notified when enforcement actions are planned in a manner that threatens effective coordination or that compromises enforcement operations. Notification of such conflicts enhances officer safety and promotes the coordination of operations in a multi-agency environment. Similarly, target deconfliction alerts investigators when there is an investigatory cross-over by enforcement agencies. Notification of duplicate targets encourages investigators to share information and resources.

There are several deconfliction systems now being utilized by HIDTAs to accomplish this task:

- Secure Automated Fast Event/Target Network (SAFETNet): SAFETNet is an event/target deconfliction system developed, owned, and operated by a consortium of 17 HIDTAs across the country. It is used by over 230 law enforcement agencies (LEAs);
- HIDTA Internet-based Information System (HIBIS): HIBIS is a web-based case management system administered by the South Florida HIDTA, which provides analysts with the ability to compartmentalize investigative information and share data internally as well as with other HIDTAs;
- Regional Information Sharing Systems (RISS): RISSIntel is information entered by RISS member agencies (law enforcement) into a database hosted by one of the six RISS (Regional Information Sharing Systems). RISSSafe is a deconfliction program available to any RISS member for event and target deconfliction; and
- Case Explorer: Case Explorer is a '.net' case management, event/case deconfliction, intelligence and tip management database that is owned and administered by the Washington/Baltimore HIDTA.

To enhance partnerships and leverage resources and data sharing between the HIDTA program and EPIC, there is an effort underway to examine how HIDTAs can share space in the EPIC Cloud[7] to expand deconfliction capabilities for agencies around the Nation. In a pilot project, the Chicago HIDTA will migrate its version of SAFETNet into the EPIC Cloud. Once the integration has been evaluated, the intent is to move the remainder of the deconfliction "middle ware" applications (other SAFETNet versions, Case Explorer, RISSSafe, and others) to the EPIC Cloud, thereby maximizing HIDTA's reach, to provide critical event and target deconfliction services to any law enforcement agency requesting the service.

To further enhance the functionality of these systems, HIDTAs have collaborated with DEA and RISS personnel to develop and implement the NVPS, a method to connect with DEA's target deconfliction system known as the National Drug Pointer Index (NDPIX). The connectivity among these systems now provides for a truly nationwide deconfliction solution.

## HIDTA Intelligence and Information Sharing Committee

The HIDTA directors have established a HIDTA Intelligence and Information Sharing Committee. ONDCP provides the committee members with guidance, recommendations, and

---

[7] The EPIC Cloud, a subset of the greater U.S. Government Cloud Computing System being established, will allow greater efficiency for accessing information sharing resources. The HIDTA program, presently in the testing phase with SAFTNet (administered by the Chicago HIDTA), is studying the viability of connecting to the EPIC Cloud for use in case/subject deconfliction.

approval as required. The Committee may establish working groups to assist in its work and may request assistance from intelligence program managers, information technology specialists, and others from the HIDTAs.

### HIDTA Intelligence Sharing

Intelligence and information-sharing initiatives continuously validate the regional drug threat and ensure the proper focus of a HIDTA's regional strategy. Specifically, the Threat Assessment is primarily used to allocate operational law enforcement task forces, initiatives, and resources to combat the illegal drug threat in the designated region. This is a process that is continually updated based on the threat. HIDTAs have the flexibility to allocate new resources, or combine current resources, to ensure the most effective enforcement.

"Actionable intelligence and information" is a term that has been used in the law enforcement community for several years and is a process that is the foundation of the HIDTA intelligence architecture. Simply stated, it refers to the use of intelligence information to drive and/or direct criminal investigations. HIDTA Intelligence and Investigative Support Centers (IISCs) and post-seizure analysis teams are able to analyze the information they collect, determine related cases, and identify new targets and trends, which inform investigations.

In addition to the HIDTA Threat Assessment, many HIDTAs prepare bulletins, alerts, and newsletters that are widely distributed throughout the HIDTA program. Specific intelligence products may:

- identify links between DTOs which are then relayed to law enforcement personnel for the targeting, investigation, and disruption or dismantlement of identified DTOs;
- cluster arrests involving similar drug packaging/stamps, e.g., heroin brand names; or link to previous arrests through database research and alert law enforcement;
- evaluate geographic commonalities by graphic depiction in maps to project areas in need of increased enforcement; and
- provide reviews and weekly progress reports on ongoing projects/investigations, as well as drug-related information found beyond HIDTA resources.

In FY 2010, $239 million was appropriated to the HIDTA program, including $50 million for intelligence and information sharing. The HIDTA program has a robust and well-established system for sharing information and intelligence within each HIDTA, between the various regional HIDTAs, and with many other law enforcement agencies not located in HIDTA-designated areas. There are 57 initiatives within the HIDTA program that focus on intelligence and information sharing, and each HIDTA has at least one such initiative. The 57 initiatives impact 11 independent cities, 491 counties included in the HIDTA program, and 45 states (South Carolina, Idaho, Minnesota, Delaware, and Alaska do not have HIDTA-designated counties).

These initiatives are directly responsible for developing information and intelligence collection requirements and for evaluating, analyzing, and disseminating law enforcement information and intelligence for the HIDTA program.

Not only do the intelligence and information-sharing initiatives and subsystems strengthen the individual HIDTAs, they facilitate the free flow of intelligence and information throughout the HIDTA program, thereby allowing for a more strategic approach to identifying drug threats.

The design and development of the HIDTA intelligence subsystem has demonstrated an ability to react quickly to emerging threats. As intelligence collection and information sharing needs change among the Federal, state, local, and tribal agencies, the participants operating within the HIDTA intelligence subsystem respond by developing and integrating efficient and effective methods of sharing collected intelligence and information.

The HIDTA program has implemented an efficient method to achieve its goals of disrupting the illegal drug market and combating illegal drug activity by leveraging additional information systems and processes. The HIDTA program continues to enhance cooperation and coordination with Department of Homeland Security (DHS)-sponsored fusion center systems. Nine IISCs and DHS fusion centers are now co-located and operating effectively and efficiently, while preventing redundant efforts.

## IV. ASSESSMENT OF DRUG ENFORCEMENT TASK FORCES IN HIDTAS

Section 707(l)(1) of the HIDTA program's authorizing legislation, as amended by Section 301 of the ONDCP Reauthorization Act of 2006, requires ONDCP to provide Congress with an assessment of drug enforcement task forces in HIDTAs.

### Reporting Requirement

The text of the reporting requirement states:

"(l) ASSESSMENT OF DRUG ENFORCEMENT TASK FORCES IN HIGH INTENSITY DRUG TRAFFICKING AREAS.— "Not later than one year after the date of enactment of this subsection, and as part of each subsequent annual National Drug Control Strategy report, the Director shall submit to Congress a report—

"(1) assessing the number and operation of all Federally funded drug enforcement task forces within each high intensity drug trafficking area; and
"(2) describing—

"(A) each Federal, state, local, and tribal drug enforcement task force operating in the high intensity drug trafficking area;

"(B) how such task forces coordinate with each other, with any high intensity drug trafficking area task force, and with investigations receiving funds from the Organized Crime and Drug Enforcement Task Force;

"(C) what steps, if any, each such task force takes to share information regarding drug trafficking and drug production with other Federally funded drug enforcement task forces in the high intensity drug trafficking area;

"(D) the role of the high intensity drug trafficking area in coordinating the sharing of such information among task forces;

"(E) the nature and extent of cooperation by each Federal, state, local, and tribal participant in ensuring that such information is shared among law enforcement agencies and with the high intensity drug trafficking area;

"(F) the nature and extent to which information-sharing and enforcement activities are coordinated with joint terrorism task forces in the high intensity drug trafficking area; and

"(G) any recommendations for measures needed to ensure that task force resources are utilized efficiently and effectively to reduce the availability of illegal drugs in the high intensity drug trafficking areas."

### Federal Task Force Report

Multi-jurisdictional task force teams are the backbone of narcotics enforcement efforts. The HIDTA program brings together Federal, state, local, and tribal law enforcement agencies into co-located, commingled task force teams to conduct joint investigations for the disruption and dismantling of drug trafficking and money laundering organizations. HIDTA task force teams collaborate with each other, as well as with non-HIDTA entities, and implement strategies to pool resources and share information. This focuses limited resources on significant threats and strengthens their ability to identify and destabilize interconnected national and transnational criminal networks. This planning and collaboration also enhances the safety of the officers involved. HIDTA initiatives also serve to reduce duplicative efforts and avoid divisive parochialism between agencies.

In addition to funding interagency investigative teams, the HIDTA program funds other types of task force initiatives to support investigative efforts. Examples of other joint HIDTA initiatives include: intelligence and information sharing, drug interdiction, technical support, crime/forensic lab programs, prosecution initiatives, and training.

Intelligence and information sharing is essential to coordinated and effective operations; therefore, each HIDTA must have at least one IISC designed to develop intelligence, share information, and provide deconfliction and technical support to enforcement initiatives. These IISCs are staffed by representatives of participating agencies who have direct on-site access to their agencies' information databases. The IISCs support and manage the reporting, analysis, and dissemination of case management and threat related information. This requires that the HIDTA work with all law enforcement agencies in preparing the required annual Threat Assessment and Strategy documents for its region. The IISCs also convey these documents and threat information to national intelligence centers, such as the El Paso Intelligence Center (EPIC) and the National Drug Intelligence Center (NDIC). Terrorism-related information and/or investigative leads are turned over to the FBI-led Joint Terrorism Task Forces (JTTF).

To ensure coordination among HIDTA and non-HIDTA task forces, every HIDTA ensures that its participating agencies' task forces deconflict targets and subjects under investigation. Deconfliction is a guiding principle of the HIDTA program. This ensures investigations do not overlap. Further, by informing agencies when critical activities associated with fluid enforcement operations occur in close proximity that could result in conflict, they protect law enforcement officers in the field. Investigators and their managers can then determine the most prudent course of action for the investigation.

Regardless of the method of funding for the participating task forces (e.g., HIDTA, Justice Action Grant/Byrne-sponsored), the 28 HIDTAs provide a coordination umbrella for Federal, state, local, and tribal drug law enforcement efforts by fostering a strategy-driven, systemic approach to integrate and synchronize efforts; facilitate efficiency, effectiveness, and cooperation among and between various agencies; and focus on outcomes and impacts. Using both formal and informal methods of coordination among drug enforcement task forces, the HIDTAs act as neutral centers to manage, deconflict, analyze, and report on drug enforcement activities in their respective regions. Informally, HIDTAs coordinate and collaborate with other drug-enforcement task forces through a variety of methods, including: drug unit commanders meetings; law enforcement coordinating committees; the Department of Justice's Organized Crime Drug Enforcement Task Force (OCDETF) case review and coordination meetings; law enforcement conferences; weekly intelligence bulletins; quarterly newsletters; and training opportunities. For example, HIDTAs regularly make training available to area drug unit personnel, to include non-HIDTA participating agencies. These trainings provide investigative tools, and promote communication, cooperation, and a strong cohesion among the investigators who train together.

*Example of a Successful HIDTA Operation*

The city of Camden, NJ, ended 2009 with its lowest rate of all major crimes since 1969. Law enforcement efforts, including the state-led Violence Reduction Initiative, the HIDTA-funded Joint Camden Task Force (JCTF), and community supported initiatives were instrumental in this noteworthy and encouraging turn around.

Led by the Camden County Prosecutor's Office, the JCTF Initiative is at the forefront in fostering cooperation among the region's law enforcement agencies. This was most evident in its pursuit of drug trafficking organizations in Operation Chili Pepper. An investigation into the shipment of marijuana through the U.S. Postal Service led members of the initiative on a two-year long journey along the drug-trafficking pipeline from Mexico to New Jersey, traversing four HIDTA regions, and leading to the dismantlement of a multi-pronged Drug Trafficking Organization (DTO). This OCDETF-designated investigation would ultimately evolve into the largest and most comprehensive case ever conducted by the JCTF, involving more than 20 law enforcement agencies. The JCTF's outstanding investigative success would not have been achieved without the active participation and coordinated efforts of four HIDTAs (Atlanta, Ohio, Philadelphia/Camden, and Southwest Border), four Federal agencies, five New Jersey prosecutor's offices, and ten local police departments.

This investigation began in February 2008 when the U.S. Postal Inspection Service (USPIS) – Philadelphia Division (South Jersey Office) – intercepted a 60-pound package of marijuana sent from McAllen, Texas, to Lindenwold, New Jersey, and referred the case to the JCTF for further investigation. Initially believed to be a marijuana-only DTO, what emerged was a picture of a criminal enterprise with marijuana and crystal methamphetamine distributions that operated largely independently of each other. Intensive follow-up investigation and surveillance revealed the true scope of the organization's operations to also include weapons sales and money laundering activities of a Transnational Criminal Organization. Investigators spent nearly two years tracking the movements of this organization. The USPIS had the ability to track and locate almost every parcel that was shipped by the McAllen, Texas-based organization. This tactic was conducted in coordination with intercepted conversations between the Delaware Valley principal targets and the Mexican sources of supply. Over a seven-month period, approximately 30 Communication Data Warrants were executed and an undercover investigator successfully infiltrated two separate DTOs. The investigation culminated in 30 arrests in November and December 2009, and the dismantlement of the DTOs.

The principals in this criminal organization are alleged to have been operating a drug pipeline that spanned from the southern Mexican state of Jalisco, through the border town of McAllen, Texas, to Columbus, Ohio, and finally to Camden and Atlantic counties in New Jersey. The investigation revealed Columbus, Ohio, to be a major distribution point for crystal methamphetamine coming to the region from both California and Mexico. The leaders of the DTO targeted in Operation Chili Pepper migrated to southern New Jersey from the Columbus, Ohio, area in an apparent effort to establish a platform for marijuana and methamphetamine trafficking regionally. The organization is alleged to have shipped marijuana in packages of up to 60 pounds through commercial parcel carriers or the postal service to recipients in various New Jersey communities including Camden, Voorhees, Lindenwold, Hammonton, Waterford and Winslow. Meanwhile, crystal methamphetamine, apparently manufactured in Mexico, was smuggled to Ohio and then transported by members of the organization to distributors in Hammonton, New Jersey. Local dealers sold the drugs in homes, at bars, or directly to individual users.

The defendants are accused of bringing approximately 4 to 6 pounds of crystal methamphetamine and 100 to 150 pounds of marijuana into New Jersey weekly. The IRS Criminal Investigations Division has so far identified $1.5 million laundered through banks across the country and funneled to banks in Texas, near the border with Mexico.

At this time, 30 suspects are in custody in New Jersey and Ohio on charges related to the conspiracy to distribute weapons and drugs. Investigators confiscated over seven pounds of crystal methamphetamine with a retail value of about $400,000. They also seized or tracked 2,000 pounds of marijuana, 1.5 kilograms of powder cocaine, and $24,000 cash. Investigators also confiscated 10 firearms including 2 automatic assault weapons and 8 vehicles.

The law enforcement collaborative effort in this case was unprecedented. The typical challenges presented in large-scale, multi-jurisdictional investigations such as Operation Chili Pepper were most efficiently overcome by the co-located team effort. The FBI assigned three full-time agents to this operation and provided invaluable translator assets for a total of seven full-time personnel. Their participation, and that of a full-time IRS agent, was integral in coordinating with Southwest Border HIDTA representatives regarding the money laundering aspects of the case. The ATF provided monetary and personnel resources for the purchase of high-powered weaponry. Pro-active information sharing and *esprit de corps* among all law enforcement partners were remarkable.

In the following section of this report, the individual HIDTAs provided descriptions of Federal, state, local, and tribal drug enforcement task forces operating in the 28 regions. Within each HIDTA task force description, there is an explanation of their efforts.

## V. INDIVIDUAL HIDTA REPORTS

To address the specific reporting requirements, individual HIDTA reports are provided. These reports are succinct descriptions of the individual HIDTAs and their responses to the Congressional report requirements. For a more comprehensive look at any particular HIDTA's performance in addressing specific drug threats, ONDCP will, upon request, provide an Annual Report, Strategy, or Threat Assessment for a HIDTA.

### *PURPOSE AND GOALS*

Per the reporting requirement in Sec. 707(k)(2)(A) of the HIDTA program authorizing legislation, this section in each individual HIDTA report highlights the specific purpose and mission for the HIDTA.

### *STRATEGY*

Per the reporting requirement in Sec. 707(k)(2)(B) of the HIDTA program authorizing legislation, this section in each individual HIDTA report highlights the specific long-term goals and objectives for the HIDTA.

### *LOCATION*

This section in each individual HIDTA report identifies the geographical location of the HIDTA, including the HIDTA-designated counties in its area of responsibility.

### *INITIATIVES*

This section in each individual HIDTA report highlights the total number of initiatives in the HIDTA and the number of enforcement and intelligence related initiatives. Support and management initiatives are not included in the breakdown. Initiatives are considered activities that implement portions of the HIDTA's Strategy, as opposed to an organization of activities or investigative efforts.

### *SHORT-TERM OBJECTIVES*

Per the reporting requirement in Sec. 707(k)(2)(B) of the HIDTA program authorizing legislation, this section in each individual HIDTA report highlights the specific short-term goals and objectives for the HIDTA. These are presented as follows for 2010:

| YEAR | DTOs Expected to be Disrupted/ Dismantled | Target Return on Investment*: Assets | Target Return on Investment: Drugs | Number of Deconflictions Expected to be Submitted | Number of Investigations Expected to be Provided Analytical Support | Number of Initiative Leads Expected to be Referred |
|------|------|------|------|------|------|------|
| 2010 | | | | | | |

**Year:** The numbers provided in this table reflect the performance targets established by the HIDTAs for 2010 and not actual results from 2010. Individual HIDTAs are not required to submit 2010 results until May 2011.

**DTOs Expected to be Disrupted/Dismantled:** *A DTO is* an organization consisting of five or more persons (1) that has a clearly defined chain-of-command and (2) whose principal activity is to generate income or acquire assets through a continuing series of illegal drug production, manufacturing, importation, transportation, or distribution activities. An organization is "dismantled" when its leadership, financial base, and supply network is incapable of operating and/or reconstituting itself. An organization is "disrupted" when the normal and effective operation of the organization is impeded, as indicated by changes in organizational leadership and/or changes in methods of financing, transportation, distribution, communications, or drug production. There is no precise way to calculate or measure whether a DTO/MLO is disrupted. This is a subjective assessment made by the case agent or initiative supervisor.

**Target Return on Investment - Assets:** Return on Investment (ROI) is the ratio between the wholesale value of cash and non-cash assets seized and the amount of HIDTA funds expended on enforcement and intelligence initiatives.

**Target Return on Investment - Drugs:** Return on Investment is the ratio between the wholesale value of drugs seized and the amount of HIDTA funds expended on enforcement and intelligence initiatives.

**Number of Deconflictions Expected to be Submitted:** Deconfliction is the process of determining if multiple law enforcement agencies are investigating the same person, crime, or organization or multiple law enforcement agencies are conducting an enforcement action (e.g., a raid, undercover operation, surveillance, or action) in close proximity to one another during a specified time period. The process includes notifying each agency of the duplication.

**Number of Investigations Expected to be Provided Analytical Support:** Analytical support means services an analyst provides to support an investigation such as Crime Pattern Analysis (showing information relating to a series of crimes), Financial Analysis (showing connections between bank accounts and individuals or entities), Association/Link/Network Analysis (showing relationships or connections among people and organizations involved in a criminal activity), Commodity Flow Analysis (showing the flow of goods, currency or services relating to a criminal act, among people ,organizations or businesses).

**Number of Initiative Leads Expected to be Referred:** A lead is the provision of sufficient information to another HIDTA or non-HIDTA entity for the purpose of enabling that entity to conduct an independent investigation; it does not matter if or when an independent investigation is opened.

## *THREAT ASSESSMENT*

As required by Sec. 707(m)(2) of the HIDTA program authorizing legislation, each individual HIDTA report highlights the Threat Assessment in its area. While each HIDTA provides an in-depth Threat Assessment annually, this section includes a short overview of the drug trends and threats in the HIDTA region. These assessments are developed through cooperation among Federal, state, local, and tribal law enforcement, as well as the National Drug Intelligence Center.

### INTELLIGENCE INITIATIVES

As required by Sec. 707(m) of the HIDTA program authorizing legislation, each individual HIDTA report identifies the HIDTA Intelligence Initiatives in its region. Each HIDTA must have, at least, one intelligence and information-sharing initiative that is responsible for developing information and intelligence collection requirements and for collecting, evaluating, collating, analyzing, and disseminating law enforcement information and intelligence for the HIDTA program. These initiatives are required to have participants from Federal and state, local, or tribal agencies.

### TASK FORCES OPERATING IN THE HIDTA REGION

As required by Sec. 707(l) of the HIDTA program authorizing legislation, each individual HIDTA report lists the name and location of each Federal, state, local, and tribal drug enforcement task force operating in the HIDTA region.

### TASK FORCE COORDINATION

As required by Sec. 707(l) of the HIDTA program authorizing legislation, each individual HIDTA report highlights how task forces coordinate with each other; the steps taken to share information among task forces; the role of the HIDTA in coordinating information sharing; and the extent of current cooperation among participants.

### HIDTA EVALUATION

As required by Sec. 707(k)(2)(B) of the HIDTA program authorizing legislation, ONDCP provides, for each HIDTA, an evaluation of the performance of the HIDTA in accomplishing its goals and objectives. It should be noted that the number of DTOs disrupted or dismantled is affected by developing cases, varying levels of DTOs, national and international scope of investigations, differing levels of sophistication and size of DTOs, and the ability to acquire resources.

# Appalachia HIDTA – Designated in 1998
## Executive Director – Frank Rapier

## *PURPOSE AND GOALS*

The goals of the Appalachia HIDTA (AHIDTA) are to measurably reduce the production and trafficking of illegal drugs and drug-related violent crime impacting the region and other areas of the United States. Although marijuana cultivation is the most significant drug threat in the region, the Appalachia HIDTA responds to the threats posed by the illicit trafficking and abuse of other drugs, as required. Central to this purpose is the development of cooperative, multi-jurisdictional law enforcement efforts involving HIDTA-funded and non-HIDTA-funded resources.

## *STRATEGY*

The AHIDTA is instrumental in fostering cooperation and collaboration among Federal, state, and local law enforcement agencies. The Executive Board, informed by a dedicated intelligence center and supported by interagency resources, develops and manages the AHIDTA Strategy and its initiatives to focus resources and efforts on the region's primary drug threats and ensures desired outcomes and impacts are achieved.

The Executive Board's ongoing efforts are dedicated to facilitating cooperation and strengthening the working relationships of the HIDTA's participating law enforcement agencies, which include 6 United States Attorneys' Offices, 7 Federal agencies, 13 state agencies, and 61 local agencies. The Board's efforts help to achieve common goals and respond to current drug threats effectively and efficiently. The AHIDTA strategy and initiatives are designed to target drug cultivation, distribution, drug-related violent crime, and to reduce drug abuse. Several task force teams focus on marijuana, a major threat to the region. Their efforts, partnered with Federal prosecutors, have been effective in reducing local marijuana cultivation operations on public lands, but the HIDTA is experiencing and beginning to respond to a different and growing threat from Mexican growers. The AHIDTA is also addressing a significant methamphetamine threat. Even as prescription monitoring systems and enforcement efforts are effectively impacting methamphetamine production and abuse, the HIDTA decision makers expect that drug trafficking organizations (DTOs) and users will modify their operations. Additionally, the AHIDTA is working with law enforcement agencies in Florida, as well as several other HIDTAs, to reduce the growing problem of diverted pharmaceuticals and pharmaceutical abuse.

## *LOCATION*

The AHIDTA operates out of London, Kentucky. It encompasses the following counties in three states:

- 28 counties in Kentucky: Adair, Bell, Breathitt, Clay, Clinton, Cumberland, Floyd, Harlan, Jackson, Jefferson, Knott, Knox, Laurel, Lee, Leslie, Letcher, McCreary, Magoffin, Marion, Owsley, Perry, Pike, Pulaski, Rockcastle, Taylor, Warren, Wayne, and Whitley;
- 30 counties in Tennessee: Bledsoe, Campbell, Claiborne, Clay, Cocke, Cumberland, Fentress, Franklin, Grainger, Greene, Grundy, Hamblen, Hamilton, Hawkins,

Jackson, Jefferson, Knox, Macon, Marion, Overton, Pickett, Putnam, Rhea, Roane, Scott, Sequatchie, Sevier, Unicoi, Washington, and White; and

- 9 counties in West Virginia: Boone, Cabell, Kanawha, Lincoln, Logan, Mason, McDowell, Mingo, and Wayne.

## INITIATIVES

The AHIDTA has 22 initiatives, which include 1 intelligence initiative, 19 investigation/interdiction/eradication initiatives, 1 management initiative, and 1 training initiative.

## SHORT-TERM OBJECTIVES

| YEAR | DTOs Expected to be Disrupted/ Dismantled | Target Return on Investment: Assets | Target Return on Investment: Drugs | Number of Deconflictions Expected to be Submitted | Number of Investigations Expected to be Provided Analytical Support | Number of Initiative Leads Expected to be Referred |
|------|------|------|------|------|------|------|
| 2010 | 79 | $2.67 | $318.88 | 4,700 | 200 | 1,309 |

## THREAT ASSESSMENT

Marijuana is a significant drug threat in Appalachia. The AHIDTA is one of the major sources of domestically grown marijuana. The AHIDTA is also under the assault of drug traffickers who are diverting prescription drugs to the region. Methamphetamine production and abuse are also above the national levels. Other dangerous drugs, including crack cocaine and powder cocaine, and drug-related violence threaten the safety of communities and are constant sources of anxiety to citizens and public servants in urban areas.

Law enforcement efforts have successfully impacted drug threats, but these efforts must address new and changing threats. The production of marijuana will increasingly be found on private land versus public land (e.g., National Forests), and Mexican DTOs will continue to establish marijuana growing operations in the Appalachia HIDTA area. And although methamphetamine/clandestine labs, dumpsites, and chemical/glassware seizures have leveled off, methamphetamine trafficking and abuse have resurged and will remain a significant threat. Clandestine manufacturers have already adapted to the legislative restrictions on the purchases of chemical precursors, such as pseudoephedrine. Law enforcement operations and prescription drug monitoring programs have made significant inroads toward diminishing the effect of pain medication diversion in the Appalachia HIDTA, but the diversion and abuse of controlled pharmaceutical drugs, particularly oxycodone from pain clinics in Florida and the Southeast United States, and hydrocodone will continue to pose a significant threat to the region.

## INTELLIGENCE INITIATIVES

The AHIDTA Intelligence and Investigative Support Center (IISC) is located in Kentucky, with supporting components in Tennessee and West Virginia. The IISC assists task force teams by providing a wide range of intelligence services and products, such as event and subject deconfliction services for officer safety and enhanced intelligence production; strategic intelligence for refined targeting and officer resource allocation; in-service analytical intelligence training; telephone toll analysis; financial analysis; threat assessments; strategic reports and organizational studies; informant/defendant debriefings; cultivating new sources of information; post-seizure and search warrant analyses; support for arrest operations; briefings for visitors to the AHIDTA; and support for trial preparations. Additionally, the IISC prepares scheduled and one-time intelligence products, assists in the preparation of management reports, coordinates the sharing and dissemination of intelligence data and information, and responds to requests for information from Federal, state, and local entities.

## TASK FORCES OPERATING IN THE HIDTA REGION

The table below highlights the Federally-funded drug enforcement task forces operating in the HIDTA region. Multiple HIDTA task forces may make up an overarching HIDTA enforcement or investigative initiative.

| TASK FORCES | LOCATIONS |
|---|---|
| Bowling Green Warren County Drug Task Force (HIDTA) | Bowling Green, KY |
| Second Judicial Drug and Violent Crime Task Force | Blountville, TN |
| West Virginia DEA HIDTA Task Force (HIDTA) | Charleston, WV |
| Metropolitan Drug Enforcement Network Team (HIDTA) | Charleston, WV |
| Tennessee Methamphetamine Task Force | Chattanooga, TN |
| DEA South Tennessee Task Force (HIDTA) | Chattanooga, TN |
| Columbia Area Drug Task Force (HIDTA) | Columbia, KY |
| Thirteenth Judicial Drug and Violent Crime Task Force | Cookeville, TN |
| TBI Middle Tennessee Task Force (HIDTA) | Cookeville, TN |
| Third Judicial Drug and Violent Crime Task Force | Greeneville, TN |
| Fifteenth Judicial Drug and Violent Crime Task Force | Hartsville, TN |
| Kentucky River Task Force (Operation UNITE) | Hazard, KY |
| Hazard Investigative Initiative (HIDTA) | Hazard, KY |
| Huntington Violent Crimes & Drug Task Force (HIDTA) | Huntington, WV |
| Eighth Judicial Drug and Violent Crime Task Force | Jacksboro, TN |
| Twelfth Judicial Drug and Violent Crime Task Force | Jasper, TN |
| First Judicial Drug and Violent Crime Task Force | Johnson City, TN |
| DEA Upper East Tennessee Task Force (HIDTA) | Johnson City, TN |
| Ninth Judicial Drug Task Force | Kingston, TN |
| Sixth Judicial Drug Task Force | Knoxville, TN |

| TASK FORCES | LOCATIONS |
|---|---|
| DEA Rocky Top Task Force (HIDTA) | Knoxville, TN |
| FBI Rocky Top Task Force (HIDTA) | Knoxville, TN |
| U.S. 119 Task Force (HIDTA) | Logan, WV |
| DEA London Task Force (HIDTA) | London, KY |
| National Forest Marijuana Investigative Initiative (HIDTA) | London, KY |
| Southeast KY OCDETF/Public Corruption Task Force (HIDTA) | London, KY |
| Cumberland Valley Task Force (Operation UNITE) | London, KY |
| Kentucky Eradication Initiative (HIDTA) | London, KY |
| Appalachia Parcel Interdiction (HIDTA) | Louisville, KY |
| Fourteenth Judicial Drug and Violent Crime Task Force | Manchester, TN |
| Big Sandy Narcotics Task Force | Prestonsburg, KY |
| Fourth Judicial Drug and Violent Crime Task Force | Sevierville, TN |
| Lake Cumberland Area Drug Task Force (HIDTA) | Somerset, KY |
| West Virginia Eradication Initiative (HIDTA) | South Charleston, WV |

## *TASK FORCE COORDINATION*

AHIDTA task force teams coordinate activities and operations with each other, other HIDTAs, and non-HIDTA task force teams and agencies. AHIDTA task force teams have long-standing relationships and frequently interact with each other through United States Attorneys' Law Enforcement Coordinating Committee training events, quarterly HIDTA state committee meetings, HIDTA conferences, annual director reviews, and other specialized training events in all three States. These venues facilitate the exchange of information and lead to working relationships that would not exist without the AHIDTA's outreach efforts. HIDTA and OCDETF goals are congruent, and HIDTA cases frequently lead to OCDETF designation.

The AHIDTA mandates its task force teams and encourages agencies to participate in target and subject deconfliction measures. This protects officers and helps agencies coordinate multiple drug investigation activities and prevents operational conflicts and safety mishaps. The AHIDTA encourages agencies that are located inside and outside of the designated area to use the Secure Automated Fast Event Tracking Network (SAFETNet), and the AHIDTA provides free training and access through the IISC. To date, more than 230 law enforcement agencies in Kentucky, Tennessee, and West Virginia, located inside and outside of the HIDTA-designated area, participate in the deconfliction program.

The AHIDTA IISC also coordinates the sharing of information for all AHIDTA initiatives, as well as other task forces, and law enforcement agencies inside and outside the HIDTA-designated areas. The IISC allows initiatives and other participants to share information concerning organizational structures of DTOs, transportation and distribution modes of operation, and other intelligence-related matters. The IISC shares intelligence with task force initiatives and law enforcement agencies received from the El Paso Intelligence Center (EPIC), the Regional Organized Crime Information Center, other HIDTAs, and other sources including other law enforcement agencies and task forces outside the Appalachia HIDTA.

## HIDTA EVALUATION

The AHIDTA task force initiatives conducted a number of investigations that are indicative of a significant positive change on drug trafficking in the region and the Nation. The investigations succeeded because of cooperation and information sharing among HIDTA member agencies, task forces and other HIDTAs, agencies and task force initiatives in other jurisdictions. The AHIDTA provided performance data to show the impact of its expenditures on identified drug trafficking threats. The data indicate that these efforts contributed to significant reductions in marijuana cultivation by local growers. Specifically, in 2009, the AHIDTA disrupted or dismantled 82 DTOs. Its law enforcement initiatives successfully disrupted and/or dismantled 85 percent of the 97 DTOs they expected to disrupt or dismantle in 2009. The 82 DTOs disrupted and/or dismantled represent 33 percent of the 250 under investigation by AHIDTA law enforcement initiatives. Of the DTOs under investigation, 173 (69 percent) operated in multiple states beyond the Appalachia HIDTA region or were involved in international operations.

## Atlanta HIDTA – Designated in 1995
## Executive Director – Jack Killorin

### *PURPOSE AND GOALS*

The mission of the Atlanta HIDTA is to measurably and accountably:

- Disrupt and dismantle drug trafficking and money laundering organizations through intelligence-driven multi-jurisdictional operations;
- Improve the safety and effectiveness of law enforcement operations; and
- Improve communication and information sharing among criminal justice, drug prevention, and drug treatment professionals in support of ONDCP objectives.

### *STRATEGY*

The Atlanta HIDTA has implemented a three-part Strategy (geographical, functional, and operational) to focus on upper and mid-level drug trafficking and money laundering organizations. Atlanta HIDTA employs state-of-the-art intelligence and telecommunications technology in addition to more traditional techniques to target investigations. Atlanta HIDTA fosters collaborative working relationships among over 40 Federal, state, and local investigative and prosecuting agencies conducting intelligence-driven operations against major drug trafficking organizations (DTOs)/money laundering organizations (MLOs).

### *LOCATION*

Atlanta HIDTA's Operations Center is in Atlanta, Georgia. As of the last quarter of 2010, Atlanta HIDTA included the following jurisdictions and enforcement initiatives in two states:

In Georgia there are two initiatives:
1) Metro Initiative, which includes the City of Atlanta, Hartsfield-Jackson Atlanta International Airport, and Fulton, Cobb, Gwinnett, Barrow, Bartow, Cherokee, Clayton, Douglas, Fayette, Forsyth, and Henry counties.
2) DeKalb Initiative, which includes DeKalb County.

In North Carolina there are four initiatives:
1) Triangle Initiative, based in Raleigh, which includes Durham, Johnston, Wake, Wayne, and Wilson Counties.
2) Triad Initiative, based in Greensboro, which includes Randolph, Guilford and Alamance Counties.
3) Piedmont Initiative, based in Charlotte, which includes Mecklenburg, Gaston, and Union Counties.
4) Asheville Initiative, which includes Buncombe, McDowell, and Henderson Counties.

## INITIATIVES

The Atlanta HIDTA has 11 initiatives, which include 1 management, 1 support (training), 1 prevention, 1 intelligence, and 7 investigation/interdiction/prosecution (the 6 enforcement/ interdiction initiatives listed above plus 1 prosecution initiative). In FY 2010, the Atlanta HIDTA received discretionary funds for prevention and highway enforcement/interdiction.

## SHORT-TERM OBJECTIVES

| YEAR | DTOs/MLOs Expected to be Disrupted/ Dismantled | Target Return on Investment: Assets | Target Return on Investment: Drugs | Number of Deconflictions Expected to be Submitted | Number of Investigations Expected to be Provided Analytical Support | Number of Initiative Leads Expected to be Referred |
|------|------|------|------|------|------|------|
| 2010 | 48 | $2 | $9 | 1,600 | 200 | 170 |

## THREAT ASSESSMENT

In 2008, Atlanta HIDTA expanded from 4 counties in the metropolitan Atlanta area to 12, and 5 added counties in the Research Triangle of North Carolina. In 2009, three counties in the Greensboro, North Carolina, area were added. In August 2010, 6 western North Carolina counties were added, for a total of 14 North Carolina counties.

The Atlanta HIDTA region is a major distribution center for DTOs, particularly Mexican DTOs, and their associated MLOs that supply the eastern United States. Interstate 85 is the major artery for this distribution. DTOs/MLOs distribute illicit drugs from the Atlanta HIDTA territories to eastern cities including Baltimore, Maryland; Boston, Massachusetts; Cincinnati and Columbus, Ohio; Columbia, South Carolina; Gainesville, Orlando, and Pensacola, Florida; Indianapolis, Indiana; Knoxville, Tennessee; Louisville, Kentucky; and Norfolk, Virginia. The supply lines reach as far as Detroit, Michigan, and New York City, New York.

## INTELLIGENCE INITIATIVES

Atlanta HIDTA's Intelligence and Investigative Support Center (IISC) has been part of Atlanta HIDTA since its founding in 1995. The IISC is located at Atlanta HIDTA's Operations Center and is supervised by a DEA Supervisory Intelligence Analyst. The IISC provides analytical intelligence (toll, link and document analyses, interviews/debriefings, administrative subpoenas, subpoena requests, profiles of suspects, database checks, etc.) and information management support to Atlanta HIDTA's law enforcement initiatives and to Domestic Highway Enforcement. The IISC also provides operational subject, case, and event deconfliction and investigative coordination for 102 Federal, state, and local law enforcement agencies. Policies guiding structure, services, security clearance access and linkage with other HIDTAs and Federal, state, and local databases are in conformance with the General Counterdrug Intelligence Plan and ONDCP policy guidance and with those of the Atlanta HIDTA Executive Board. The Atlanta Metro HIDTA's IISC is linked through RISSNET to all HIDTA programs (task force and intelligence centers) employing this virtual private network.

## *TASK FORCES OPERATING IN THE HIDTA REGION*

The table below highlights the Federally-funded drug enforcement task forces operating in the HIDTA region. Multiple HIDTA task forces may make up an overarching HIDTA enforcement or investigative initiative.

| TASK FORCES | LOCATIONS |
|---|---|
| Metro Task Force (HIDTA) | Atlanta, GA |
| DeKalb Task Force (HIDTA) | Decatur, GA |
| Triangle Initiative (HIDTA) | Durham, NC |
| Triad Initiative (HIDTA) | Greensboro, NC |
| Piedmont Initiative (HIDTA) | Charlotte, NC |
| DEA Task Force (DEA) | Charlotte, NC |
| Asheville Initiative (HIDTA) | Asheville, NC |
| Tactical Diversion Squad (DEA) | Atlanta, GA |
| West Metro Regional Drug Enforcement Office (Byrne/JAG) | Carrollton, GA |
| OCDETF Strike Force (OCDETF/DOJ) | Atlanta, GA |

## *TASK FORCE COORDINATION*

There are significant formal and informal coordination mechanisms among all relevant task forces in the Atlanta HIDTA area, regardless of Federal funding. Many of these mechanisms are enhanced or enabled by the Atlanta HIDTA. Informally, participants know each other from operational contacts, periodic meetings, and HIDTA/OCDETF/Law Enforcement Coordinating Committee-sponsored training and conferences. Agencies participating in one task force often have officers assigned to other task forces, thereby promoting information exchange and coordination. HIDTA-sponsored deconfliction services promote event and target coordination among task forces and agencies. Executives from agencies with personnel participating in HIDTA initiatives serve on the HIDTA Executive Board, thereby promoting information exchange and coordination. The Atlanta HIDTA task force groups exchange information regularly with narcotics units and task forces in the area where active cases are under investigation and with area units; and task forces regularly contact the IISC to develop or coordinate leads. The IISC publishes and distributes intelligence bulletins to the area narcotics investigation units and task forces.

All area task forces are interviewed by the Atlanta HIDTA IISC in preparing the required annual Threat Assessment. This information is then shared with the agencies interviewed and with the Atlanta HIDTA Executive Board. The Executive Board is comprised of the heads of the participating investigative and prosecutorial agencies in the HIDTA. In addition, area narcotics enforcement units attend periodic conferences and drug unit commander meetings, including those sponsored by the Atlanta HIDTA and OCDETF.

## HIDTA EVALUATION

The Atlanta HIDTA's area of operations encompasses the primary as well as many secondary distribution hubs for DTOs/MLOs operating in the eastern part of the United States. Over the past several years, this activity has spread throughout north Georgia and into central and western North Carolina. To target this threat, the HIDTA expanded between 2008 and 2010, to include 14 counties in North Carolina and 12 counties in Georgia.

In 2009, the Atlanta HIDTA disrupted or dismantled 57 DTOs/MLOs, compared to 51 the prior year, surpassing its target objective of 40 DTOs. The increase in DTOs/MLOs dismantled and disrupted is due to the geographical expansion of the HIDTA and internal restructuring to enhance investigative efforts. The HIDTA's ROI increased 27 percent from $19.10 in cash, assets, and drugs seized for every HIDTA dollar spent in 2008 to $24.21 in 2009. Domestic Highway Enforcement contributed significantly by seizing over $40 million in assets and drugs (wholesale value).

Atlanta HIDTA's Intelligence Support Center provided analytical support to over 1,300 investigations in 2009. Improvements in the Center's electronic/telecommunications surveillance capabilities in 2009 increased its ability to provide analytical support.

To improve the safety and effectiveness of law enforcement, Atlanta HIDTA's training initiative provided 44,195 hours of training to sworn officers and staff from over 300 different law enforcement agencies. Also, the deconfliction staff trains law enforcement throughout the state, resulting in deconflictions increasing from 1,008 in 2007 to 4,101 in 2009.

To improve communication between law enforcement, treatment providers, and drug demand reduction professionals, the Atlanta HIDTA hosts an annual prevention conference that is a unique opportunity for these professionals to "compare notes" and learn from one another. Each year, the HIDTA conducts a survey of treatment professionals in its area of operation focused on the drugs of abuse across the demographics of persons seeking treatment. During the conference, this is compared with information developed by law enforcement concerning illicit trafficking. The conference is highly regarded because it reveals developing trends, changes, or anomalies that better prepare the community to set priorities, prepare for coming issues, and build relationships across the community involved with drug abuse.

# Central Florida HIDTA – Designated in 1998
## Executive Director – William Fernandez

## *PURPOSE AND GOALS*

The mission of the Central Florida HIDTA (CF HIDTA) is to improve the quality of life in Central Florida by reducing drug availability and crime through the effective disruption and dismantling of DTOs impacting Central Florida and other areas of the United States.

## *STRATEGY*

The CF HIDTA will continue to foster cooperative and effective working relationships between the Office of the U.S. Attorney, eight Federal agencies, and eight state and local agencies to achieve the common goals of dismantling or disrupting DTOs and reducing the demand for drugs.

## *LOCATION*

The CF HIDTA operates out of Sanford, Florida. It encompasses a seven-county area including Pinellas, Hillsborough, Polk, Osceola, Orange, Seminole, and Volusia Counties.

## *INITIATIVES*

The CF HIDTA has 15 initiatives, which include 1 management, 1 training support, 1 prevention, 1 intelligence, and 11 investigation/investigation/interdiction initiatives.

## *SHORT-TERM OBJECTIVES*

| YEAR | DTOs Expected to be Disrupted/ Dismantled | Target Return on Investment: Assets | Target Return on Investment: Drugs | Number of Deconflictions Expected to be Submitted | Number of Investigations Expected to be Provided Analytical Support | Number of Initiative Leads Expected to be Referred |
|------|------|------|------|------|------|------|
| 2010 | 44 | $5 | $25.35 | 1,810 | 105 | 682 |

## *THREAT ASSESSMENT*

The passage of the Combat Methamphetamine Epidemic Act of 2005 (Title VII of P.L. 109-177) had the immediate positive impact of reducing the number of clandestine laboratories encountered by the CF HIDTA. However, smurfing[8] has since reversed the trend, and the number of laboratories encountered is expected to continue to increase. Mexican DTOs were first observed trafficking methamphetamine in the CF HIDTA region in 2007, and it is expected that their market share will increase. Cocaine will continue to be the primary drug problem, with prescription drug diversion and abuse following closely behind. Drug-related violence will

---

[8] "smurfing" refers to the action of going from store-to-store purchasing the maximum limit allowable under the law of pseudoephedrine and ephedrine products and then pooling these products, which will then be provided to a meth producer.

continue to increase, continuing a disturbing trend. Indoor marijuana grow houses will continue to proliferate in Central Florida, due to the enormous profits which can be gained from this activity. Rogue pain clinics that illegally dispense medications are a growing threat in the region.

## *INTELLIGENCE INITIATIVES*

The ONDCP funds the Central Florida Intelligence and Investigative Support Center (CFIISC) as an initiative of the CF HIDTA. The CFIISC was created with the designation of the HIDTA in 1998 to provide co-located multi-agency intelligence support to regional drug law enforcement agencies to enhance their ability to dismantle and disrupt drug trafficking organizations.

The mission of the CFIISC is to actively collect, analyze, and disseminate information on the composition, scope, and dynamics of money laundering, drug trafficking, distribution, and drug-related violent crime organizations; and to provide clarity and an understanding of the organized criminal elements operating throughout Central Florida. The CFIISC provides deconfliction services to 72 Federal, state, and local law enforcement agencies.

The CFIISC serves as the central processing hub of information in support of effective investigative enforcement efforts to reduce drug trafficking, money laundering, and drug-related violent criminal activity affecting Central Florida and other areas of the United States.

The success of the CFIISC is measured through assessments of the previously mentioned investigative efforts and the extent to which major and secondary organizations involved in these criminal activities have been disrupted or dismantled. Additional assessments are made through the coordinated and cooperative efforts of Federal, state, and local law enforcement agencies to address the specific criminal activity.

## *TASK FORCES OPERATING IN THE HIDTA REGION*

The table below highlights the Federally-funded drug enforcement task forces operating in the HIDTA region. Multiple HIDTA task forces may make up an overarching HIDTA enforcement or investigative initiative.

| TASK FORCES | LOCATIONS |
|---|---|
| Pinellas County (HIDTA) | Largo |
| Colombian/South American DTO (HIDTA) | Tampa |
| DEA HIDTA Methamphetamine Task Force (HIDTA) | Tampa |
| Polk County HIDTA Task Force (HIDTA) | Bartow |
| DEA Tampa State and Local Task Force (DEA) | Tampa |
| Tactical Diversion Squad (DEA) | Tampa |
| DEA Orlando State and Local Task Force (DEA) | Orlando |
| Osceola County Investigative Bureau (HIDTA) | Kissimmee |
| Metropolitan Bureau Of Investigation (HIDTA) | Orlando |
| IRS/Secret Service Financial Crimes Task Force (IRS) | Orlando |

| TASK FORCES | LOCATIONS |
|---|---|
| ICE Financial Money Laundering Task Force (ICE) | Orlando |
| City County Investigative Bureau (HIDTA) | Sanford |
| DEA HIDTA Heroin Task Force (HIDTA) | Heathrow |
| DEA Mex/Poly Task Force (HIDTA) | Heathrow |
| US Marshals Fugitive Apprehension Strike Team, East/West (HIDTA) | Orlando/Tampa |
| Volusia Bureau of Investigation (HIDTA) | Daytona |

## *TASK FORCE COORDINATION*

The CF HIDTA funds 10 drug task forces and 1 fugitive apprehension task force. The CF HIDTA is overseen by a balanced (Federal/state and local) Executive Board made up of participating law enforcement officials. All task forces utilize the CFIISC for deconfliction of cases, subjects, and activities. All law enforcement agencies in the area are encouraged to utilize the CFIISC for information sharing and deconfliction.

CF HIDTA task forces meet and are evaluated quarterly. They routinely coordinate activities with other regional task forces, as well as other HIDTA task forces nationwide. All HIDTA task forces are asked to be vigilant in obtaining and sharing information relating to national security. CF HIDTA task forces strive to meet an ever-changing drug threat through the re-direction of their efforts when needed. The annual Threat Assessment serves as a guideline when a change in focus is needed, and is shared with other regional task forces.

## *HIDTA EVALUATION*

Although the CF HIDTA will continue to focus its primary investigative efforts on organizations trafficking cocaine and other traditional drug threats, it has taken positive steps to address an increased threat of indoor marijuana cultivation, an increase in methamphetamine labs, and pharmaceutical diversion in its region.

In 2009, the CF HIDTA disrupted or dismantled 36 DTOs, compared to 50 the prior year. The decrease in the number of DTOs disrupted or dismantled is due to several long-term and complex investigations which were closed in 2010. A preliminary review of CF HIDTA performance data for 2010 indicates the HIDTA exceeded its 2010 DTO targets. The CF HIDTA continues to achieve an excellent return on investment of approximately $30 for every dollar spent on investigations.

# Central Valley California HIDTA – Designated in 1999
## Executive Director – William Ruzzamenti

## PURPOSE AND GOALS

The mission of the Central Valley California HIDTA (CVC HIDTA) is to reduce the manufacture or cultivation, trafficking, and distribution of marijuana, methamphetamine, precursor chemicals, and other dangerous drugs by attacking and dismantling the large-scale and often violent organizations responsible through the implementation of cooperative and innovative strategies. The goals of the CVC HIDTA are to reduce drug availability by disrupting and dismantling DTOs, and to improve the efficiency and effectiveness of the region's law enforcement organizations.

## STRATEGY

The CVC HIDTA applies traditional law enforcement methodologies and techniques that have proved effective against DTOs. Nearly 150 Federal, state, county, and city law enforcement members representing 39 agencies comprise the CVC HIDTA initiatives. The integration and coordination of task force efforts are supported by a network of criminal intelligence analysts and integrated intelligence centers.

## LOCATION

The CVC HIDTA operates out of Sacramento, California. The ten counties that comprise the CVC HIDTA region include Kern, Kings, Madera, Merced, Shasta, Stanislaus, San Joaquin, Fresno, Tulare, and Sacramento.

## INITIATIVES

The CVC HIDTA has 16 initiatives, which include 1 management; 1 training; 2 intelligence and 12 investigation and highway enforcement initiatives.

## SHORT-TERM OBJECTIVES

| YEAR | DTOs Expected to be Disrupted/ Dismantled | Target Return on Investment: Assets | Target Return on Investment: Drugs | Number of Deconflictions Expected to be Submitted | Number of Investigations Expected to be Provided Analytical Support | Number of Initiative Leads Expected to be Referred |
|------|------|------|------|------|------|------|
| 2010 | 88 | $2.21 | $4,000 | 9,900 | 2,111 | 103 |

## THREAT ASSESSMENT

The CVC HIDTA's greatest drug problems are related to methamphetamine, marijuana, cocaine, and heroin. The 10-county region is a leading producer of outdoor- and indoor-grown sensimilla marijuana and methamphetamine. Outdoor marijuana growing usually takes place in national forests and remote public lands. Large cannabis plots are usually tended by illegal aliens, many of whom are armed. They pose a grave danger to hikers, campers, and forest workers. In 2009, approximately 7.5 million marijuana plants were eradicated in the state; this amounted to 70 percent of the Nation's total marijuana eradication. There were over 1.3 million cannabis plants eradicated in CVC HIDTA counties alone. Organized bands of "smurfers" roam the region purchasing thousands of pseudoephedrine tablets from pharmacies.[9] These are sold to methamphetamine laboratory operators. The CVC HIDTA dismantled 6 superlabs in 2009, nearly half of the total for California (13). A superlab is defined as a lab that is capable of producing more than ten pounds of methamphetamine in a single cycle.

This area is a national drug production and transshipment hub. According to intelligence reports, Mexico-based DTOs produce and/or smuggle into the Central Valley of California heroin, cocaine, marijuana, and methamphetamine for transportation to domestic drug markets. Asian-centric DTOs produce marijuana, and distribute ecstasy around the country. Over 3 tons of marijuana that originated in California was seized on the Nation's highways during 2009, according to the National Seizure System. HIDTA initiatives report the vast majority of all DTOs operating in the Central Valley HIDTA counties are comprised of foreign nationals. DTOs comprised of individuals of Vietnamese descent operated the indoor grow houses which were eradicated in Sacramento, Elk Grove, and surrounding communities during 2009.

## INTELLIGENCE INITIATIVES

The IISC's mission of providing tactical and strategic intelligence services to the HIDTA participating agencies and Executive Board is accomplished under the leadership of a DEA Supervisor and California DOJ managers. The IISC operates from a central intelligence office in Sacramento, and also places analysts in other offices in Fresno, Bakersfield, Modesto, and Sacramento. Decentralization of services is needed because the HIDTA initiatives span a geographic area of over 300 miles. Critical event deconfliction services for the CVC HIDTA initiatives are provided by the Western States Information Network (WSIN). The HIDTA's analysts are supplemented with intelligence analysts from the California National Guard.

The Marijuana Intelligence Fusion Center began in 2005 and has become an essential function of the CVC HIDTA's intelligence subsystem. The mission of the Fusion Center is to provide tactical and strategic intelligence support to drug investigations; to collect and analyze intelligence and investigative information about marijuana producing DTOs; to identify the structure, membership, interrelationships, and operations of DTOs; and to provide this intelligence and information to enforcement agency investigators and managers.

---

[9] "smurfers": numerous individuals going from store to store purchasing the maximum limit of pseudoephedrine and ephedrine products at each store and then pooling their purchases.

## TASK FORCES OPERATING IN THE HIDTA REGION

The table below highlights the Federally-funded drug enforcement task forces operating in the HIDTA region. Multiple HIDTA task forces may make up an overarching HIDTA enforcement or investigative initiative.

| TASK FORCES | LOCATIONS |
|---|---|
| Fresno Area Meth Task Force (HIDTA) | Fresno County |
| Fresno Area Surveillance Team (HIDTA) | Fresno County |
| Merced Mariposa Task Force (HIDTA) | Merced County |
| Sacramento Area Intelligence Narcotic Task Force (HIDTA) | Sacramento County |
| Stanislaus San Joaquin Meth Task Force (HIDTA) | Stanislaus |
| Southern Tri-County Drug Task Force (HIDTA) | Kern County |
| Central Valley Marijuana Investigative Team (HIDTA) | Fresno County |
| Northern States Marijuana Investigative Team (HIDTA) | Shasta County |
| Mountain and Valley Marijuana Investigative Team (HIDTA) | Sacramento County |
| Shasta Marijuana Eradication Team (HIDTA) | Shasta County |
| Shasta Domestic Highway Enforcement (HIDTA) | Shasta County |
| Shasta Interagency Narcotics Task Force (JAG-Byrne) | Shasta County |
| Fresno Domestic Highway Enforcement (HIDTA) | Fresno County |
| Joint Fugitive Task Force (HIDTA) | Fresno County |
| IISC (HIDTA) | Sacramento County |
| Marijuana Intelligence Fusion Center (HIDTA) | Sacramento County |
| DEA Multi-agency Drug Task Force | Sacramento |
| Tactical Diversion Squad (DEA) | Sacramento |
| FBI Operation Safe Streets Task Force | Redding |
| FBI Operation Safe Streets Task Force | Sacramento |
| FBI Operation Safe Streets Task Force | Stockton |
| FBI Operation Safe Streets Task Force | Modesto |
| FBI Operation Safe Streets Task Force | Bakersfield |
| Madera Narcotics Enforcement Team (Byrne Grant) | Madera |
| Merced Multi-Agency Narcotics Enforcement Team (Byrne Grant) | Merced |
| Kings County Narcotics Task Force (Byrne Grant) | Hanford |

## TASK FORCE COORDINATION

CVC HIDTA task forces routinely coordinate their investigations and tactical deployments when their operations enter into an adjoining jurisdiction, via in-person communications or through the WSIN deconfliction system. Using this multi-state deconfliction system is essential to task force operations. Investigative subjects and critical/tactical events are posted in WSIN as routine operating procedures. Coordination is generally achieved through information sharing, leveraging of resources, sharing of analytical resources, pooling of analysts, shared computer networks and software, and enhanced training opportunities. Up to 39 percent of the case/subject entries have been found to be already on record and of interest to other investigators or agencies. CVC HIDTA initiatives coordinate with other HIDTAs regarding cross-country transportation investigations and meet quarterly to share investigative information.

CVC HIDTA initiatives are comprised of multi-jurisdictional agencies at the local, state, and Federal level. These agencies include city police departments, county sheriff's offices, the U.S. Marshals Service, the Bureau of Land Management, the National Guard, DEA, FBI, California Bureau of Narcotics Enforcement, California Bureau of Investigation and Intelligence, the U.S. Forest Service, and the National Park Service. Information sharing between HIDTA initiatives takes place at regularly scheduled meetings where investigative activity is discussed with the team commanders.

The CVC HIDTA Executive Board has members from the local, state and Federal agencies. Local sheriff offices and police departments, the IRS, FBI, ICE, DEA, National Park Service, ATF, U.S. Attorneys, and the U.S. Marshals Service are all represented. The Executive Board meets on a regular basis to evaluate funding, training, and effectiveness of the initiatives. The Executive Board is continually kept apprised of changing threats and needs of the area enabling them to disseminate that information among their own agencies. The board members also bring pertinent information from their agencies to the HIDTA.

Training programs are open to all agencies in the region. Terrorism-related information programs have alerted regional agencies and drug task forces of the importance of sharing information with the JTTF. Executive level discussions are in-process concerning co-locating the HIDTA's intelligence groups with the regional JTTF assessment center. The HIDTA's incoming information is researched through the files of the EPIC database, which includes DHS records.

## HIDTA EVALUATION

ONDCP will continue to work with the CVC HIDTA to appropriately focus its resources against methamphetamine as well as other drugs such as marijuana. To ensure compliance with ONDCP and HIDTA regulations, the CVC HIDTA conducts an annual inspection of its initiatives.

In 2009, the HIDTA disrupted or dismantled 88 DTOs and seized drugs with a value of over $ 26.8 billion. The majority of this seizure value is attributed to the marijuana eradicated by CVC HIDTA initiatives.

# Chicago HIDTA – Designated in 1995
## Executive Director – Kurt Schmid

### PURPOSE AND GOALS

The mission of the Chicago HIDTA is to enhance and coordinate drug control efforts among Federal, state, and local law enforcement agencies in its geographic area of responsibility, the surrounding region, and other affected areas of the country.

### STRATEGY

The Chicago HIDTA continues to foster cooperative and effective working relationships among Federal, state, and local law enforcement agencies in order to eliminate or reduce drug trafficking and its harmful consequences. This includes coordinated efforts to reduce the production, manufacturing, distribution, transportation, and chronic use of illegal drugs, as well as the attendant money laundering of drug proceeds.

### LOCATION

The Chicago HIDTA operates out of Chicago, Illinois. It encompasses four counties in the State of Illinois: Cook, (City of Chicago), Grundy, Kendall, and Will.

### INITIATIVES

The Chicago HIDTA has 12 initiatives, which include 1 Management, 1Training, 1 Intelligence, and 9 Investigation/Interdiction initiatives.

### SHORT-TERM OBJECTIVES

| YEAR | DTOs Expected to be Disrupted/ Dismantled | Target Return on Investment: Assets | Target Return on Investment: Drugs | Number of Deconflictions Expected to be Submitted | Number of Investigations Expected to be Provided Analytical Support | Number of Initiative Leads Expected to be Referred |
|------|------|------|------|------|------|------|
| 2010 | 76 | $4 | $7 | 15,700 | 70 | 438 |

### THREAT ASSESSMENT

Chicago is not only one of the largest consumer markets for cocaine, heroin, marijuana, and other illicit drugs, but it also serves as a national-level transshipment hub and distribution center for these drugs to other areas of the country. The distribution and abuse of cocaine, followed by heroin and marijuana, are the primary drug threats in the Chicago HIDTA region. Intelligence and ongoing cases indicate that large quantities of these drugs are transported to the area by Mexican DTOs and criminal groups, principally from locations along the Southwest border. In 2009, Chicago HIDTA initiatives reported the seizure of 1,116 kilograms of cocaine, 143 kilograms of heroin, and 10,678 kilograms of marijuana. Mexican DTOs and criminal groups dominate the wholesale transportation and distribution of cocaine, heroin, and marijuana; they typically obtain these drugs directly from DTOs operating in Mexico and provide them to street gang leaders in the region for retail-level distribution. Street gangs are the primary retail distributors of illicit drugs. These gangs regularly engage in violent criminal activities to protect their drug supplies, distribution territories, and illicit drug proceeds. Street gangs are continuing their incursion into outlying areas and are becoming increasingly problematic for suburban law enforcement. In addition, the Chicago metropolitan area has one of the highest rates of drug-use prevalence in the United States. The most recent data available from the Illinois Department of Human Services, Office of Alcoholism and Substance Abuse (DASA), indicates that the HIDTA region accounted for almost half (53.6 percent) of all treatment provider services received by patients in Illinois in 2009.

## *INTELLIGENCE INITIATIVES*

The mission of the Chicago HIDTA IISC is to facilitate the interaction and sharing of information to support multi-agency efforts to further drug-related and/or criminal investigations. The operational mission of the IISC is to provide actionable, accurate, detailed, and timely tactical, investigative, and strategic criminal intelligence to HIDTA initiatives, HIDTA participating agencies, and other law enforcement agencies as appropriate, enabling a more effective and efficient utilization of valuable investigative resources.

Functions of the ISC include: the collection, compilation, and analysis of information regarding illicit drug and associated criminal activities, the dissemination and exchange of value-added counter drug intelligence products, a regional pointer event and target deconfliction system, an "all source" counterdrug information gateway accessible to all law enforcement agencies, case and trial support to Federal and state counterdrug and related prosecutions, the coordination of counterdrug and related law enforcement training and technical assistance to law enforcement counterdrug efforts.

The Management Information System (MIS) is a subsystem of the IISC; its mission is to provide the HIDTA enforcement and intelligence initiatives with state-of-the-art resources for intelligence gathering and analysis. These resources include access to relevant information through a myriad of Federal, state, municipal, and public information stores; software for analysis and presentation of case data; custom-built databases for storage and organization of law enforcement data; innovations of analytical methodologies created from MIS staff and analyst collaborations; and wider availability of HIDTA resources via network infrastructure.

## *TASK FORCES OPERATING IN THE HIDTA REGION*

The table below highlights the Federally-funded drug enforcement task forces operating in the HIDTA region. Multiple HIDTA task forces may make up an overarching HIDTA enforcement or investigative initiative.

| TASK FORCES | LOCATIONS |
| --- | --- |
| Joliet Metropolitan Area Narcotics Squad (HIDTA) | Romeoville |
| Intelligence and Investigative Support Center (HIDTA) | Cook County |
| Consolidated Priority Organization Target Initiative Task Force (HIDTA) | Cook County |
| Money Laundering and Financial Crimes Initiative Task Force (HIDTA) | Cook County |
| Package Interdiction Initiative Task Force (HIDTA) | Cook County |

| TASK FORCES | LOCATIONS |
|---|---|
| Regional Drug Trafficking Organization Initiative/Violent Crimes Task Force (HIDTA) | Cook County |
| Street Narcotics and Gangs Initiative Task Force (HIDTA) | Cook County |
| Tri-County Multi-Jurisdictional Counterdrug Enforcement Initiative Task Force (HIDTA) | Cook County |
| Violent Gang Conspiracy Group Initiative Task Force (HIDTA) | Cook County |
| Multi Jurisdictional Financial Enforcement Group Initiative Task Force (HIDTA) | Cook County |
| Domestic Highway Enforcement/Narcotics Interdiction Team (HIDTA) | Cook County |
| Tactical Diversion Squad (DEA) | Chicago |
| Safe Streets Task Force on Gangs – Tactical (FBI) | Cook County |
| Safe Streets Task Force on Gangs – 1 (African American Gangs) (FBI) | Cook County |
| Safe Streets Task Force on Gangs – 2 (Hispanic Gangs) / (FBI) | Cook County |
| Safe Streets Task Force on Gangs / West RA (non-Chicago) (FBI) | Cook County |
| Will County Violent Crimes Task Force (FBI) | Cook County |
| Will County CPAT (Cooperative Police Assistance Team) (FBI) | Cook County |

## TASK FORCE COORDINATION

Five of the above HIDTA-funded initiatives/task forces (the IISC, the Money Laundering and Financial Crimes Initiative Task Force, the Violent Gang Conspiracy Group Initiative Task Force, the Multi Jurisdictional Financial Enforcement Group Initiative Task Force, and the Domestic Highway Enforcement/Narcotics Interdiction Team) are co-located on a single, secure floor in a Chicago office building. The IISC includes analysts from the Cook County Sheriff's Department, DEA, the Chicago Police Department, the FBI, and the Illinois National Guard. This co-location and diversity helps to foster information sharing among law enforcement agencies. All task force initiatives within the Chicago HIDTA are required to cooperate and interact with the IISC. Chicago HIDTA also conducts quarterly information-sharing meetings with initiative supervisors. Timely intelligence bulletins and other relevant regional law enforcement information are shared electronically through an extensive contact list, and intelligence is routinely shared with the Statewide Terrorism and Intelligence Center. Chicago HIDTA initiatives are encouraged to seek OCDETF designation and funding when an investigation is multi-jurisdictional, focuses on an organization involved with drug trafficking and/or a money laundering, and shows a conspiracy.

All HIDTA initiatives and numerous law enforcement agencies in the region are interviewed in preparing the required annual Threat Assessment resulting in correlation and sharing of information. HIDTA-funded initiatives, as well as the Chicago Police Department, are mandated to utilize the Chicago HIDTA SAFETNet target and event deconfliction system. This system is also used by 234 other law enforcement agencies in the region. Chicago also serves as the SAFETNet node for HIDTAs in Milwaukee, WI; Lake County, IN; Cleveland, OH; and the Statewide Terrorism & Intelligence Center in Springfield, Illinois. All HIDTA initiatives/task forces are continually monitored and assessed by the Executive Board utilizing the HIDTA program's PMP system.

FBI task forces regularly use the services of the Chicago HIDTA IISC. The HIDTA region also includes the FBI's Chicago Terrorist Task Force (CTTF), whose mission is to prevent, detect, deter, and investigate attacks perpetrated by domestic and international terrorists in the Northern District of Illinois. Founded in 1981, the CTTF investigates the activities of both international and domestic terrorist organizations. The CTTF also investigates all criminal activities, including the acquisition by terrorists of funds, weapons, explosives, false identifications, and other means.

Additionally, the CTTF works with all Federal, state, and local agencies, as well as the private sector, to establish appropriate responses to terrorist attacks. The CTTF is comprised of Chicago Police Detectives, Illinois State Police Investigators, as well as Agents of the FBI, the U.S. Secret Service, the ATF, the U.S. Customs Service, and the IRS.

## HIDTA EVALUATION

The Chicago HIDTA's area of responsibility constitutes one of the Nation's most active illegal drug distribution centers. Coupled with a severe challenge presented by large and well-organized "street gangs," the Chicago HIDTA has recognized the need to expand its total number of initiatives and to be more inclusive by involving more Federal agencies. It is seeking to enhance its efforts in this area.

The HIDTA Executive Board is more enthusiastically engaged in oversight, allocation of resources, response to emerging threats, and operations than ever before in the HIDTA's history. The Executive Director is aggressively expanding and enhancing the information and intelligence-sharing capabilities of the HIDTA. These two actions will aid the Chicago HIDTA in addressing the multiple threats it faces.

In 2009, the HIDTA disrupted or dismantled 53 DTOs or MLOs. In August, 2009 a lengthy Chicago HIDTA investigation into a DTO responsible for large scale cocaine and heroin distribution resulted in the indictment of 36 defendants in the United States and Mexico. "Operation Buzzkill" was "the most significant drug importation conspiracy ever charged in Chicago," according to Patrick Fitzgerald, U.S. Attorney for the Northern District of Illinois. The seizures in this investigation totaled 2061 kilograms of cocaine, 411 pounds of methamphetamine, 58.5 kilograms of heroin, $22,352,701, 25 properties, 27 vehicles, 22 weapons, and miscellaneous jewelry and electronics. Prosecutors are also seeking the forfeiture of up to $1.8 billion in drug proceeds.

# Gulf Coast HIDTA – Designated in 1996
## Executive Director – Tony Soto

### PURPOSE AND GOALS

The specific mission of the Gulf Coast HIDTA is to reduce illicit drug availability and its harmful consequences within its designated areas by creating and maintaining intelligence-driven task forces, and supporting infrastructure designed to target, disrupt, and eliminate DTOs impacting the region and beyond.

### STRATEGY

The Gulf Coast HIDTA works to promote an effective working relationship among and between the GC HIDTA law enforcement initiatives by designing and deploying an infrastructure that fosters information sharing and ensures a coordinated response to the drug threat, as well as realizes an environment through which the participating Federal and state/local agencies may achieve the goals of disrupting and dismantling DTOs and reducing the demand for drugs by focusing on specific drug threat elements unique to their respective areas.

### LOCATION

The Gulf Coast HIDTA operates out of Metairie, Louisiana. It encompasses the following counties in five states:

- Alabama—Baldwin, Jefferson, Madison, Mobile, Montgomery, and Morgan;
- Arkansas—Benton, Jefferson, Pulaski, and Washington;
- Louisiana—Bossier, Caddo, Calcasieu, East Baton Rouge, Jefferson, Lafayette, Orleans, and Ouachita Parishes;
- Mississippi—Hancock, Harrison, Hinds, Jackson, Lafayette, Madison, and Rankin; and
- Tennessee—Shelby

### INITIATIVES

The GC HIDTA has 30 initiatives, which include 1 management, 1 training, 2 intelligence, and 26 investigation/interdiction initiatives.

### SHORT-TERM OBJECTIVES

| YEAR | DTOs Expected to be Disrupted/ Dismantled | Target Return on Investment: Assets | Target Return on Investment: Drugs | Number of Deconflictions Expected to be Submitted | Number of Investigations Expected to be Provided Analytical Support | Number of Initiative Leads Expected to be Referred |
|---|---|---|---|---|---|---|
| 2010 | 238 | $6.48 | $15.63 | 3,400 | 11,225 | 1,536 |

The Gulf Coast HIDTA is a partner/participant in the Blue Lightning Operation Center (BLOC), a U.S. Immigrations and Customs Enforcement program that provides real-time tactical intelligence and information to Federal, state and local law enforcement engaged in drug law enforcement and interdiction throughout the eight states of Louisiana, Mississippi, Alabama, Arkansas, Georgia, North Carolina, South Carolina, and Tennessee.

## *THREAT ASSESSMENT*

The Gulf Coast HIDTA is a geographically diverse area consisting of 26 HIDTA-designated counties/parishes in the States of Alabama, Arkansas, Louisiana, Mississippi, and Tennessee. The drug which continues to pose the greatest threat in the GC HIDTA is cocaine, along with its derivative, crack. Law enforcement intelligence indicates that cocaine/crack is transported into the Gulf Coast HIDTA by Mexican poly-DTOs and subsequently distributed by local drug-trafficking groups. Methamphetamine is ranked, overall, as the second-most serious threat. In Arkansas and Mississippi, methamphetamine surpasses cocaine/crack as the primary threat. Each state has enacted and begun enforcement of provisions designed to regulate the sale of methamphetamine precursors. Significantly, Mississippi enacted House Bill (HB) 512 in July 2010, designating ephedrine and pseudoephedrine Schedule III drugs. Consequently, prescriptions are required for all medications containing these methamphetamine precursors.

Diverted pharmaceuticals obtained through internationally-based Internet pharmacies, Mexican DTOs, and pain management clinics remain a significant threat across the Gulf Coast HIDTA. Overdose deaths and injuries from oxycodone, methadone, and their combination with other drugs, such as Soma, remain high and, in some cases, surpass those of street drugs such as heroin. Violent crime continues to impact the safety and quality of life of the citizens in the Gulf Coast HIDTA. Violent drug trafficking groups have returned to the storm-ravaged areas of Louisiana and Mississippi, leading to a series of violent crimes and related social problems. A 2009 survey found that 20 percent of the 25 most dangerous metropolitan areas of the United States are located in the Gulf Coast HIDTA.

## *INTELLIGENCE INITIATIVES*

The mission of the Investigative Support Network (ISN) is to implement the Gulf Coast HIDTA Strategy by addressing drug trafficking modalities noted in the annual Threat Assessment and facilitating the effective and efficient sharing of information between and among Gulf Coast HIDTA participant agencies, non-participating agencies within the Gulf Coast HIDTA, and other HIDTA enforcement entities nationwide. Its operational mission is to provide the full spectrum of intelligence products to law enforcement agencies, thereby enabling effective and efficient use of drug investigative resources.

The Network Coordination Group (NCG), the Technical Operations Group (TOG), the Title III Wire Intercept Center and the IT Systems Administrators are co-located at the Louisiana Operations Center in Metairie, LA. Intelligence Support Teams (ISTs) are co-located within the State Operations Center in Jackson, MS; the Alabama Bureau of Investigation (ABI) Fusion Center in Montgomery, AL; the GC HIDTA Major Investigations Team (MIT) in Little Rock, AR; the Louisiana State Police (LSP) Fusion Center in Baton Rouge, LA; and the GC HIDTA initiative in Shelby County, Tennessee. The BLOC/HIDTA Watch Center is located in Gulfport, Mississippi. The BLOC/HIDTA Watch Center, while part of the HIDTA's Intelligence Subsystem, is a separate initiative and, consequently, reports staffing and budgeting items independent of the ISN.

The NCG functions as the central coordination component through which the entire ISN intelligence sub-system communicates. The NCG communicates directly with other ISN components, including the ISTs, TOG, the IT Systems Administrators, and BLOC/HIDTA Watch Center in Gulfport, Mississippi to ensure a coordination of efforts. Real-time communication, data collection, and sharing and dissemination of information are achieved through connectivity via the Gulf Coast HIDTA Wide Area Network (WAN).

The ISTs are composed of analysts from Gulf Coast HIDTA participating agencies, HIDTA-funded contract analysts, and National Guard personnel. The principal function of each team is to provide HIDTA initiatives and participating agencies with tactical and investigative intelligence support for active investigations. The NCG supervisor provides direction to and oversight of the ISTs. Each IST is tasked with providing a full range of intelligence products and services including the collection, analysis, and dissemination of drug intelligence targeting DTOs. Analytical techniques routinely employed include, but are not limited to, tactical wiretap support, telephone toll analysis, document analysis, and flow charts.

Additional responsibilities include coordinating the development of threat assessments for both its area of responsibility and the Gulf Coast HIDTA Threat Assessment. The ISTs also work with NDIC analysts in the preparation of threat assessments and other products. The ISTs are analytical extensions of the ISN. Thus, the ISN outputs apply to the ISTs and the ISTs contribute to the completion of the ISN outputs.

The TOG supports wire intercept capabilities for the Gulf Coast HIDTA and assists the investigative teams by providing technical support for intelligence and operational purposes on a case-by-case basis. The team also maintains an inventory of HIDTA-supplied equipment, and assists in the evaluation and coordination of equipment requests.

### TASK FORCES OPERATING IN THE HIDTA REGION

The table below highlights the Federally-funded drug enforcement task forces operating in the HIDTA region. Multiple HIDTA task forces may make up an overarching HIDTA enforcement or investigative initiative.

| TASK FORCES | LOCATIONS |
|---|---|
| Little Rock Major Investigations/Mobile Deployment Team (HIDTA) | Little Rock, AR |
| U.S. Marshal's Service Fugitive Task Force (HIDTA) | Little Rock, AR |
| Northwest Arkansas Major Investigations Team (HIDTA) | Fayetteville, AR |
| 4TH Judicial District Drug Task Force (Byrne) | Fayetteville, AR |
| Madison/Morgan Counties Drug Task Force (HIDTA/Byrne) | Huntsville, AL |
| Jefferson County HIDTA Task Force (HIDTA) | Birmingham, AL |
| Alabama Operations Center (HIDTA) | Montgomery, AL |
| Mobile/Baldwin Major Investigations Team (HIDTA) | Mobile, AL |
| Mobile/Baldwin Street Enforcement Team (HIDTA/Byrne) | Mobile, AL |
| Metro New Orleans Major Investigations Team (GC HIDTA) | Metairie, LA |

| TASK FORCES | LOCATIONS |
|---|---|
| Metro New Orleans Mobile Deployment Team (HIDTA) | Metairie, LA |
| City of New Orleans Major Investigations Team (HIDTA) | Metairie, LA |
| Multi-Agency Safe Neighborhood Task Force (HIDTA/Safe Streets) | Metairie, LA |
| Project STAR (HIDTA) | Harvey, LA |
| New Orleans Gang Task Force (HIDTA/Safe Streets) | New Orleans, LA |
| Tactical Diversion Squad (DEA) | New Orleans, LA |
| Mid-Louisiana Major Investigations/Interdiction Team (HIDTA) | Baton Rouge, LA |
| Southwest Louisiana Major Investigations/Financial Team (HIDTA) | Lafayette, LA |
| Caddo/Bossier Drug Task Force (HIDTA) | Shreveport, LA |
| Northwest Louisiana Violent Crimes Task Force (HIDTA/Safe Streets) | Shreveport, LA |
| Monroe Metro Drug Task Force (HIDTA/Byrne) | Monroe, LA |
| Calcasieu Parish Combined Anti-drug Team (HIDTA/Safe Streets) | Lake Charles, LA |
| Multi-Jurisdictional Drug Task Force (Byrne) | Gretna, LA |
| Mississippi Operations Center Major Investigations Team (HIDTA) | Pearl, MS |
| Mississippi Operations Center Mobile Deployment Team (HIDTA) | Pearl, MS |
| North Mississippi Major Investigations Team (HIDTA) | Oxford, MS |
| Oxford/Lafayette County Task Force (Byrne) | Oxford, MS |
| Tri-County Major Investigation Team (HIDTA) | Gulfport, MS |
| Coastal Narcotics Enforcement Team (Byrne) | Gulfport, MS |
| Jackson County Major Investigations Team (HIDTA/Safe Streets) | Pascagoula, MS |
| Inter-Local Narcotics Task Force (Byrne) | Pascagoula, MS |
| Shelby County HIDTA Drug Task Force (HIDTA) | Memphis, TN |

## *TASK FORCE COORDINATION*

Gulf Coast HIDTA initiatives are required to submit all of their targets and planned operations to SAFETNet, which not only links them to HIDTA initiatives nationwide, but also to agency-specific databases such as DEA's National Drug Pointer Information System (NDPIX). Non-HIDTA task forces and agencies are encouraged to participate in the HIDTA-sponsored deconfliction. The Gulf Coast HIDTA provides deconfliction services to 89 participating Federal, state, and local agencies and 26 non-participating agencies. Gulf Coast HIDTA initiatives regularly meet with Federal, state, and local counterparts in their respective areas of responsibility to coordinate and share information.

Gulf Coast HIDTA initiatives are encouraged to share information regarding local, regional, and national DTOs. This is accomplished through deconfliction, as well as regional meetings of task force commanders. The HIDTA Executive Board is comprised of heads of Federal, state, and local agencies operating in its five-state area. The Executive Board is regularly informed of ongoing operations conducted by all initiatives funded by the GC HIDTA.

The Gulf Coast HIDTA provides funding toward standing and maintaining its intelligence subsystem. The intelligence subsystem includes funding a network of intelligence analysts strategically located throughout a four-state area to ensure the efficient collection, analysis, and dissemination of information to all law enforcement entities within the area. The dissemination of information is not only accomplished within the HIDTA, but it is also shared nationally through the circulation of its products which include threat assessments, information bulletins, and officer safety alerts. All HIDTA intelligence products are posted on the FBI-sponsored Law Enforcement Online (LEO) website, which is available to all Joint Terrorism Task Forces (JTTFs) throughout the United States. Specific information generated by Gulf Coast HIDTA initiatives is routinely forwarded to the appropriate JTTF.

## *HIDTA EVALUATION*

CY 2009 statistical accomplishments show significant improvement over CY 2008 in a number of areas and exceeded performance targets in almost every category.

Enforcement initiatives disrupted or dismantled 249 DTOs and MLOs operating in their designated areas and beyond, a 15 percent increase over the previous year. Just as significant was at the HIDTA's effectiveness in disrupting and dismantling international and multi-state DTOs operating in the area. As a result of increased focus on the most serious DTOs, in 2009 GC HIDTA initiatives disrupted or dismantled 161 DTOs, which were international or multi-state in scope. The average cost for every DTO dismantled or disrupted was below the national HIDTA program average.

Equally important was the success in removing the profits obtained by DTOs through their illegal activities. In 2009, GC HIDTA initiatives seized over $28 million in assets from drug traffickers in currency, real property, jewelry, weapons, and other items of value. The GC HIDTA realized a combined return-on-investment of $16.39 for every dollar invested.

## Hawaii HIDTA – Designated in 1999
## Executive Director – Larry Burnett

### PURPOSE AND GOALS

At the crossroad of the Pacific and gateway into the continental United States, the Hawaii HIDTA's participating agencies work together through enhanced coordination and integrated initiatives to disrupt and dismantle illicit drug distribution, production, money laundering, transportation, and trafficking within the region.

### STRATEGY

The Hawaii HIDTA has a clear-cut mission for its law enforcement and intelligence components. The Hawaii HIDTA fosters cooperative and effective working relationships among all 24 of Hawaii's Federal, state, and local law enforcement agencies. These relationships are embodied in the co-located and commingled law enforcement personnel who are strategically aligned into task forces that focus on long-term and short-term multi-jurisdictional investigations, complex money laundering investigations, violent offenders and fugitives, border interdiction, and marijuana eradication. Additionally, the Hawaii HIDTA invests heavily in a robust IISC and a Fusion Center. The Hawaii HIDTA intelligence-led policing approach pulls together targeted information into an analytical intelligence cycle so priorities can be established and the most pressing law enforcement threats can be dealt with in a focused/planned manner.

### LOCATION

The Hawaii HIDTA operates out of Honolulu, HI. It encompasses the City and County of Honolulu (the Island of Oahu), Maui County (the Islands of Maui, Molokai and Lanai), Hawaii County (the Big Island of Hawaii), and Kauai County (the Island of Kauai).

### INITIATIVES

The Hawaii HIDTA has 15 initiatives, which include 1 management, 1 training, 2 support, 4 intelligence, 2 interdiction, and 5 investigative initiatives.

### SHORT-TERM OBJECTIVES

| YEAR | DTOs Expected to be Disrupted/ Dismantled | Target Return on Investment: Assets | Target Return on Investment: Drugs | Number of Deconflictions Expected to be Submitted | Number of Investigations Expected to be Provided Analytical Support | Number of Initiative Leads Expected to be Referred |
|---|---|---|---|---|---|---|
| 2010 | 43 | $4.77 | $295.15 | 13,500 | 50 | 180 |

### THREAT ASSESSMENT

The trafficking and abuse of crystal methamphetamine and a resurgence of cocaine, along with the production/cultivation of marijuana, pose the greatest illicit drug threats to the state.

Crystal methamphetamine, cocaine, and marijuana are much more frequently associated with violence and other forms of social disruption than other illicit drugs, including heroin, MDMA, steroids, and diverted pharmaceuticals, which are available in lesser quantities, and also pose a threat to the region. Often, these drugs are present alongside crystal methamphetamine and marijuana during police raids as well as autopsies in cases of drug-related deaths. According to the National Drug Intelligence Center, four out of five state and local law enforcement agencies in the region indicated that the greatest drug threat in their respective areas of responsibility was crystal methamphetamine.

Violence associated with illicit drug trafficking extracts an expensive toll on Hawaii's resources, families, and neighborhoods. Drug abuse contributes to domestic violence, child endangerment, and hospital emergency room visits. For example, Matthew Higa was sentenced to life in prison in May 2010 for the murder of Cyrus Belt, a 23-month old toddler who was left under his care. Higa threw the boy off a bridge onto a busy freeway. The boy's mother testified in court that she left her son with Higa, who was high on methamphetamine, while she went out to shoplift and get high on methamphetamine herself.

Criminal groups and DTOs are usually international or multi-state in scope, with ample opportunity to traffic drugs to, through, and from the area using Hawaii's exceptionally high volume of international and domestic air and/or ocean traffic. Hawaii is ranked among the highest in the Nation for methamphetamine abuse per capita, and consistently comes in fourth place or higher for annual marijuana production. Hawaii is forty-seventh in the Nation for land mass; imparting a dubious first-place ranking in available land-to-marijuana cultivation ratio.

## *INTELLIGENCE INITIATIVES*

The Hawaii HIDTA IISC has four components which provide investigative support, criminal intelligence, strategic intelligence, and the facilitation of communication and information sharing among initiatives, task forces, community stakeholders, decision makers, and participating law enforcement agencies. The IISC houses the Investigative Case Support Initiative (ICS), the Pacific Regional Informational Clearing House Initiative (PAC CLEAR), the Criminal Intelligence and Violent Crime Gang Initiative (CIU-Gang), and the HIDTA's Communications and Information Sharing Program. These four components provide all of the case support, annual report, annual threat assessment, strategy, event deconflictions, and case activation.

The CIU-Gang focuses on criminal intelligence gathering and analysis. It enhances criminal intelligence analysis within the Hawaii HIDTA by facilitating the sharing of information from the Criminal Intelligence Units of the four county police departments and State corrections with the other elements of the IISC, enforcement task forces, and other HIDTA participating Federal, state, and local law enforcement agencies. CIU-Gang determines the scope/threat level and provides a comprehensive intelligence picture of illicit drug trafficking and crime activities of organized criminal gangs, prison gangs, Outlaw Motorcycle Gangs (OMG), and drug distribution gangs. The analysis of the gangs also includes the crimes they commit, other problems they present, and localities they affect. The information and intelligence collected through CIU-Gang is disseminated through a collaborative approach to law enforcement for suppression and enforcement strategies when dealing with major organized crime gangs. This initiative facilitates intelligence-led policing aimed at the dismantling or disruption of major gang DTOs. The CIU-Gang interfaces with RISSIntel and the national Gang Database through the Western States Information Network (WSIN).

The ICS is the nucleus of the Hawaii HIDTA intelligence program. The ICS supports the HIDTA mission by collecting, evaluating, analyzing, and disseminating timely information in support of investigative case activity relating to drug importation, drug distribution, money laundering, drug-related violent crime, and drug-related firearm trafficking. The ICS provides a full range of core investigative support to enforcement task forces and Federal/state prosecuting attorneys. The IISC supports the HIDTA mission by collecting, evaluating, analyzing, and disseminating timely intelligence on drug importation, drug distribution, money laundering, drug-related violent crime, and drug-related firearm trafficking. The ICS provides operational and tactical case support to investigations being conducted by HIDTA participating agencies, appropriate non-HIDTA law enforcement and other official intelligence money laundering, drug-related violent crime, and drug-related firearm trafficking and other official intelligence entities. ICS support includes telephone toll and pen register analysis (analysis of phone call records), link analysis (analysis of connections among targets), event analysis (analysis of illegal activity or law enforcement action), post seizure analysis, financial investigative analysis and development of new analytical techniques. The ICS analysts are closely coupled to the agents and officers in the investigative and interdiction task forces, often working hand in hand during the investigative and prosecution process.

PAC CLEAR is awaiting accreditation by the Department of Homeland Security (DHS) as a State/Regional Fusion Center. The mission of Fusion Centers is to protect the people of the United States from terrorism and other criminal activity through effective collaboration and dissemination of critical threat information and intelligence among first responders and those involved in the homeland security effort, including law enforcement, emergency services, and homeland security. In addition to exploiting existing databases, PAC CLEAR analysts take advantage of input from a variety of sources including agents, officers, investigators, analysts, researchers, and community stakeholders. This information is also utilized in close coordination with the National Drug Intelligence Center (NDIC) and the El Paso Intelligence Center (EPIC), among others. PAC CLEAR is designed to access and collect varied-formatted information. PAC CLEAR provides data consolidation through analysis and fusion. Intelligence reports or projects are disseminated using existing Federal, state, and local networks, HIDTA's intranet, and RISS ATIX. As a node on the nationwide RISS Project, the intelligence and informational products generated are accessed by task forces, law enforcement, first responders, critical stakeholders, and other HIDTAs nationwide. Information and intelligence support includes trend and pattern analysis and the collection, analysis, and dissemination of information concerning the composition, scope, magnitude and dynamics, both internal and external, of the regional illicit drug problem and the resulting trends and threats to the public's safety.

PAC CLEAR also has primary responsibility for PMP input/maintenance and the production of the HIDTA's annual reports, threat assessments, and strategy. It serves as a regional strategic information clearinghouse for empirical and statistical data relating to illicit drug trafficking and abuse. PAC CLEAR consolidates and provides decision makers in law enforcement, public office, and community stakeholders with accurate, fact-based information to enhance operational efficiency and planning effectiveness.

All Hawaii HIDTA initiatives, and HIDTAs nationwide, link together through the RISSnet project. WSIN maintains the RISSnet gateway and a comprehensive intelligence database linked to all other RISSnet databases, giving initiatives nationwide access. Hawaii HIDTA is provided with 24/7 Watch Center protection and assistance, and deconfliction services (through the WSIN and NIN Watch Centers). In exchange, the HIDTA provides the WSIN Coordinator and staff with office space, parking, phones, postage, copier access, etc. Deconfliction services not only ensure officer safety but reduce duplication of effort and promote coordination and information sharing among participating agencies. WSIN, by Executive Board mandate and written policy, provides case and subject deconfliction for all law enforcement agencies operating within the State of Hawaii. WSIN is a RISS ATIX and PAC CLEAR facilitator, providing resources to enhance coordination and promote information development and dissemination among participating/supporting partners in drug control efforts.

## TASK FORCES OPERATING IN THE HIDTA REGION

The table below highlights the Federally-funded drug enforcement task forces operating in the HIDTA region. Multiple HIDTA task forces may make up an overarching HIDTA enforcement or investigative initiative.

| TASK FORCES | LOCATIONS |
|---|---|
| HI Impact Group 1 Task Force (HIDTA) | City and County of Honolulu (Oahu) |
| HI Impact Group 3 Task Force (HIDTA) | City and County of Honolulu (Oahu) |
| HI Impact Maui Task Force (HIDTA) | Maui County |
| HI Impact Kona Task Force (HIDTA) | Hawaii (Big Island) County |
| HI Impact Hilo Task Force (HIDTA) | Hawaii (Big Island) County |
| HI Impact Kauai Task Force (HIDTA) | Kauai County |
| Domestic Interdiction Task Force (HIDTA) | Honolulu International Airport: Operating Statewide |
| Foreign Interdiction Task Force (HIDTA) | Honolulu International Airport |
| Parcel Interdiction Task Force (HIDTA) | Honolulu International Airport |
| Rapid Reduction Drug Unit (HIDTA) | City and County of Honolulu |
| Project Safe Neighborhoods (HIDTA) | City and County of Honolulu |
| Money Laundering & Asset Forfeiture Task Force (HIDTA) | City and County of Honolulu |
| Marijuana Task Force (HIDTA) | City and County of Honolulu |
| Fugitive Task Force (HIDTA) | City and County of Honolulu |
| Hawaii Narcotics Task Force (JAG) | Encompasses Maui, Kauai, and Hawaii Counties |
| Statewide Marijuana Eradication Task Force (DCSEP) | Maui County, Kauai County, Hawaii County and the City & County of Honolulu |

## TASK FORCE COORDINATION

The Hawaii HIDTA Executive Board stresses equal partnerships among the participating agencies, and is the coordinating body for drug investigations within the State of Hawaii (the only HIDTA encompassing an entire State). Although the SME and HNTF task forces are non-HIDTA funded, they coordinate and report activities on a monthly basis to a Hawaii HIDTA program analyst. All task forces, whether Hawaii HIDTA-sponsored or Justice Action Grant (JAG)/Byrne sponsored, coordinate with each other in the generation of threat assessment surveys.

Additionally, a Hawaii HIDTA task force commander serves as a coordinator between the HNTF and Hawaii HIDTA enforcement task forces. The coordinator hosts a quarterly drug unit commanders meeting which is intended to facilitate the exchange of information and address issues of mutual concern. The task forces often work together on OCDETF prosecutions through investigative or resource sharing. The Hawaii HIDTA director, along with participating agency heads, coordinates with the OCDETF Assistant United States Attorney in evaluating all OCDETF proposals.

All law enforcement task forces, whether receiving JAG/Byrne or HIDTA funding in Hawaii, are mandated to use WSIN and part of the DOJ sponsored RISSnet, for coordination, case activation, and critical event/subject deconfliction. All other law enforcement components within the State of Hawaii, whether Federally funded or not, voluntarily use WSIN for deconfliction services and information sharing. Additionally, the drug task forces share information through the various components of the Hawaii HIDTA IISC.

The Hawaii HIDTA IISC maintains a 24/7 Watch Center, through an exchange of services with WSIN. The Watch Center coordinates all case activation, critical event/subject deconfliction, and communication activities. Within the Hawaii HIDTA IISC, the Investigative Case Support unit and the PAC CLEAR coordinate the reporting, analysis, and dissemination of information among the task forces. The CIU-Gang unit within the IISC coordinates the sharing of information among the different island police department intelligence units. The Hawaii HIDTA plays a central role in providing training to the task forces, to ensure the latest information and enforcement techniques are shared and coordinated.

The heads of all Federal, state, and local law enforcement agencies in Hawaii participate, either as a voting or advisory member, on the Hawaii HIDTA Executive Board. The Executive Board ensures information is shared among its membership.

The Hawaii HIDTA Executive Board has an established written policy and procedure mandating that the PAC CLEAR Fusion Center, the Hawaii HIDTA IISC and the Hawaii HIDTA task forces turn over and coordinate any terrorism-related information and/or investigative leads to the FBI led JTTF. JTTF analysts have access to the IISC.

## HIDTA EVALUATION

ONDCP will continue to help the Hawaii HIDTA improve its information sharing capacity, including the expansion of their PAC CLEAR program, which is designated as Hawaii's only Fusion Center by the Department of Homeland Security. In 2009, the HIDTA disrupted or dismantled 55 DTOs, compared to 48 the prior year. Hawaii HIDTA task forces focus on organizations causing the most harm to Hawaii HIDTA communities. For every dollar spent on law enforcement and intelligence activities by the Hawaii HIDTA, a return on investment (ROI) of $262.19 in drug seizures and an ROI of $2.23 in asset seizures was realized; for a total overall return-on-investment of $264.42.

## Houston HIDTA – Designated in 1990
## Executive Director – Stan Furce

### PURPOSE AND GOALS

The mission of the Houston HIDTA is to disrupt the market for illegal drugs through the creation and maintenance of intelligence-driven task forces targeting major DTOs, money laundering organizations, and drug gangs. Further, the Houston HIDTA will enhance and help coordinate efforts among Federal, State, and local law enforcement agencies.

### STRATEGY

Continue to foster cooperative and effective working relationships among Federal, State, and local agencies that participate and/or operate in the Houston HIDTA area to achieve the common goals of disrupting and dismantling DTOs, and reducing the demand for drugs.

### LOCATION

The Houston HIDTA operates out of Houston, Texas. The 17 counties that comprise the Houston HIDTA region include: Aransas, Brooks, Fort Bend, Galveston, Hardin, Harris, Jefferson, Jim Wells, Kenedy, Kleberg, Liberty, Montgomery, Nueces, Orange, Refugio, San Patricio, and Victoria. The City of Houston is also part of the HIDTA.

### INITIATIVES

The Houston HIDTA has 13 initiatives, which include 1 management, 3 intelligence, 8 investigation/interdiction initiatives, and 1 training initiative.

### SHORT-TERM OBJECTIVES

| YEAR | DTOs Expected to be Disrupted/ Dismantled | Target Return on Investment: Assets | Target Return on Investment: Drugs | Number of Deconflictions Expected to be Submitted | Number of Investigations Expected to be Provided Analytical Support | Number of Initiative Leads Expected to be Referred |
|------|------|------|------|------|------|------|
| 2010 | 94 | $3.07 | $12.73 | 11,600 | 380 | 23,402 |

The Houston HIDTA funds four analysts that provide support to the Texas Narcotics Information System (TNIS), which is led by the Texas Department of Public Safety and located in Austin, Texas. The TNIS provides state-wide drug related intelligence support and accounts for 3,500 of the 11,600 expected deconflictions, 200 of the 380 investigations expected to receive analytical support, and 22,000 of the expected lead referrals.

### THREAT ASSESSMENT

The threat from illicit drug trafficking and associated violence within the Houston HIDTA remains high, in large part due to its close proximity to the Southwest Border Area, as well as its role as an international transportation hub with major airports, seaports, and national highway infrastructure. As a result, the Houston HIDTA region is one of the most significant distribution and transshipment areas for the variety of illegal drugs trafficked from Mexico into the United States. It is also a primary consolidation point for bulk cash smuggled back across the border. Therefore, Houston is one of the principal centers for drug activity in the country. Seizure data from the Texas Department of Public Safety indicates that they interdicted drug and cash shipments destined for 36 states in 2010, as well as the Republic of Mexico. Within the Houston HIDTA, 40% percent of the DTOs operate internationally; 15% operate regionally; and 45% are local. Most Houston HIDTA DTOs are considered to be poly-drug distributors, trafficking more than one drug type. Cocaine was trafficked most frequently (76%), followed by marijuana (59%), methamphetamine (41%), heroin (9%), and pharmaceutical or designer drugs (8%). Mexican DTOs account for the majority of the 446 identified drug trafficking organizations operating in the region. The Gulf Cartel, along with its long standing enforcer group, Los Zetas, has traditionally been the primary threat to the region. The role played by Los Zetas, however, has evolved. Now, the Gulf Cartel and Los Zetas are considered to be separate cartels. Los Zetas have expanded their operations, becoming a more powerful presence and an increasing threat to the Houston HIDTA.

Houston has experienced an increase in pharmaceutical diversion activities over the past several years, including the presence of rogue pain clinics operating in the area, heightening the level of threat posed to the region and beyond. In addition to the imminent threat posed by the vast supply of illegal drugs moving through the Houston HIDTA, drug-related violence continues to escalate, especially among the region's gangs. Gangs within the Houston HIDTA continue to grow in strength and number. Their violence, often spurred by drug-related turf issues is increasingly brutal, heightening the severity of the impact of the drug trade in the region. Gangs now have a younger, more violent membership. This increased violence, especially toward law enforcement, heightens the level of threat to the Houston HIDTA. Gang recruitment is at an all-time high. The Texas Department of Public Safety released a statement to the media warning parents that Mexican cartels and transnational gangs are recruiting in Texas schools. The Houstones pose the greatest threat in terms of their strength and number. However, criminal illegal immigrants such as Mexican and Central American gangs pose the greatest threat in terms of their propensity for violence within the Houston HIDTA. The Texas Syndicate, Mexican Mafia, and the Hermanos de Pistoleros Latinos (HPL) are also a significant threat to the region. According to interviewed gang investigators, for the first time in ten years, there has been some noticeable disruption of security threat group (STG) gangs through joint law enforcement efforts.

## INTELLIGENCE INITIATIVES

The mission of the Houston Intelligence Support Center (HISC) is to provide accurate and timely intelligence analysis to law enforcement agencies regarding drug-related criminal activity within the Houston HIDTA. The HISC, formerly known as the Joint Drug Intelligence Group (JDIG), was first funded by HIDTA in 1992. The FBI has used Houston as a model for its Field Intelligence Groups. The HISC provides strategic, organizational, and tactical intelligence on DTOs operating in the Houston HIDTA region using the full gamut of analytical techniques. To accomplish the mission, the HISC uses two major squads consisting of five teams that provide and supervise intelligence and analytical support to the law enforcement community. The five teams are:

- Intelligence Research Team (IRT);
- Analytical Case Support Team (ACST);
- Case Development Team (CDT);
- Strategic Intelligence Team (SIT); and
- The HISC Management Team

The IRT is comprised of law enforcement and contract and military analysts who use Federal, State, local, and commercial databases to identify and locate criminal suspects associates, organizations, businesses, and property. The IRT responds to requests from any law enforcement agency. The IRT analysts produce intelligence summaries that are a result of the analytical process and the identifying and resolution of intelligence gaps. In addition, the IRT provides case and subject deconfliction on all intelligence requests. The IRT interacts with other HIDTA initiatives practically every day. During CY 2009, 34 percent of the IRT's workload was in support of HIDTA initiatives and 98 percent was in support of HIDTA agencies.

The ACST supports the intelligence development phase of cases pursued by members of Houston HIDTA Initiatives or Southeastern Texas law enforcement agencies. One HISC ACST analyst is embedded with the Texas Coastal Corridor Initiative located in Corpus Christi. ACST analysts collate and condense raw research information into a single comprehensive product focusing on the relevant facts regarding the criminal subjects, their criminal activities, and their drug trafficking organization. ACST analysts forward the resultant research package to the requester to supplement any ongoing investigation. If the operational agency or initiative requests further assistance, the analyst who developed the original research package may be assigned to provide ongoing case support that continues through the prosecution phase. ACST members also assist the Case Development Team with their research and case development.

The CDT, also known as the proactive squad, employs investigators and analysts to develop leads for new cases and to refer actionable intelligence packages to HIDTA Initiatives and to other law enforcement agencies. The case development process includes identifying a potential target, and performing analytical research, surveillance, and interviews of witnesses and informants. Additionally, the CDT proactively develops informants throughout the community to assist the HISC with its intelligence collection capability. Some CDT case referrals have a short turn-around time and often result in arrests and seizures that have a direct and immediate impact on the community. Other CDT cases require a substantial investigative and intelligence effort in order to fully identify and assess the scope of the targeted criminal conspiracy. The CDT routinely interacts with the ACST and the IRT during case development, and ACST analysts typically support CDT investigations. However, if there is no analyst assigned to a specific investigation, the investigator from the CDT will interact with the IRT in order to develop a case. The CDT will normally disseminate the investigative and intelligence work product to other HIDTA initiatives. In the case referral scenario, the CDT will usually interact before, during, and after the referral of the investigation. During CY 2009, 80% of CDT case referrals went to HIDTA agencies with 50% going to HIDTA Initiatives.

The SIT has a nucleus of two analysts who develop and publish actionable intelligence research based on its value to the HIDTA community. SIT analysts use survey instruments, intelligence research, and interviews to identify unusual trends or circumstances involving DTOs operating in the Houston HIDTA region. Furthermore, the SIT proactively compares national trends to current and historical data regarding Houston-based drug traffickers. The SIT is responsible for collecting, drafting, and publishing the intelligence and information gathered from the annual HIDTA Threat Assessment surveys. SIT team members provide information to the Houston HIDTA law enforcement community about new trends and patterns of DTOs operating in the Houston HIDTA area. In addition to the annual threat assessment, the SIT identifies and responds to contemporary trends and threats in the Houston HIDTA region as evidenced by the 2010 Pharmaceutical Threat Assessment and the comprehensive 2010 Gang Threat Assessment. These documents provide succinct details of the threat environment, criminal organizations, and criminal activity trends that assist the HIDTA community and others in the development of enforcement strategies. The 2010 Gang Threat Assessment has been posted on several law enforcement web sites including the Texas Attorney General's Gang Resource System (GRS) where it has been downloaded over 200 times in November and December.

The HISC Management Team provides oversight of operational intelligence collection activities, intelligence research and development, administrative reporting, fiscal management, and personnel supervision on behalf of the HIDTA Executive Board and its Intelligence Subcommittee. The center is co-managed by an FBI ASAC and a Houston Police Department Supervisor.

In 2010, the CDT continued developing actionable intelligence and referring leads to other HIDTA initiatives, resulting in multiple arrests and seizures by the recipient agencies.

In late 2010, the HISC established a regional clearinghouse for cartel intelligence. Fifty-eight representatives from 8 federal, state, and local law enforcement agencies attended an initial planning meeting to develop goals and objectives for the clearinghouse. The clearinghouse will be used to collect information on known and suspected cartels from investigations ranging from routine patrol encounters to complex narcotics investigations. Its goals will be to develop leads for new and existing cases and to look at cartel activity regionally rather than on a case-by-case basis. The HISC cartel clearinghouse team will deconflict, analyze, and process the information and refer actionable intelligence packages as needed to the law enforcement community. The collected information will also be used to identify and fill intelligence gaps and to view regional cartel activity from a broad perspective.

In March 2007, the HISC hosted a 60-day pilot program that provided state-of-the-art computerized analysis of telephone records obtained through standard investigative techniques. The highly successful pilot turned into a full time program beginning in August 2007 and has since expanded nationally, with regional centers in Atlanta, Houston, and Los Angeles. This program has been successfully used by numerous HIDTAs across the country to locate dropped phones during wire-tap investigations, to locate suspects, and to quickly find pertinent links between the target and other members of a respective DTO.

In 2006, the HISC created a database designed to capture and exploit intelligence obtained from phone numbers found on business cards, scraps of paper, hotel stationery, or any other venue observed during enforcement operations. Houston HIDTA initiatives populate this pointer system database with telephone numbers typically overlooked or thrown in the trash. This database is available for all law enforcement in the Houston HIDTA region. In 2007, the HISC developed and implemented a standardized case support system among analysts supporting long-term investigations.

The "Case Support Package (CSP)" has seven components: a Case Synopsis, an

Organizational Chart, a Timeline, Biographical Sheet on all significant members of the organization, a Deconfliction Report, a Link Chart of Significant Telephone Analysis, and Analyst Observations. The seven components are a framework that provides guidance and consistency for all assigned cases. The CSP was developed to facilitate information sharing and dissemination and to prevent information "stove piping" for non-FBI cases worked by HISC analysts. The CSP fosters a consistent work product among analysts, provides an automatic checklist for case support, and is a training tool for new analysts. The CSP is also designed to assist analysts in keeping accurate statistical information needed for the HIDTA monthly and annual reports. The CSP is continuing to evolve.

## *TASK FORCES OPERATING IN THE HIDTA REGION*

| TASK FORCES | LOCATIONS |
|---|---|
| Major Drug Squads (HIDTA) | Houston |
| Truck, Air, Rail and Port (HIDTA) | Houston |
| Targeted Narcotics Enforcement Team (HIDTA) | Houston |
| Texas Costal Corridor Initiative (HIDTA) | Corpus Christi |
| The Methamphetamine Initiative Group (HIDTA) | Houston |
| Ft. Bend Enforcement Team (HIDTA) | Stafford |
| Houston Money Laundering Initiative (HIDTA) | Houston |
| Gangs and Non-Traditional Gang Squad (HIDTA) | Houston |
| OCDETF Strike Force (OCDETF) | Houston |
| Multi-agency Gang Task Force (FBI) | Houston |
| Tactical Diversion Squad (DEA) | Houston |
| Corpus Christi Violent Crimes Task Force (FBI) | Corpus Christi |

## *TASK FORCE COORDINATION*

It is the policy of the Houston HIDTA Executive Board that all participating agencies deconflict all events, whether or not they are related to a HIDTA initiative, through the HIDTA event deconfliction initiative, the Narcotic Operations Control Center. Area agencies that do not participate in the HIDTA also deconflict drug and other events. Case/subject deconfliction through the Houston HIDTA ISC is generally done by HIDTA Initiatives and Houston-area agencies. The HIDTA provided deconfliction services to 37 Federal, state, and local law enforcement agencies.

The Houston HIDTA ISC is collocated with the FBI JTTF in Houston, and sharing is routine and institutionalized. The manager of the FBI Field Intelligence Group is also the Houston HIDTA ISC Commander. His Deputy is a Houston Police Department Sergeant. The OCDETF Strike Force is in the DEA office and shares information daily with the Major Drug Squads, a HIDTA Initiative at DEA. It also shares information on an ad hoc basis with other HIDTA Initiatives, especially Ft. Bend Enforcement Team. DEA has formal task forces in Corpus Christi, Galveston, and Beaumont, Texas. The Corpus Christi task force is collocated with TCCI and shares information constantly. The others work with HIDTA ad hoc. The FBI violent crimes task force in Corpus Christi works closely and shares personnel with GANGS, a HIDTA Initiative. The FBI task force is not strictly a drug task force, but it has a drug nexus.

Other FBI and ATF task forces operating in the area that have a drug nexus to varying degrees include the Houston Asian Organized Crime Task Force; JTTF (4 RAs), Houston, Beaumont, Bryan/College Station, Corpus Christi Violent Crime Fugitive Task Force; Houston Coastal Safe Streets Task Force; Southeast Texas Safe Streets Task Force, Texas City, Texas; and the Counter Terrorism Intelligence Group, Houston. The ATF also has a VCIT task Force in Houston and three Project Gunrunner groups that operate in the area. Other than deconfliction, the cooperation with these task forces is ad hoc and frequent.

## *HIDTA EVALUATION*

The initiatives and efforts of the Houston HIDTA program are primarily focused on drug trafficking threats that impact other areas of the country. They have enabled investigative initiatives to successfully destabilize drug trafficking and money laundering organizations that are connected with organizations in numerous States.

The effects of the continuing trafficking of illicit drugs in the Houston HIDTA region are felt throughout the country. Analysis of verified intelligence and of telephone records obtained through court orders and subpoenas reveals Houston connections to traffickers in all 50 States and many foreign countries. This supports the National Drug Intelligence Center's (NDIC) statement that Houston is potentially the most significant cocaine distribution center in the United States. Despite impressive law enforcement accomplishments, Houston-based DTOs or their cells still manage much of the Nation's drug supply. Accordingly, Houston HIDTA initiatives target some of the most important DTOs and MLOs in the world. Houston HIDTA initiatives continue to make major inroads against these organizations.

HIDTAs reduce drug availability by targeting, disrupting, or dismantling major DTOs; arresting and prosecuting traffickers; and seizing their drugs and profits. In 2009, the HIDTA disrupted or dismantled 118 DTOs. Of the 445 DTOs identified, 319 were under investigation; 234, or 73% of those under investigation operated beyond the Houston HIDTA region in multiple states, or were involved in international operations. Of the 84 DTOs disrupted, 62, or about 74% were multi-state or international in scope. Of the 34 DTOs that were totally dismantled, 24, or about 71% were multi-state or international in scope.

## Lake County HIDTA – Designated in 1996
## Executive Director – Charles Porucznik

### *PURPOSE AND GOALS*

The mission of the Lake County HIDTA is to reduce drug availability and use by creating intelligence-driven drug task forces (initiatives) aimed at eliminating or reducing domestic drug trafficking and its harmful effects through the enhancement and coordination of drug trafficking enforcement efforts among Federal, state, and local law enforcement agencies.

### *STRATEGY*

The HIDTA works with eighteen state and local jurisdictions, six law enforcement initiatives, and several Federal agencies in bringing a coordinated law enforcement effort to the county to combat drug trafficking.

### *LOCATION*

The Lake County HIDTA operates out of Crown Point, Indiana. It has one county in the State of Indiana: Lake County. In early 2009, the Lake County HIDTA relocated into a stand-alone commercial building and now all but two investigative initiatives are co-located on the same floor.

### *INITIATIVES*

The Lake County HIDTA has nine initiatives, which include one management, one training, one intelligence, and six investigation/interdiction initiatives.

### *SHORT-TERM OBJECTIVES*

| YEAR | DTOs Expected to be Disrupted/ Dismantled | Target Return on Investment: Assets | Target Return on Investment: Drugs | Number of Deconflictions Expected to be Submitted | Number of Investigations Expected to be Provided Analytical Support | Number of Initiative Leads Expected to be Referred |
|------|------|------|------|------|------|------|
| 2010 | 23 | $1 | $3 | 3,000 | 800 | 81 |

### *THREAT ASSESSMENT*

Cocaine, particularly crack, poses the greatest drug threat to the region. Cocaine is transported from Mexico, the Southwest border and Chicago to, and through, Lake County, Indiana by Mexican DTOs. Street gangs in the northern section of the county protect their drug trade with violence and firearms. Heroin availability is increasing in the county. Marijuana is the most widely available and abused illicit drug in the county. A study by the Lake County Drug Free Alliance revealed marijuana is being smoked regularly by more Lake County high school students than tobacco. Methamphetamine availability and abuse are low in Lake County. Pharmaceutical drug diversion has increased, consistent with national trends. The increased abuse of prescription drugs is fueled by a lack of social stigma associated with pharmaceutical drugs. The availability of the three most diverted drugs in Lake County (hydrocodone, oxycodone, and methadone) is stable.

## INTELLIGENCE INITIATIVES

The Intelligence and Investigative Support Center (IISC) is the hub of Lake County HIDTA operations. The initiative was started in 1997 with the creation of the HIDTA. The IISC is jointly managed by the DEA and the Indiana State Police. The IISC is staffed by HIDTA analysts, DEA personnel, and the Indiana National Guard. The IISC provides accurate, detailed, and timely drug and non-drug intelligence to both HIDTA initiative partners, as well as other Lake County law enforcement agencies. The IISC provides both event and case subject deconfliction to HIDTA initiatives and outside agencies in Lake County. It is co-located in the HIDTA facilities with all of the other HIDTA initiatives except the Gang Response Investigative Team. The IISC has expanded with a variety of software and hardware improvements that make it a legitimate interagency intelligence center. Examples of this are: the regional gang database created and managed by the HIDTA; participation in SAFETNet, a deconfliction system currently linked to four regional HIDTAs that is connected to the 18 other HIDTAs and the National Virtual Pointer System; the creation of a hardware and software link at the IISC which allows the two primary data systems used in the County by Police and Correctional facilities to interface; and deploying I2 Analyst Notebook and ArcView graphics and mapping programs. In 2009, the priorities were to increase quality case support activities, while adding strategic and predictive intelligence capabilities. In late 2009, a new digital evidence section came on-line to assist with computer and cell phone forensics. The Lake County HIDTA continues to participate in the area's Major Crimes Task Force.

## TASK FORCES OPERATING IN THE HIDTA REGION

The table below highlights the Federally-funded drug enforcement task forces operating in the HIDTA region. Multiple HIDTA task forces may make up an overarching HIDTA enforcement or investigative initiative.

| TASK FORCES | LOCATIONS |
|---|---|
| DEA Task Force Group 56 (state and local task force) | Merrillville |
| Lake County Combined Task Force (HIDTA) | Crown Point |
| Gang Response Investigative Team Initiative (HIDTA) | Gary |
| Lake County Drug Task Force (Local task force) | Crown Point |
| Hotel Interdiction and Truck Stop Initiative (HIDTA) | Crown Point |
| Marshal's Fugitive Task Force (HIDTA) | Hammond |
| Firearms Interdiction Regional Enforcement Initiative (HIDTA) | Crown Point |
| Domestic Highway Enforcement Initiative (HIDTA) | Lowell |

## TASK FORCE COORDINATION

The Lake County Drug Task Force (LCDTF) coordinates with a number of other Lake County HIDTA initiatives. If LCDTF's operations encounter large amounts of drugs or any weapons, they will contact and coordinate with either the Lake County Combined Task Force (LCCTF), a DEA-led initiative, or the Firearms Interdiction Regional Enforcement Task Force (FIRE, an ATF-led initiative). LCDTF works with the Lake County HIDTA's IISC on certain operations and event/subject deconflictions, and with the Internal Revenue Service, Postal Inspectors, Immigration Customs Enforcement, and other agencies to effectively carry out their operations. The Lake County HIDTA IISC provides deconfliction services to 24 Federal, state, and local law enforcement agencies.

The Lake County HIDTA IISC assists all of the task forces with case support and analysis, critical event/subject deconfliction, and any requests for information, as well as the dissemination of information among the task forces. The Lake County HIDTA Regional Gang Database is an Internet-based system that allows any Federal, state, or local officer to check if someone is a gang member within the region. The IISC coordinates the activity within the database. The sharing of information among the task forces is usually done through the IISC, when permitted by the requesting unit. The Lake County HIDTA plays a central role in providing training to the task forces, to ensure the latest information and enforcement techniques are shared and coordinated.

The Federal, state, and local law enforcement agencies in Lake County participate, either as voting or advisory members, on the Lake County HIDTA Executive Board. The Executive Board ensures information is shared among its membership.

The IISC and the Lake County HIDTA task forces turn over and coordinate any terrorism-related information and/or investigative leads to the JTTF.

## HIDTA EVALUATION

The Lake County HIDTA continues to seek ways to enhance its overall performance and is currently developing new capabilities to attack its regional threats. It has established an initiative that will focus on Suspicious Activity Reports (SAR) and attacking illegal drug proceeds. The HIDTA is also expanding its interdiction operations along the many major highways that run through its area of responsibility.

During 2009, the FBI and DEA led initiatives targeting DTOs through the use of Title III investigations. Intercepted telephone calls determined that cocaine availability was significantly impacted by law enforcement efforts at the Mexican border, and as such, availability dropped in Northwest Indiana. Numerous conversations were intercepted indicating cocaine was difficult to get out of Mexico. Therefore, this significantly impacted the HIDTA's ability to dismantle DTOs, resulting in lower percentages than expected. In 2009, the HIDTA expected to disrupt or dismantle 42 DTOs; the actual number was 13, or 31 percent of the expected result. In comparison, the 2008 numbers were 37 expected, 20 disrupted or dismantled, or 54 percent of the expected results.

As noted earlier, the Lake County HIDTA relocated into a new stand-alone commercial building. This relocation has enabled all but two investigative initiatives to be co-located on the same floor which enhances cooperation and coordination of investigations.

In response to an increased money laundering threat, the Executive Board also authorized a new IRS-led money laundering initiative, staffed additionally by the Secret Service and the Indiana State Police.

# Los Angeles HIDTA – Designated in 1990
## Executive Director – Roger Bass

### PURPOSE AND GOALS

It is the mission of the Los Angeles HIDTA (LA-HIDTA) to measurably reduce drug trafficking, thereby reducing the impact of illicit drugs in this and other areas of the country. This mission is to be accomplished through the use of multi-jurisdictional (Federal, state, and local), co-located, and co-mingled law enforcement and intelligence initiatives designed to attack, disrupt, and dismantle major drug trafficking and money laundering organizations operating in and through the LA-HIDTA region.

### STRATEGY

By design, the LA-HIDTA Strategy provides a comprehensive, dynamic law enforcement/intelligence plan which combines and coordinates regional drug control efforts in areas where they can have the most significant impact upon the threat. By Executive Board direction, this HIDTA consists of seven major operational task forces comprised of co-located Federal, state, and local law enforcement agencies and three intelligence initiatives. It is their collective purpose to effectively and efficiently work within the Strategy to identify and target the major DTOs which operate at the higher levels of the illegal narcotic "food chain," in order to measurably reduce drug trafficking and its impact in this and other areas of the country.

### LOCATION

The LA-HIDTA operates out of Los Angeles, California. Its designated geographic area covers the four counties of Los Angeles, Orange, Riverside, and San Bernardino.

### INITIATIVES

The LA-HIDTA has 13 initiatives, which include 1 management, 1 training, 3 intelligence, 1 prosecution, and 7 investigation/interdiction initiatives.

### SHORT-TERM OBJECTIVES

| YEAR | DTOs Expected to be Disrupted/ Dismantled | Target Return on Investment: Assets | Target Return on Investment: Drugs | Number of Deconflictions Expected to be Submitted | Number of Investigations Expected to be Provided Analytical Support | Number of Initiative Leads Expected to be Referred |
|------|------|------|------|------|------|------|
| 2010 | 136 | $3.49 | $20.94 | 221,141 | 1,435 | 340 |

## THREAT ASSESSMENT

Mexican DTOs and criminal groups control the wholesale distribution of illicit drugs in the LA-HIDTA region. They supply illicit drugs to distributors within the region and to distributors in most other significant drug markets throughout the country. Their influence is so profound that the LA-HIDTA region has become one of the most significant illicit drug distribution centers in the United States for cocaine, heroin, marijuana, methamphetamine, MDMA, and PCP. Sources of the investigations for most of the open DTO cases in the LA-HIDTA at the end of 2010 are Mexican nationals.

Additionally, the Mexican DTOs and criminal groups based in the LA-HIDTA region are increasing their control over illicit drug distribution in many drug markets, most recently in east coast drug markets that have long been controlled by other trafficking groups, which further enhances the role of the region as a national-level drug distribution center. It clearly is a staging area for Mexican DTOs and some that have national presence.

The geographic, cultural, social, economic diversity and general affluence of the population within the four county area (12th largest economy in the world) have helped make the LA-HIDTA a huge market for drug use and distribution. At the same time, the highly developed transportation routes and the proximity to the United States/Mexico border have made the LA-HIDTA a primary distribution, storage, and supply hub for illicit drugs destined for all the major metropolitan areas in the United States. Further, the large rural and remote desert areas make the LA-HIDTA an ideal location for clandestine manufacturing of methamphetamine. However, the majority of methamphetamine encountered in the LA-HIDTA is manufactured in Mexico.

## INTELLIGENCE INITIATIVES

It is the primary mission of the Los Angeles County Regional Criminal Information Clearinghouse (LACRCIC, or more commonly known as LA CLEAR) to ensure officer safety and operational efficiency by providing advanced technology, intelligence, and enhanced information sharing to all law enforcement agencies. As part of the LA-HIDTA Intelligence Support System, the LA CLEAR was created to provide an IISC for law enforcement agencies operating within the LA-HIDTA. The LA CLEAR is a member of the LA-HIDTA Intelligence Support System (ISS). The LA-HIDTA ISS is comprised of the three HIDTA-funded intelligence initiatives. These three intelligence initiatives make up the LA-HIDTA IISC. The LA CLEAR has electronic connectivity with all HIDTA initiatives and other agencies. The center provides a variety of services to both HIDTA-funded initiatives and other law enforcement agencies operating within the LA-HIDTA. The LA CLEAR is made up of the following components:

- A 24 hour, 7 day a week Intelligence & Deconfliction Watch Center (War Room);
- The War Room use of the California State Intelligence Index (CSII) database, the Regional Information Sharing System Intelligence database (RISSIntel) as pointer systems, and national connectivity through the Regional Information Sharing System Network pointer system (RISS.NET), facilitate the sharing of information between law enforcement agencies operating within and outside the LA-HIDTA;

- An Analytical Unit that is comprised of an Investigative Analysis Section (Case Support); and a Research Analysis Section (Post Seizure Analysis and Domestic Highway Enforcement).
  - The Analytical Unit provides agencies with all types of operational, tactical, and analytical products, including telephone toll analysis, link analysis, charts, graphs, wire tap support, and targeting analysis.
  - The Analytical Unit also produces quarterly trend reports that have strategic analysis on enforcement trends, price/purity updates, lab seizure data and clandestine laboratory trend information.
  - The Analytical Unit has access to the CSII and RISS Intel databases, law enforcement databases, commercial databases such as Autotrak and Lexis-Nexus, as well as access to EPIC and DEA NADDIS.
- In addition, the LA CLEAR also has a Special Operations Support Unit that provides electronic intercept support through an on-site 50 station digital electronic intercept and surveillance center.
  - The Special Operations Support Unit also provides high tech equipment, support and training to law enforcement agencies operating in the LA-HIDTA with pole cameras, vehicle tracking devices, pager intercepts, and other equipment.
  - The Special Operations Support Unit has technicians on call 24 hours a day to assist law enforcement agencies with installing or repairing any of the above mentioned equipment.
- The LA CLEAR has a 120 seat training facility that doubles as a command post with sufficient telephone and data lines to support large operations.
- The LA CLEAR also has a 24 station computer training lab where classes are presented on a variety of programs including Pen-Link, Analyst's Notebook, etc.
- The LA CLEAR also has an Information Systems Support Unit that supports the over 160 computers, 20 servers, and 150 software applications on-site at LA CLEAR. This unit also maintains the HIDTA Node and is a RISS Node within RISS.net information-sharing highway.
- LA CLEAR provides both focused intelligence and deconfliction services to 512 Federal, state, local law enforcement agencies and task forces in California and Nevada.

## TASK FORCES OPERATING IN THE HIDTA REGION

The table below highlights the Federally-funded drug enforcement task forces operating in the HIDTA region. Multiple HIDTA task forces may make up an overarching HIDTA enforcement or investigative initiative.

| TASK FORCES | LOCATIONS |
|---|---|
| Southern California Drug Task Force (HIDTA) | Los Angeles County |
| Los Angeles Interagency Metropolitan Police Apprehension Crime Task Force (HIDTA/BJA) | Los Angeles County |
| Los Angeles County Sheriff's Department Multijurisdictional Meth Enforcement Team (BJA) | Los Angeles County |

| TASK FORCES | LOCATIONS |
|---|---|
| Southwest Border Task Force (DEA) | Los Angeles County |
| Tactical Diversion Squad (DEA) | Los Angeles |
| Los Angeles Regional Criminal Information Clearinghouse (HIDTA/BJA) | Los Angeles County |
| Pacific Southwest Regional Fugitive Task Force (HIDTA) | Los Angeles, Orange, Riverside, San Bernardino Counties |
| Joint Regional Intelligence Center (DHS) (HIDTA) | Los Angeles County |
| Los Angeles Joint Terrorism Task Force (FBI) | Los Angeles County |
| Regional Methamphetamine Task Force (HIDTA) | Los Angeles County |
| Regional Narcotics Suppression Program (HIDTA) | Orange County |
| Regional Methamphetamine Task Force (HIDTA/BJA) | Orange County |
| Orange County Sheriff's Department Domestic Highway Enforcement Team (BJA) | Orange County |
| Orange County Joint Regional Intelligence Center (DHS/FBI) | Orange County |
| Orange County Joint Terrorism Task Force (FBI) | Orange County |
| Inland Regional Narcotic Enforcement Team (HIDTA) | San Bernardino County |
| Regional Methamphetamine Task Force (HIDTA) | San Bernardino County |
| San Bernardino County Marijuana Eradication Team (BJA) | San Bernardino County |
| San Bernardino County West-End Narcotic Enforcement Team (BJA) | San Bernardino County |
| San Bernardino County High Desert Task Force (BJA) | San Bernardino County |
| San Bernardino Joint Terrorism Task Force (FBI Lead) | San Bernardino County |
| Inland Crackdown Allied Task Force (HIDTA) | Riverside County |
| Inland Narcotic Clearing House (HIDTA) | Riverside County |
| Regional Methamphetamine Task Force (HIDTA) | Riverside County |
| Riverside County Marijuana Eradication Team (BJA) | Riverside County |
| Coachella Valley Narcotic Task Force (BJA) | Riverside County |
| Allied Riverside Cities Narcotic Enforcement Team (BJA) | Riverside County |
| Palm Springs Narcotic Enforcement Team (DEA) | Riverside County |
| Riverside Joint Terrorism Task Force (FBI) | Riverside County |

## TASK FORCE COORDINATION

The LA-HIDTA facilitates cooperation and joint efforts among more than 72 Federal, state, and local law enforcement agencies, involving over 720 personnel participating in the LA-HIDTA Task Force and Intelligence initiative.

LA-HIDTA's ISS brings a working memorandum of understanding (MOU) between intelligence initiatives, enhances lines of communication, and defines areas of responsibility. The plan also brings an enhanced level of intelligence resources to the LA-HIDTA law enforcement community. Law enforcement's intelligence needs are addressed regardless of which component of the ISS is initially contacted for service. The ISS then focuses on defining viable targets and providing meaningful case support, based on major drug trafficking intelligence information that has been gathered by the ISS and various law enforcement elements within the region.

The LA-HIDTA Task Force then applies all necessary investigative resources to identify, prioritize, target, and dismantle the major poly-DTOs found operating in the LA-HIDTA on a regional, national, and international level. All task forces, in concert with the ISS, review ongoing cases. The goal is to re-evaluate their targets' viability and redistribute resources, if necessary, to ensure maximum impact and overall success. Case, subject, and event "all crimes" deconfliction are major components of these efforts.

The LA-HIDTA uses the California State Intelligence Index (CSII) to collect, disseminate, and coordinate all investigations that are categorized as any narcotic, gang, or terrorism crimes, as well as major felonies, or Part 1 Crimes, as categorized by the FBI. Field events, primarily involving undercover law enforcement investigators, are also coordinated through a system similar in concept to an air traffic control system. Communication with investigators is continuous and transcends jurisdictional boundaries.

The U.S. Federal Central District's Regional Terrorism Threat Assessment Center (RTTAC) has been identified as the Joint Regional Intelligence Center (JRIC). The JRIC serves as a coordination center of terrorism intelligence for the JTTFs and FBI Field Intelligence Groups (FIGs) within the LA-HIDTA region. In order to enhance efficiency in 2010, the JRIC and JDIG have combined into one intelligence effort and the JRIC is now considered to be one of the LA-HIDTA's three intelligence initiatives. The JRIC is co-led by personnel from the FBI and local agencies which are represented on the LA-HIDTA Executive Board. In order to enhance communications and joint use between personnel, the FBI S.C.I.F. is located in the JRIC. To share secure communications, analysts and managers assigned to the JRIC, along with the other two LA-HIDTA Intelligence initiatives have access to the California Joint Regional Information Exchange System (Cal JRIES) as well as FBI's Law Enforcement On-Line (LEO) system. Additionally, appropriate law enforcement intelligence bulletins are passed between the LA-HIDTA Intelligence and Investigative Support Centers and the JRIC.

All law enforcement agencies, task forces (to include all JTTFs) and intelligence centers within the LA-HIDTA, as well as all HIDTA task force teams within the State of Nevada, utilize the LA CLEAR to perform all case deconfliction and event deconfliction. Additionally, LA CLEAR performs the "off hour" (5:00 PM to 8:00 AM) phone-in tips and leads coverage; monitors state and Federal terrorism information-sharing databases; and monitors public news television channels covering local, regional, national, and international events, for both the State Bureau of Investigation and Intelligence Operations Center (BII/IOC) and for the Northern California Regional Threat Assessment Center (NC-RTTAC).

## *HIDTA EVALUATION*

In order to streamline its intelligence initiatives, the LA-HIDTA has developed an Intelligence Architecture Plan that defines the intelligence responsibilities and priorities within the HIDTA, effectively bringing together its intelligence projects into what today is called the Intelligence Support System (ISS). It optimizes valued resources and enhances coordination of effort including the sharing of information.

In 2009, after prioritizing 317 identified DTOs, the HIDTA specifically targeted 315 for immediate enforcement action. Of the 315 organizations targeted by the LA-HIDTA initiatives, 207 were dismantled or severely disrupted compared to 154 the prior year. Additionally, over 127.6 tons of dangerous drugs were seized by LA-HIDTA Initiatives.

## Michigan HIDTA – Designated in 1997
## Executive Director – Abraham L. Azzam

### *PURPOSE AND GOALS*

The mission of the Michigan HIDTA is to reduce drug trafficking, related violent crimes, and money laundering in the HIDTA Region. This will be accomplished through the coordination and sharing of intelligence, a unified law enforcement effort, and community cooperation that will improve the quality of life in the State of Michigan.

### *STRATEGY*

The Michigan HIDTA Strategy is the Executive Board and Executive Director's response to the drug threat in the Michigan HIDTA region as detailed in the 2009 and 2010 *Michigan HIDTA Drug Market Analysis*. The Strategy is a comprehensive solution to the specific threats in the Michigan HIDTA Region. It is the Executive Board's plan to accomplish the HIDTA program mission to disrupt and dismantle drug trafficking and money laundering organizations in the most effective and efficient manner. The Michigan HIDTA has adopted a three-tiered enforcement strategy. The initiatives attack the threat in the region at Level 1) street level dealers in response to community concerns, Level 2) mid-level dealers and priority targets, and Level 3) major drug and money laundering organizations identified in the HIDTA's Threat Assessment.

The HIDTA's approach to accomplishing its mission and attacking the threat in the region is through a united response from Federal, state, local, and tribal partners, taking full advantage of their knowledge, skills and expertise. Through co-location, interagency cooperation, and consolidation of strategic and tactical information, the HIDTA fosters a comprehensive response to illicit drug trafficking by bringing together all available law enforcement resources in a united front. Cooperative working relationships have been nurtured over many years by the Executive Board and Executive Director to ensure that enhanced communication, collaboration and information sharing support intelligence driven investigations.

### *LOCATION*

The Michigan HIDTA operates out of Detroit, Michigan. It is comprised of 10 counties, 6 in eastern Michigan (Genesee, Macomb, Oakland, Saginaw, Washtenaw and Wayne) and 4 in western Michigan (Allegan, Kalamazoo, Kent and Van Buren). The population of the Michigan HIDTA counties is approximately six million people and includes the major drug markets of Detroit, Flint, Saginaw and the Grand Rapids-Kalamazoo area.

### *INITIATIVES*

The Michigan HIDTA supports many initiatives distributed as follows: 1 management and coordination, 1 training, 2 operational support, 1 investigative support and deconfliction, 2 fugitive apprehension, 4 interdiction, and 19 investigative initiatives that focus on drug trafficking and money laundering organizations.

## SHORT-TERM OBJECTIVES

| YEAR | DTOs Expected to be Disrupted/ Dismantled | Target Return on Investment: Assets | Target Return on Investment: Drugs | Number of Deconflictions Expected to be Submitted | Number of Investigations Expected to be Provided Analytical Support | Number of Initiative Leads Expected to be Referred |
|---|---|---|---|---|---|---|
| 2010 | 167 | $10 | $38.32 | 12,500 | 356 | 342 |

## THREAT ASSESSMENT

The Michigan HIDTA region is located between major drug markets in Chicago and New York City, shares an international border with Canada and has 3 of the 25 busiest commercial land ports in the United States. The Detroit and Port Huron border crossings are major transshipment points for large quantities of club drugs and high potency Canadian indoor-grown marijuana. The region is also a major importation and distribution center for cocaine, heroin, marijuana, BC Bud and MDMA (Ecstasy). Cocaine and crack cocaine continue to pose a significant threat in the region. The availability and abuse of heroin are increasing, with a marked rise in heroin use by young, suburban Caucasians. Marijuana continues to be the most widely abused drug in our region. The exploitation of the Michigan Medical Marijuana Act has become a major problem for law enforcement in the region. Methamphetamine continues to be a problem in western and rural Michigan. Michigan ranks fifth in the Nation in the number of methamphetamine-related events reported to the National Seizure System. Diverted controlled prescription drugs are widely abused in the region. Detroit has become a source city for OxyContin which is smuggled south to Kentucky and other states.

## INTELLIGENCE INITIATIVES

Supervisors from the DEA, FBI, Michigan State Police, the Detroit Police Department and the Michigan HIDTA co-manage the Investigative Support and Deconfliction Center. They meet on a regular basis to discuss current trends and to update each other on agency operations. This commitment provides an open environment with a free sharing of information across agency boundaries. Throughout the Michigan HIDTA, more than 100 law enforcement agencies participate in deconfliction and intelligence sharing services.

## TASK FORCES OPERATING IN THE HIDTA REGION

The table below highlights the Federally-funded drug enforcement task forces operating in the HIDTA region. Multiple HIDTA task forces may make up an overarching HIDTA enforcement or investigative initiative.

| TASK FORCES | LOCATIONS |
|---|---|
| Balkan Organized Crime | Oakland County |
| Bay Area Narcotics Enforcement Team | Saginaw and Bay County |
| Combined Hotel Interdiction Enforcement Team | Wayne County |
| County of Macomb Enforcement Team | Macomb County |
| DEA Dangerous Drugs Group 2 | Wayne County |

| TASK FORCES | LOCATIONS |
|---|---|
| Tactical Diversion Squad (DEA) | Detroit |
| DEA Detroit Enforcement Group 6 | Wayne County |
| DEA Group 19 | Wayne County |
| Detroit Fugitive Apprehension Team | Oakland, Wayne County |
| Detroit Transportation Interdiction Unit DEA Group 7 | Wayne County |
| Domestic Highway Enforcement | Ingham County |
| Downriver Area Narcotics Organization | Wayne County |
| FBI DPD Conspiracy One Organized Crime Task Force | Wayne County |
| Financial Investigation Initiative DEA Group 9 | Wayne County |
| Firearms Investigation Team | Wayne and Genesee County |
| Flint Area Narcotics Group | Genesee County |
| Forensic Enhancement | Wayne and Ingham County |
| Grand Rapids Fugitive Task Force | Kent County |
| Livingston and Washtenaw Narcotics Enforcement Team | Livingston and Washtenaw County |
| Methamphetamine Training | Ingham County |
| Metropolitan Enforcement Team | Kent County |
| Michigan State Police Technical Support | Ingham County |
| Oakland County Narcotics Enforcement Team | Oakland County |
| REDRUM | Wayne County |
| Southwest Enforcement Team | Kalamazoo and Calhoun County |
| Violent Crimes Task Force | Wayne County |
| West Michigan Enforcement Team | Allegan and Ottawa County |
| Western Wayne Narcotics | Wayne County |

## TASK FORCE COORDINATION

The initiatives listed above comprise all of the task forces supported by the Michigan HIDTA. They coordinate their activities through direct communication, case and event deconfliction conducted by the Michigan HIDTA Investigative Support and Deconfliction Center (ISDC), at Task Force Commander meetings coordinated by the Michigan HIDTA and through their initiating Federal, state, and local agencies. Each member agency of the Michigan HIDTA Executive Board utilizes the (ISDC) for deconfliction and case support purposes.

The Michigan HIDTA produces its annual Threat Assessment in conjunction with the National Drug Intelligence Center (NDIC). This assessment provides information on DTOs, MLOs, firearms trafficking, violent crime, terrorist groups, drug trafficking trends, production techniques, gangs, drug-related homicides, and information regarding threats along the Canadian Border. Timely intelligence bulletins and relevant regional law enforcement information is shared electronically through an extensive contact list and directly with the Michigan Intelligence Operations Center (MIOC). The Michigan HIDTA houses components of the State and Detroit/Southeast Michigan Fusion Center.

The Michigan HIDTA is involved in highway interdiction through a comprehensive Domestic Highway Enforcement initiative. The El Paso Intelligence Center's, National Seizure System (NSS) is utilized by this initiative to gather and share data nationwide with other HIDTAs and other agencies. The (NSS) is also utilized by Michigan HIDTA initiatives involved with methamphetamine lab seizures.

Also housed at the Michigan HIDTA are representatives from the ATF, ICE and the Michigan National Guard Counter Drug Program. These agents/analysts work in conjunction with our DEA, FBI, Detroit Police Department and Michigan State Police supervisors, agents and officers, for day-to-day intelligence gathering/sharing, dissemination and case support, and regularly communicate with task force participants.

## HIDTA EVALUATION

The Michigan HIDTA is an excellent example of "agency buy-in" from its law enforcement partners. This is best demonstrated by the small budgets requested by each of our initiatives because participating agencies continue to support the mission by providing the majority of administrative, financial, and operational support required to maintain an effective and efficient initiative. As a result, the Michigan HIDTA has been able to support more initiatives with "added value" funding than many other HIDTAs receiving similar funding.

The Michigan HIDTA continues to monitor emerging threats within its area of responsibility and is quick to respond to them by shifting resources when appropriate. This rapid response to new threats is demonstrative of the HIDTA's increasing capability to conduct intelligence-led enforcement operations, and is an excellent example of the HIDTA's progress in rapidly and effectively addressing new threats before they reach crisis level.

During CY 2009, Michigan HIDTA initiatives disrupted or dismantled 149 DTOs or MLOs, confiscated more than 87 million dollars in illegal drugs, seized more than 26 million dollars in currency and other drug related property or assets, and dismantled 265 clandestine methamphetamine laboratories in HIDTA counties. The Michigan HIDTA removed $28.66 in illegal drugs from the marketplace and seized $8.74 in cash and other assets from drug traffickers for every Michigan HIDTA dollar spent on criminal investigations, intelligence gathering and investigative support activities.

**Midwest HIDTA – Designated in 1996**
**Executive Director – David Barton**

*PURPOSE AND GOALS*

The mission of the Midwest HIDTA is to reduce drug availability in critical and identified markets by creating and supporting intelligence-driven enforcement task forces whose activities are aimed at eliminating or reducing domestic drug trafficking. This is accomplished by enhancing and coordinating drug control efforts among Federal, state, and local enforcement agencies. Central to this mission is cooperative, multi-jurisdictional law enforcement task forces, interagency collaboration, and the sharing of accurate and timely information and intelligence among participating agencies.

*STRATEGY*

The Midwest HIDTA has developed a cohesive and comprehensive regional program focused on reducing and disrupting the importation, distribution, and manufacturing of illegal narcotics. Midwest HIDTA Drug Task Forces maintain an aggressive posture toward enforcement activities. The Midwest HIDTA has identified primary and secondary threat areas, defined drug importation and transportation corridors, and identified areas of local drug production. Investigators then conduct complex, in-depth, multi-jurisdictional OCDETF, Priority Target Organization, Special Operations Division, Regional Priority Organization Target, Consolidated Priority Organization Target, and Drug Trafficking Organization investigations with an emphasis on dismantling organizations and reducing drug-related violence. Investigations target the highest-level of drug trafficking and money laundering organizations utilizing undercover operations and surveillance of command and control communications. These investigations are intelligence driven and are conducted in a spirit of cooperation among Federal, state, and local counterparts in a task force environment.

*LOCATION*

The Office of the HIDTA Director, as the primary management and coordination initiative of the Midwest HIDTA is co-located with the Investigative Support Center in Kansas City, Missouri. The Director's field program staff assists and provides coordination support to regional task forces and HIDTA initiatives. Field staff offices are located within donated office space in four of the six states that are involved in the Midwest HIDTA program. The Midwest HIDTA encompasses the following counties in seven states:
- Illinois: Rock Island;
- Iowa : Black Hawk, Linn, Marshall, Muscatine, Polk, Pottawattamie, Scott, and Woodbury;
- Kansas: Barton, Cherokee, Crawford, Finney, Franklin, Johnson, Labette, Leavenworth, Miami, Saline, Sedgwick, Seward, Shawnee, and Wyandotte;
- Missouri: Boone, Buchanan, Cape Girardeau, Christian, Clay, Cole, Franklin, Greene, Jasper, Jackson, Jefferson, Marion, Platte, Scott, St. Charles, Texas, and St. Louis (City of St Louis);
- Nebraska: Dakota, Dawson, Dodge, Douglas, Gage, Hall, Jefferson, Lancaster, Madison, Platte, Sarpy, and Scott's Bluff;

- North Dakota: Burleigh, Cass, Grand Forks, Morton, Ramsey, Richland, Walsh, and Ward;
- South Dakota: Beadle, Brookings, Brown, Clay, Codington, Custer, Lawrence, Lincoln, Meade, Minnehaha, Pennington, Union, and Yankton.

## *INITIATIVES*

The Midwest HIDTA has 51 initiatives, which include 1 management, 1 training, 2 support, 1 prosecution, 42 investigation/interdiction, and 4 intelligence initiatives.

## *SHORT-TERM OBJECTIVES*

| YEAR | DTOs Expected to be Disrupted/ Dismantled | Target Return on Investment: Assets | Target Return on Investment: Drugs | Number of Deconflictions Expected to be Submitted | Number of Investigations Expected to be Provided Analytical Support | Number of Initiative Leads Expected to be Referred |
|------|------|------|------|------|------|------|
| 2010 | 324 | $3.60 | $16.75 | 23,015 | 5,549 | 7,603 |

## *THREAT ASSESSMENT*

The Midwest HIDTA region continues to be a fertile environment for the importation, manufacturing, and distribution of narcotics. Overall, methamphetamine trafficking is the greatest problem faced by the HIDTA. However, densely populated urban areas in the region continue to experience major problems with all drugs, especially crack cocaine. Along with cocaine, methamphetamine and marijuana continue to be popular in the large urban cities of St. Louis, Kansas City, Des Moines, and Omaha. Heroin is prevalent in large urban communities and surrounding suburbs of St. Louis and Kansas City. The diversion of prescription drugs and medications through "pill mills" and fraudulent Internet transactions is an emerging and dangerous threat. MDMA, GHB, and other dangerous drugs known as "club drugs" are also present in most urban areas.

Law enforcement agencies indicate that Mexican DTOs dominate wholesale drug distribution and transportation. Small cities and rural areas are affected by methamphetamine on a wider scale than large cities; however that gap continues to narrow. All areas continue to see methamphetamine supplied through local production by small clandestine laboratories, facilitated by precursor chemical dealers, and pseudoephedrine smurfing operations.[10]

Competing gangs and other DTOs continue to use violence to solidify and maintain their hold on drug trafficking within their areas of influence. Cooperative local, state, and Federal law enforcement efforts throughout the Midwest HIDTA region have met with noteworthy success in identifying, targeting, and prosecuting active DTOs and gang members involved in violent drug-related activity. Drug trafficking analysis indicates that high level DTOs have been taking root in the region. Many DTOs in the Midwest region are poly-drug operations. The larger urban areas of St. Louis, Kansas City, Des Moines, and Omaha continue to be drug transportation and

---

[10] "smurfing" refers to the action of going from store-to-store purchasing the maximum limit allowable under the law of pseudoephedrine and ephedrine products and then pooling these products which will then be provided to a meth producer.

distribution hubs for the region. Along with drugs, these cities are also in the crossroads of the Nation's highways and are important transit points for movement of DTOs' financial profits returning to the western United States and Mexico.

## INTELLIGENCE INITIATIVES

The Midwest HIDTA Intelligence and Investigative Support Center (IISC), operational since 1998, is located in Kansas City, Missouri and co-managed by the DEA and the Kansas City, MO Police Department. The initiative is a multi-agency coalition that consists of Federal, state, and local agencies in the seven-state Midwest HIDTA region. The IISC, electronically linked to task force locations and key state agencies in each State, collects and analyzes information from all Midwest HIDTA task forces, as well as other participating task forces and agencies. The IISC provides event and subject deconfliction services, multi-source name checks, investigative case support, toll analysis, charting, and graphic work, as well as post-seizure and trend/predictive analysis. The IISC also provides continual evaluation of drug threats to the region, to identify changes in smuggling patterns and trends. The Watch Center is currently manned by elements of the Missouri and Kansas National Guard as well as the Kansas City, Missouri Police Department. By improving the exchange of intelligence and information through more efficient coordination and communications, the IISC enhances the ability of Federal, state, and local law enforcement agencies to identify, arrest, and prosecute key members of DTOs and individuals involved in the clandestine manufacturing of narcotics. Trend and predictive analysis developed by the IISC assists the Midwest HIDTA Executive Board in utilizing its limited resources more efficiently. Event and subject deconfliction is fully implemented in major metropolitan areas through remote access and the Watch Center. The IISC has expanded these services to other areas and further growth and improvements with the interface with Chicago and Southwest Border HIDTAs will occur during the year.

## TASK FORCES OPERATING IN THE HIDTA REGION

The table below highlights the Federally-funded drug enforcement task forces operating in the HIDTA region. Multiple HIDTA task forces may make up an overarching HIDTA enforcement or investigative initiative.

| TASK FORCES | LOCATIONS |
|---|---|
| Cedar Rapids DEA Task Force (HIDTA) | Linn County, IA |
| Des Moines DEA Task Force (HIDTA) | Polk County, IA |
| Fargo DEA Task Force (HIDTA) | Cass County, ND |
| Franklin County Narcotics Enforcement Unit (HIDTA/JAG) | Franklin County, MO |
| Garden City DEA Task Force (HIDTA) | Finney County, KS |
| Grand Forks County Task Force (HIDTA) | Grand Forks County, ND |
| III Corp Drug Task Force (HIDTA/JAG) | Dodge County, NE |
| Iowa Interdiction Support (HIDTA/JAG) | Polk County, IA |
| Jackson County Drug Task Force (HIDTA/JAG) | Jackson County, MO |
| Jefferson County Municipal Enforcement Group (HIDTA/JAG) | Jefferson County, MO |

| TASK FORCES | LOCATIONS |
| --- | --- |
| Kansas City DEA Interdiction TF (HIDTA) | Platte County, MO |
| Kansas City FBI Squad I (HIDTA) | Jackson County, MO |
| Kansas City Metropolitan Enforcement Initiative (HIDTA/JAG) | Jackson County, MO |
| Kansas City Street Crimes Task Force (HIDTA) | Jackson County, MO |
| Kansas City/Overland Park DEA Task Force (HIDTA) | Johnson County, MO |
| Kansas Interdiction Support (HIDTA) | Shawnee County, MO |
| Lincoln-Lancaster Drug Task Force (HIDTA/JAG) | Lancaster County, NE |
| Metro Area Safe Trails Task Force (HIDTA/JAG) | Burleigh County, ND |
| Midwest HIDTA IISC (HIDTA) | Platte County, MO |
| Missouri Interdiction and Information Exchange (HIDTA) | Cole County, MO |
| Muscatine Task Force (HIDTA/JAG) | Muscatine County, IA |
| MUSTANG (HIDTA/JAG) | Boone County, MO |
| Nebraska Interdiction Support (HIDTA) | Lancaster County, NE |
| North Dakota Interdiction (HIDTA) | Burleigh County, ND |
| Omaha Metro Drug Task Force (HIDTA) | Douglas County, NE |
| Pennington County Drug Task Force (HIDTA) | Pennington County, SD |
| Quad Cities Metropolitan Enforcement Group (HIDTA) | Rock Island County, IL |
| Sioux Falls Task Force (HIDTA) | Minnehaha County, SD |
| South Dakota Interdiction (HIDTA) | Pierre, SD |
| Southeast Kansas Drug Enforcement Task Force (HIDTA) | Crawford County, KS |
| Southeast Missouri Drug Task Force (HIDTA/JAG) | Cape Girardeau County, MO |
| Springfield DEA Task Force (HIDTA) | Green County, MO |
| St. Charles County Drug Task Force (HIDTA/JAG) | St. Charles County, MO |
| St. Louis County Multi Drug Enforcement Task Force (HIDTA/JAG) | St. Louis County, MO |
| Tactical Diversion Squad (DEA) | Kansas City, MO |
| Tactical Diversion Squad (DEA) | St. Louis, MO |
| St. Louis DEA Intelligence Group (HIDTA) | St. Louis City, MO |
| St. Louis DEA Major Investigations and Conspiracy Group (37) (HIDTA) | St. Louis City, MO |
| St. Louis DEA Violent Traffickers Task Force (HIDTA) | St. Louis City, MO |
| St. Louis FBI Combined Enforcement Task Force (HIDTA) | St. Louis City, MO |
| Tri-City Drug Task Force (HIDTA) | Hall County, NE |
| Tri-State Sioux City DEA Task Force (HIDTA/JAG) | Woodbury County, IA |
| Wichita DEA Task Force (HIDTA) | Sedgwick County, KS |
| WING Drug Task Force (HIDTA/JAG) | Scottsbluff County, NE |
| Rural Area Interdiction Detail Task Force (JAG) | Buchanan County, IA |

| TASK FORCES | LOCATIONS |
|---|---|
| Southeast Iowa Narcotics Task Force (JAG) | Burlington, IA |
| South Central Iowa Drug Task Force (JAG) | Centerville, IA |
| North Central Iowa Narcotics Task Force (JAG) | Cerro Gordo County, IA |
| Iowa Great Lakes Task Force (JAG) | Clay County, IA |
| S.W. Iowa Narcotics Enforcement Task Force (JAG) | Council Bluffs, IA |
| Northeast Iowa Drug Task Force (JAG) | Decorah, IA |
| Career Criminal & Drug Prosecution Support Task Force (JAG) | Dept. of Justice, IA |
| Dubuque Area Drug Task Force (JAG) | Dubuque County, IA |
| Johnson County Multi-Agency Drug Task Force (JAG) | Iowa City, IA |
| Lee County Narcotics Task Force (JAG) | Keokuk, IA |
| Mid Iowa Drug Task Force (JAG) | Marshall County, IA |
| Southeast Iowa Inter-Agency Drug Task Force (JAG) | Ottumwa, IA |
| Mid-Iowa Narcotics Enforcement Task Force (JAG) | Polk County, IA |
| Scott County Drug Task Force (JAG) | Scott County, IA |
| Central Iowa Drug Task Force (JAG) | Story County, IA |
| Washington/Louisa Narcotics Enforcement Team (JAG) | Washington County, IA |
| Tri-County Drug Task Force (JAG) | Washington County, IA |
| Southeast Multi-County Agency (JAG) | Wahpeton, ND |
| Stutzman County Task Force (JAG) | Jamestown, ND |
| South Sakakawea Narcotics Task Force (JAG) | Sakakawea, ND |
| North Missouri Drug Task Force (JAG) | Adair County, MO |
| East Central Drug Task Force (JAG) | Audrain County, MO |
| Southwest Missouri Drug Task Force (JAG) | Barry County, MO |
| North County Municipal Enforcement Group (JAG) | Bridgeton, MO |
| Buchanan County Drug Strike Force (JAG) | Buchanan County, MO |
| Lake Area Narcotics Enforcement Group (JAG) | Camden County, MO |
| Clay County Drug Task Force (JAG) | Excelsior Springs, MO |
| COMET (Combined Ozarks Multi-Juris. Enforcement Team) (JAG) | Greene County, MO |
| Nitro Task Force (JAG) | Ground County, MO |
| South Central Drug Strike Force (JAG) | Howell County, MO |
| Jasper County Drug Task Force (JAG) | Jasper County, MO |
| Lafayette County Narcotics Unit (JAG) | Lafayette County, MO |
| Mineral Area Drug Strike Force (JAG) | Leadington, MO |
| Northeast Missouri Narcotics Task Force (JAG) | Monroe, MO |
| Mid-Missouri Multi-Jurisdictional Drug Task Force (JAG) | Morgan County, MO |
| Bootheel Drug Task Force (JAG) | Pemiscot County, MO |

| TASK FORCES | LOCATIONS |
|---|---|
| Platte County Multi-Jurisdictional Enforcement Group (JAG) | Platte County, MO |
| Community Narcotics Enforcement Team (JAG) | St. Clair County, MO |
| Metro Multi-Jurisdictional Undercover Drug Program (JAG) | St. Louis, MO |
| Central Nebraska Cooperation for Drug Enforcement (JAG) | North Platte, NE |
| Regional Apprehension Program (JAG) | York, NE |
| Southeast Area for Drug Enforcement (JAG) | Beatrice, NE |
| Special Narcotics Abuse Reduction Effort (JAG) | Columbus, NE |
| DCI Statewide Drug Task Force (JAG) | Pierre, SD |
| Southwest Kansas Drug Task Force (JAG) | Liberal, KS |

## TASK FORCE COORDINATION

The Midwest HIDTA plays a central role in assuring coordination and cooperation with HIDTA-designated initiatives, and to a lesser degree, with agencies and task forces that voluntarily participate. Many efforts are underway outside of HIDTA in state and local agencies to further enhance the capabilities of information exchange. All HIDTA enforcement drug task forces in the Midwest HIDTA share information with the HIDTA IISC and actively participate in the HIDTA Intelligence Coordination Plan. Non-HIDTA task forces utilize the IISC and SAFETNet or their own agency or state programs. Over 1,700 remote users are managed on the secure internal VPN. (In this region, OCDETF has no full-time enforcement task force infrastructure. Coordination is accomplished on a case-by-case basis.) The HIDTA provides the only formal coordination plan in the region. During 2011 Midwest HIDTA will continue to liaison and cooperate with the 11 individual DHS funded state and local fusion, or threat integration centers in the Midwest HIDTA region.

The Midwest HIDTA IISC coordinates information sharing through several integrated groups. The DEA St. Louis Intelligence Group helps gather, analyze, and evaluate information for the St. Louis DEA regional enforcement area. The initiative electronically connects Firebird, Merlin, and Midwest HIDTA VPN to facilitate the exchange of information and intelligence products. The St. Louis DEA Regional Wire Intercept Initiative provides a regionally based telecommunications interception strategy for Federal, state, and local law enforcement agencies. Intelligence gained and distributed through the use of this investigative tool greatly enhances the ability to expand investigations. Additionally, the ATF's Regional Intelligence Group is co-located within the Midwest HIDTA IISC facility. This group provides intelligence support and assistance within the Kansas City division area of Missouri, Kansas, Nebraska, and Iowa. This co-location enhances the coordination of intelligence relating to firearms, gun tracing, domestic terrorism, and violent drug trafficking offenders.

All HIDTA task forces are required to use the HIDTA SAFETNet deconfliction system. All other task forces in the seven-state HIDTA area, whether Federally funded or not, have the ability to voluntarily use SAFETNet to enhance officer safety and event deconfliction. Currently, 399 task forces or agencies in the Midwest HIDTA region participate or have access to SAFETNet. SAFETnet also connects to the National Virtual Pointer System (NVPS), assuring interface with NDPIX and 11 other HIDTA deconfliction systems.

The intelligence subsystem deploys and implements dual purpose all-crime intelligence systems to help law enforcement agencies share, analyze, and disseminate criminal intelligence. The use of RISS and other technology makes it possible to connect multiple HIDTAs together. Midwest HIDTA is a NODE on this secure Virtual Private Network (VPN) system, and continues to develop and host intelligence resources for HIDTA agencies and task forces.

## *HIDTA EVALUATION*

The Midwest HIDTA leadership is keenly focused on the performance of initiatives and task forces. The HIDTA has developed tools to identify primary and secondary drug threat areas to enable agencies at local, regional, and headquarters levels to work together to develop customized plans and focus needed resources on specific identified problems. These tools help target specific drug threats in the HIDTA, which faces significant challenges due to the compartmentalization of drug networks and various business plans of multiple DTOs. The HIDTA Strategy tracks very well with the specific drug threats identified in the HIDTA Threat Assessment and the Drug Market Analysis produced by the NDIC. Performance data provided in the Midwest HIDTA's most recent Annual Report indicate that the initiatives are targeting and impacting identified drug threats. Additionally, ONDCP recently conducted an on-site review of HIDTA initiatives, which verified the Executive Board, HIDTA staff, and task force commanders have instituted procedures to monitor and evaluate the performance and funding of the initiatives.

Several multi-year investigations culminated in 2009 when the HIDTA disrupted or dismantled 340 DTOs, compared to 477 the prior year. There was a large spike in the number of DTOs/MLOs disrupted or dismantled during 2008 resulting from the ONDCP designation of four new Missouri counties in late 2006 (Franklin, Jefferson, Boone and Cole) and the subsequent establishment of four new task force teams in the newly designated counties. Of the 794 DTOs the Midwest HIDTA task forces investigated in 2009, 301 were identified as local, 400 as multi-state, and 93 as international in scope.

# Milwaukee HIDTA – Designated in 1998
## Executive Director – Edward Polachek

## PURPOSE AND GOALS

The mission of the Milwaukee HIDTA is to substantially reduce drug-related activity through enhanced intelligence processes and coordinated law enforcement, prosecutions, and demand reduction efforts.

## STRATEGY

The Milwaukee HIDTA will continue to foster cooperative and effective working relationships among the 21 local, state, and Federal participating member agencies to achieve the common goals of disrupting and dismantling DTOs, and reducing the demand for drugs. Through Milwaukee HIDTA enforcement initiatives working within the seven member counties, investigative emphasis is placed upon the targeting of DTOs that pose the most significant threats, primarily those with ties to the Southwest and Northern borders (multi-state and international). In addition, the initiatives work cooperatively with counties bordering the HIDTA region, other HIDTAs, and law enforcement agencies via Domestic Highway Enforcement to develop multi-pronged investigations.

## LOCATION

The Milwaukee HIDTA operates out of Milwaukee, Wisconsin. It encompasses the seven counties of Brown, Dane, Kenosha, Milwaukee, Racine, Rock, and Waukesha.

## INITIATIVES

The Milwaukee HIDTA has 11 initiatives, which include 1 management, 1 training, 1 support, 1 prevention, 1 prosecution, 1 intelligence, and 5 investigation/interdiction initiatives.

## SHORT-TERM OBJECTIVES

| YEAR | DTOs Expected to be Disrupted/ Dismantled | Target Return on Investment: Assets | Target Return on Investment: Drugs | Number of Deconflictions Expected to be Submitted | Number of Investigations Expected to be Provided Analytical Support | Number of Initiative Leads Expected to be Referred |
|---|---|---|---|---|---|---|
| 2010 | 48 | $.87 | $6.71 | 2,200 | 1,750 | 208 |

## THREAT ASSESSMENT

Heroin abuse and resultant overdose deaths have increased dramatically in the past few years as a result of prescription abuse acting as a gateway and increasing availability of the product. It is rated as a major threat by law enforcement because of the likelihood of overdosing and death for users. Cocaine availability has fallen over the past few years, but it continues to be a large money maker for DTOs operating in this area. High-potency marijuana, both indoor and outdoor grown, is readily available, commands a high price ($3,000 - $5,000 per pound) and is imported directly from Mexico, California, and Canada. It is becoming a major money producer for DTOs that are bringing it to the region in dramatically increasing volumes. Distribution of MDMA from Canada fluctuates in the area. Drug-related violence and violent crime by gangs will continue to pose a serious threat to the Milwaukee HIDTA region.

## *INTELLIGENCE INITIATIVES*

The Intelligence and Investigative Support Center (IISC) was originally called the HIDTA Investigative and Technical Support (HITS) Center and was the first initiative formed with the creation of the Milwaukee HIDTA in 1998. It represents a unique combination of civilian criminal intelligence analysts, WI National Guard Drug Control Program analysts, FBI and DEA analysts, local law enforcement officers acting as technical surveillance officers, law enforcement supervisors (local and Federal), and university criminal justice seniors working as Interns. Overall, this is a combination that brings a breadth of skill to this fast-evolving area variously dubbed "intelligence-led policing," but in reality this is a team approach of skilled analysts working with investigators to find and analyze information and turn it into "actionable intelligence" that leads to operational successes.

The mission of the IISC is to provide accurate and timely information that has been analyzed by trained criminal intelligence analysts and is now "actionable intelligence" to law enforcement agencies regarding drug-related criminal activity within the Milwaukee HIDTA area. In addition, the IISC also supplies technical assistance for the vast array of surveillance equipment utilized for enforcement operations. It continues to provide strategic, organizational, and tactical intelligence on DTOs operating in the Milwaukee HIDTA region using a full array of analytical software such as Pen-Link and I2.

To accomplish the mission, the IISC recently implemented a team approach methodology. Within the IISC are five separate teams of analysts comprised of a team leader and other analyst(s) assigned to the team. The team leader is selected on the basis of experience, skill, and leadership ability, and is responsible for managing team efforts in supporting analytical casework. This approach further encourages analyst development by allowing less experienced analysts to learn new analytical skill sets under the mentorship of the team leader. The IISC supports the overall mission by collecting, evaluating, analyzing, and disseminating timely intelligence on drug distribution, drug-related firearm trafficking, homeland security targets, money laundering, and violent crime organizations and their members. The Milwaukee HIDTA intelligence subsystem is comprised of two components, the IISC and the Technical Support Unit (TSU). These intelligence components provide a full range of tactical, operational, and strategic intelligence support to HIDTA initiatives, participating agencies, and other appropriate law enforcement and intelligence community entities. There is an ever-expanding exchange of tactical, operational, and strategic intelligence between Milwaukee HIDTA and other HIDTAs throughout the country. The core intelligence subsystem functions include:

- Event Deconfliction;
- Case/Subject Deconfliction; and
- Post Seizure Analysis.

The Milwaukee HIDTA IISC functions as a key factor in implementing the HIDTA Strategy, and supports the HIDTA initiatives throughout the year as they execute strategic activities to accomplish the targeted outcomes. Tactical and operational intelligence, as facilitated by IISC personnel, provides the requisite coordination between initiatives and agencies to achieve efficient and effective results, as mandated by the national HIDTA program goals. Full-time, co-located multi-agency personnel and databases provide the infrastructure. The IISC activities have been extremely successful performing the following key functions on behalf of the Milwaukee HIDTA initiatives and participating agencies:

- Facilitating connectivity between and/or among local, state, and Federal law enforcement agencies, criminal databases, as well as other intelligence databases, HIDTA IISCs, national intelligence centers, and open source databases;
- Title-III and PEN register capabilities have proven to be an effective investigative tool and have enabled HIDTA initiatives to disrupt and dismantle major DTOs operating within and outside of the HIDTA region. Several cases were referred to FBI and DEA offices outside of the HIDTA region for additional investigation;
- Developing drug threat and needs assessments; specialized interdiction reports highlighting trafficking trends from across the country that involved subjects from Wisconsin;
- Encouraging reporting agency drug seizures to the National Drug Seizure system at EPIC;
- Author and disseminate intelligence bulletins related to DHE seizures for the States of Wisconsin and Minnesota;
- Providing a variety of analytical tools/graphical depiction capability for use by Milwaukee HIDTA law enforcement initiatives and participating agencies;
- Coordinating Wisconsin National Guard – Drug Control Program resources to law enforcement initiatives and area law enforcement; and
- Collecting, analyzing, and disseminating all DHE seizure data for the State of Wisconsin in support of the National I-90/94 Corridor DHE Project.

The Milwaukee HIDTA IISC is continually seeking new ways to provide intelligence support to member agencies and other law enforcement groups outside the HIDTA region. The IISC analysts have been a source of expertise for other departments as they attempt to increase their intelligence capabilities. By instituting mentoring and training opportunities for other departments, the ability to significantly disrupt or dismantle drug trafficking groups and other criminal entities is enhanced.

### TASK FORCES OPERATING IN THE HIDTA REGION

The table below highlights the Federally-funded drug enforcement task forces operating in the HIDTA region. Multiple HIDTA task forces may make up an overarching HIDTA enforcement or investigative initiative.

| TASK FORCES | LOCATIONS |
|---|---|
| DEA Task Force for Southern WI (DEA) | Southeastern WI |
| Northeast Drug task Force (HIDTA) Includes Brown County MEG | Brown County |
| South Central Drug Task Force (HIDTA) Includes Dane County MEG | Rock and Dane Counties |

| TASK FORCES | LOCATIONS |
|---|---|
| REACT (HIDTA)<br>Includes MEG Units from Waukesha, Racine, Kenosha | Waukesha, Racine and Kenosha Counties |
| Drug Gang (HIDTA) | Milwaukee |
| Fugitive (HIDTA) | Throughout Southeast WI |

## *TASK FORCE COORDINATION*

The Milwaukee Metropolitan Enforcement Group (MMEG) is co-located with the HIDTA, but operates under its own Executive Board policies and is responsible for small to mid-level drug investigations in Milwaukee County. As cases get more complex they are turned over to one of the HIDTA initiatives. The remaining Multi-Jurisdictional Enforcement Group (MEG) units (Kenosha, Racine, and Waukesha) are part of the REACT Initiative to better coordinate information flow on cases, deconflict investigations and share resources in an efficient manner. Each is responsible to its local Executive Board and under REACT to the HIDTA Executive Board for coordination of long term investigations. Again, as their cases develop beyond their own geographic boundaries, they flow to REACT or DEA task force, as appropriate. The DEA task force focuses on major drug trafficking investigations throughout approximately 40 counties in the southern portion of Wisconsin.

Three HIDTA investigative initiatives are co-located in the HIDTA facility in Milwaukee and, as such, are directly involved with information sharing through the HIDTA systems in the IISC. The Northeast and South Central Drug Task Forces are located in Green Bay, Madison and Janesville respectively, but are all connected to the IISC for information sharing and analytical support. One initiative, the Regional Enforcement Activity for Current Threats (REACT) focuses on interdiction (packages, highway, and heroin); another, the Drug Gang Task Force (DGTF) focuses on violent DTOs/gangs throughout southeast Wisconsin; and the third (Fugitive) focuses on apprehension of fugitives and participates in all HIDTA operations. Many of the targets of the Fugitive task force are predominately drug traffickers and murderers.

The Milwaukee HIDTA Executive Board is composed of representatives of all 21 member agencies and is committed to a results/impact-driven strategy that emphasizes demonstrated results, as certified in the PMP developed exclusively by HIDTA directors to demonstrate the value-added by cooperative, multi-agency intelligence-led investigations of major DTOs. The HIDTA initiatives have an Operations Coordinator, who is one of the task force supervisors charged with coordinating the investigations within the HIDTA to ensure maximum use of limited resources.

Coordination of all information is accomplished through the HIDTA IISC and through the use of a common automated case management system (Automated Criminal Investigation Secure System, or ACISS) operated by the State of Wisconsin, Department of Justice, Division of Criminal Investigation (DCI). Criminal Intelligence Analysts from the HIDTA regularly meet with each of the task forces to gather and share information of an intelligence nature. All participate in the HIDTA's annual Threat Assessment, quarterly investigator meetings, i.e. the Southeast Law Enforcement Coordination Team (SELECT), where additional information is shared and training is provided on new investigative/analytic techniques or legal updates.

The HIDTA IISC supervisor and Deputy Director, along with the initiative supervisors, conduct meetings that address the targeting of DTOs.

All information is available for sharing not only within the Milwaukee HIDTA, but through a RISS connection to the State of Wisconsin, and through the NVPS. All targets are deconflicted nationally. Regional events are deconflicted via SAFETNet through the Chicago HIDTA server. This service is provided to all the MEGs and law enforcement across southern Wisconsin. The ACISS, is open to other HIDTAs across the country with approval from the Milwaukee HIDTA IISC Managers, and is currently utilized by the following HIDTAs: Chicago, Midwest, Lake County, Ohio, Michigan, New York/New Jersey, Washington/ Baltimore, and Atlanta.

All units provide information to and receive information from the Fusion Center - Wisconsin State Information Center (WSIC) in Madison, the Southeast Terrorism Alert Center (STAC) in Milwaukee, and the FBI JTTF in Milwaukee. The HIDTA IISC has an FBI Analyst assigned to ensure the flow of information is uninterrupted, as many of the international cases with which HIDTA initiatives are involved with, identify money laundering and arms smuggling operations that could have a terrorism nexus.

## *HIDTA EVALUATION*

The Milwaukee HIDTA program is quickly becoming the recognized focal point for multi-agency enforcement operations in and around the metropolitan Milwaukee area.

The program continues to report and provide solid evidence that a majority of DTOs working within its designated HIDTA region are interconnected with national and international drug trafficking networks and has taken innovative and aggressive steps to develop multi-HIDTA efforts tasked with attacking the threats. The HIDTA's management has made great strides in increasing its interaction and collaboration with other HIDTA programs and agencies in order to destabilize national and transnational drug trafficking networks.

In 2009, the HIDTA disrupted or dismantled 57 DTOs, compared to 36 the previous year. The continued increase in investigative success for 2009 into 2010 is a direct result of several key factors such as: increased utilization of the IISC and the increasing sophistication of analytical tools at the disposal of trained intelligence analysts. In addition the incorporation of outlying counties (Kenosha, Racine, Waukesha, and newly added Rock and Brown), investigative units have added to a more global investigative approach throughout the State. Increased efficiency of investigations has occurred through increased information sharing and deconfliction participation.

## Nevada HIDTA – Designated in 2001
## Executive Director – Kent Bitsko

### PURPOSE AND GOALS

The mission of the Nevada HIDTA (NV HIDTA) is to reduce the manufacture, trafficking, and distribution of methamphetamine, precursor chemicals, and other dangerous drugs by attacking and dismantling large-scale and violent drug trafficking organizations. The goals of the NV HIDTA are to reduce drug availability by disrupting and dismantling drug trafficking organizations (DTOs), reduce the harmful consequences of drug trafficking, and improve the efficiency and effectiveness of the region's law enforcement organizations.

### STRATEGY

The NV HIDTA is instrumental in fostering cooperation between Federal, state, local, and tribal and agencies. The Executive Board facilitates cooperation and collaboration among 17 Federal, state and local agencies that participate in the HIDTA. Having all of the law enforcement agencies in Clark and Washoe Counties working closely together and the executive board of the NV HIDTA aggressively managing the direction of the initiatives, the HIDTA is able to redirect resources very quickly thus mitigating the effectiveness of the DTOs. This, coupled with becoming involved in drug prevention, has given HIDTA multiple tools to combat the harmful effects of the drug traffickers.

During 2009 and 2010, the NV HIDTA Executive Board structured HIDTA initiatives to improve collaboration and coordination among law enforcement agencies. The relationships that have been built will enhance the effectiveness and efficiency of ongoing efforts to attack DTOs operating in Clark and Washoe Counties. Enforcement task force teams will focus on methamphetamine, the number one threat to the Nevada HIDTA region. Additionally, the Pharmaceutical Narcotic Enforcement Team (PharmNet) was expanded by adding two additional DEA agents and an additional local detective to reduce the distribution of diverted pharmaceuticals. Furthermore, NV HIDTA officials have observed a significant increase in heroin trafficking and abuse during the past three years with seizures going from 1 kg in 2007 to 12.6 kg in 2009 and 14 kg through the first three quarters of 2010. As a result, all NV HIDTA task force teams were directed to pay special attention to heroin DTOs and the Special Investigations Unit (SIU) and Northern Nevada Drug Task Force (NNDTF) will both concentrate on heroin distribution groups.

Drug prevention initiatives were also added to the NV HIDTA Strategy. The HIDTA has partnered with the Las Vegas Metropolitan Police Department (LVMPD) and Safe Village Prevention Coalition to help the young people, who are living in one of the lower socioeconomic areas of Las Vegas, stay off drugs. The NV HIDTA has also added the Western Nevada Safe Trails Task Force (WNSTTF) initiative to create inroads to the tribal community.

### LOCATION

The NV HIDTA operates out of Las Vegas, Nevada. It encompasses two counties in the State of Nevada: Clark and Washoe.

## INITIATIVES

The NV HIDTA funds 17 initiatives, which include 1 management, 1 training, 1 prosecution, 1 intelligence, 1 prevention, and 12 enforcement initiatives.

## SHORT-TERM OBJECTIVES

| YEAR | DTOs Expected to be Disrupted/ Dismantled | Target Return on Investment: Assets | Target Return on Investment: Drugs | Number of Deconflictions Expected to be Submitted | Number of Investigations Expected to be Provided Analytical Support | Number of Initiative Leads Expected to be Referred |
|---|---|---|---|---|---|---|
| 2010 | 76 | $6.64 | $7.19 | 13,900 | 140 | 529 |

## THREAT ASSESSMENT

The distribution and use of methamphetamine pose the most significant drug threat to the NV HIDTA region. According to NV HIDTA intelligence, most of the methamphetamine available in the region is supplied by Mexican DTOs that transport the drug to the region from sources of supply in Mexico, Arizona, and California. Methamphetamine availability varies throughout the NV HIDTA region. This variability is most likely associated with different domestic source areas that supply methamphetamine to markets in the region. Underscoring this threat, in the last three months of 2010, Nevada HIDTA task forces have made two large methamphetamine seizures. The first was a Domestic Highway Enforcement stop in Washoe County on I-80 that resulted in the seizure of 17 pounds of methamphetamine, and the second resulted from an investigation by the Clark County Gang Task Force that led to the arrest of 2 suspects and seizure of 19 pounds of methamphetamine. Marijuana is the most widely available and frequently used drug in the Nevada region. NV HIDTA officials have reported a significant increase in the number of indoor grows in the Clark County portion of the NV HIDTA, with over 115 indoor grows discovered by HIDTA task forces or local law enforcement in the area during the first 10 months of 2010. NV HIDTA has also reported an increase of diverted pharmaceuticals available on the streets of Las Vegas and in the numerous nightclubs. The abuse and distribution of these drugs is not limited to these venues, but they contribute significantly to the rapidly expanding problem in the NV HIDTA. There has also been a significant increase in the availability and use of heroin in the area. The heroin seizures in the NV HIDTA have been on the increase for the past three years, including a 12-pound seizure that occurred in November of 2010. Intelligence indicates the young people who are users of opiate-based pharmaceuticals are turning to heroin because it is cheaper and easier to get.

## INTELLIGENCE INITIATIVES

The mission of the NV HIDTA Intelligence and Investigative Support Center (IISC) focuses on the production of comprehensive and timely intelligence products, which are both tactical and strategic in scope. These intelligence products enhance enforcement task force operations and inform regional and national policy makers. Deconfliction services are provided in cooperation with LA CLEAR, the Los Angeles HIDTA intelligence center. Nevada membership in LA CLEAR is funded through the NVHIDTA. LA CLEAR provides all event deconfliction, while the NV HIDTA IISC complements LA CLEAR with subject/case deconfliction services. The Nevada IISC and HIDTA enforcement personnel maintain the ability to interact with each other on a daily basis as the IISC is co-located with 6 of the 12 HIDTA enforcement task forces within the DEA Las Vegas District Office. HIDTA enforcement teams utilize the IISC to cross check names, addresses, and phone numbers on a daily basis and the results are typically shared within 24 hours. The IISC's in-house DEA indices system allows analysts to check information against DEA-wide toll and intelligence records.

The IISC produces case-support products for the task force teams' most prolific investigations. The IISC's involvement in every major NV HIDTA-funded investigation led to 88 IISC "referrals" to other HIDTAs and agencies.

The significance of the IISC's tactical support is not only reflected by the preceding numerical data, but also in its timely and comprehensive strategic products. The IISC's exposure to a wide array of cases has increased its opportunities for intelligence collection and analyses. In 2009, the IISC's commitment to strategic products generated seven intelligence bulletins that included assessments of unique concealment methods and changes to regional trends within MDMA trafficking and distribution.

## TASK FORCES OPERATING IN THE HIDTA REGION

The table below highlights the Federally-funded drug enforcement task forces operating in the HIDTA region. Multiple HIDTA task forces may make up an overarching HIDTA enforcement or investigative initiative.

| TASK FORCES | LOCATIONS |
|---|---|
| Clark County Gang Task Force (HIDTA) | Clark County |
| Regional Offender Drug Enforcement Organization (HIDTA) | Clark County |
| Money Laundering & Asset Removal Task Force (HIDTA) | Clark County |
| Nevada Fugitive Investigative Strike Team (HIDTA) | Clark County |
| Nevada Interdiction Task Force (HIDTA) | Clark and Washoe Counties |
| Northern Nevada Drug Task Force (HIDTA) | Washoe County |
| Pharmaceutical Narcotic Enforcement Team (HIDTA) | Clark County |
| Safe Streets Gang Task Force (HIDTA) | Clark County |
| Southern Nevada Joint Meth Task Force (HIDTA) | Clark County |
| Southern Nevada Drug Task Force (HIDTA) | Clark County |
| Special Investigations Unit (HIDTA) | Clark County |
| Western Nevada Safe Trails Task Force (HIDTA) | Washoe County |
| Tactical Diversion Squad (DEA) | Las Vegas |

## TASK FORCE COORDINATION

All Federally funded drug enforcement task forces in the HIDTA region that specifically target illegal drugs are funded by the HIDTA program. All of the task forces within the NV HIDTA are required to cooperate and interact with the IISC. Every agency in the southern part of the State are required to run all of their deconfliction cases and subjects through LA CLEAR. The Washoe County Task Forces utilize the Regional Information Sharing System (RISS) for their deconfliction service.

All Nevada HIDTA task forces use the HIDTA ISC to do their case analytical support. This results in the information being available to all of the task forces. The other drug units that operate within the confines of the NV HIDTA area (but not funded through HIDTA) use LA CLEAR for their event and subject deconfliction.

There is no terrorism task force within the NV HIDTA. The NV HIDTA has an intelligence analyst assigned to the Southern Nevada Fusion Center. The NV HIDTA director is a member of the Southern Nevada Fusion Center's Board of Governance, and the HIDTA IISC manager is on the steering committee. These organizational structures facilitate the flow of information between the HIDTA and the Southern Nevada Fusion Center.

Information-sharing meetings are facilitated by the IISC on a weekly basis and are attended by detectives and agents assigned to the individual HIDTA task forces. An initiative managers meeting is held bimonthly. These meetings further encourage information sharing.

## HIDTA EVALUATION

The NV HIDTA reported data demonstrating improved outcomes, compared to 2008 data. The number of intelligence referrals to other agencies and other HIDTAs increased from 324 in 2007 to 1,016 in 2009 — an indication that collaboration and coordination with other initiatives, agencies, and HIDTAs has improved. The Executive Board is managing the performance of NV HIDTA task force initiatives, and modifies the funding of the initiatives according to their performance, as well as the new challenges that have emerged in the NV HIDTA region. For example, during 2009, the NV HIDTA reported a surge in heroin seizures both in the northern part of Nevada and in the Las Vegas area. Intelligence indicates there is a significant percentage of young people who are addicted to pharmaceuticals, and they are turning to heroin due to its increased availability and lower price. The price of one dose of heroin is $10, while one dose of Oxycodone is $17-$20.

In 2009, the HIDTA disrupted or dismantled 91 DTOs, compared to 110 the previous year. The reduction in the number of DTOs disrupted or dismantled is consistent with the elements that characterize the NV HIDTA. Many of the organizations identified during 2009 were cells of more extensive international and regional DTOs. By targeting the largest DTOs, and more specifically the methamphetamine DTOs, the NV HIDTA should achieve maximum impact on both the regional and national drug market.

# New England HIDTA – Designated in 1999
## Executive Director – J. T. Fallon

## *PURPOSE AND GOALS*

The mission of the New England (NE) HIDTA is to reduce drug availability by creating intelligence-driven drug and financial crimes task forces aimed at eliminating or reducing domestic drug trafficking and its harmful consequences through enhancing and helping to coordinate drug trafficking control efforts among Federal, state, and local agencies.

## *STRATEGY*

The NE HIDTA provides an agency-neutral program to balance regional law enforcement efforts, and coordinates a strategy to address the regional threat and national priorities. It continues to foster effective working relationships among six U.S. Attorneys' Offices, nine Federal law enforcement agencies, and scores of state and local law enforcement agencies. The 18-member NE HIDTA Executive Board approves the Strategy, as well as the Threat Assessment, budget, and initiatives. NE HIDTA task force initiatives are staffed with co-located Federal, state, and local law enforcement officers. Each task force initiative has a stated mission, strategy, objectives, and performance targets. The NE HIDTA Executive Board, Operations Subcommittee, Intelligence Subcommittee, and Management and Coordination initiative coordinate the integration of all initiatives to ensure a unified effort in achieving goals and objectives. Coordination and partnership with the OCDETF program are fostered, as are partnerships with non-HIDTA agencies and organizations.

## *LOCATION*

The NE HIDTA operates out of Methuen, Massachusetts. It encompasses 13 counties, in 6 states:

- Massachusetts (Essex, Hampden, Middlesex, Plymouth, Suffolk, Worcester);
- Connecticut (Fairfield, Hartford, New Haven);
- Rhode Island (Providence);
- Vermont (Chittenden);
- Maine (Cumberland); and
- New Hampshire (Hillsborough)

## *INITIATIVES*

The NE HIDTA has 19 initiatives, which include 1 management, 1 training, 1 intelligence, 1 prevention, and 15 investigation/interdiction initiatives.

## SHORT-TERM OBJECTIVES

| YEAR | DTOs Expected to be Disrupted/ Dismantled | Target Return on Investment: Assets | Target Return on Investment: Drugs | Number of Deconflictions Expected to be Submitted | Number of Investigations Expected to be Provided Analytical Support | Number of Initiative Leads Expected to be Referred |
|------|------|------|------|------|------|------|
| 2010 | 146 | $6.84 | $6.89 | 7,300 | 84 | 692 |

## THREAT ASSESSMENT

The distribution and abuse of heroin and diverted controlled prescription drugs pose the greatest drug threat to the New England HIDTA region. The use of opioid-based and other controlled prescription drugs (CPDs) will continue to rise, leading to the continued use of heroin as the (cheaper) drug of choice. The Northern border vulnerabilities will continue to be exploited, and the violent crime rate of the major metropolitan areas of New England will continue to be a major cause of concern for state and local law enforcement. This increased crime rate can largely be attributed to poly-drug DTOs and gangs.

Opioid abuse is associated with high levels of violent crime and property crime, and accounts for 70 percent of all illicit drug-related treatment admissions and the majority of poison center hotline calls, hospital visits, and drug-related deaths in the region. Controlled prescription opioid abusers fuel the heroin abuse problem in the region due to the fact that an increasing number of these abusers are switching to heroin because of its higher potency and greater affordability. Cocaine, particularly crack cocaine, is commonly abused in some parts of the New England region, mainly inner-city neighborhoods of major cities. Crack cocaine availability has expanded in many northern New England cities largely because criminal groups and street gangs from southern New England and the New York City metropolitan area have increased distribution in those areas of the region. Violence between these street gangs is increasing as they compete for territory in a lucrative drug market area. Marijuana abuse is pervasive throughout the New England region, with Mexican marijuana and high-potency marijuana from regional domestic and Canadian suppliers readily available. New York City-based Colombian DTOs are the primary wholesale suppliers of heroin and cocaine in the New England region. Dominican DTOs are significant transporters and distributors of retail-level quantities of cocaine, marijuana, heroin, and controlled prescription drugs in the region. Mexican DTOs have increased their operations in the New England HIDTA region and are now significant wholesalers of heroin, cocaine, and marijuana.

## INTELLIGENCE INITIATIVES

The mission of the New England HIDTA Intelligence and Investigative Support Center (IISC) is to proactively collect, evaluate, collate, analyze, and disseminate detailed and relevant all-source information concerning DTOs, specifically Dominican and Colombian Trafficking Organizations, Consolidated Priority Organization Targets (CPOT) and Regional Priority Organization Targets (RPOT) impacting New England and other areas of the country. The IISC provides investigators with tactical all-source information, which supports cases on a daily basis, with special emphasis on cases being worked by other HIDTA initiatives. The IISC also provides strategic intelligence support, which assists investigators in probing major conspiracies, projecting potential criminal drug operations, and producing estimates of future major drug activities. This provides agencies with the necessary information to prioritize investigations and enforcement operations. The IISC Watch Center provides deconfliction services to minimize investigative conflicts between agencies. Sixty-eight New England law enforcement agencies participate in deconfliction services.

The IISC is co-managed by an FBI Supervisory Special Agent and a Sergeant with the Massachusetts State Police. The IISC is co-located in Maynard, MA in a joint venture with the Commonwealth Fusion Center. This space is paid for by the Massachusetts State Police. The IISC utilizes advanced computer technology to assist in the collation, analysis, retrieval, and dissemination of all the collected data. This information includes, but is not limited to: Dominican and Colombian DTOs, emerging border/coastal threats, narco-terrorism, and other organized trafficking groups operating along the New England/Canada border and the New England coastline. Connectivity to other HIDTAs and other HIDTA task forces is achieved through the use of Virtual Private Network (VPN) technology, while the IISC has utilized an intranet/internet solution to connect to non-HIDTA task forces in other states. The IISC furthers this goal through implementation of a RISS node for the IISC. The IISC is committed to the General Counterdrug Intelligence Plan, which mandates that all HIDTAs affiliate with the RISS.NET for information-sharing purposes.

A priority of the IISC is providing Federal, state, and local law enforcement with event and target deconfliction services through the IISC's web-based deconfliction system. Communication to the New England HIDTA IISC is by voice telephone and facsimile transmission, with some remote entry by task forces. Subsequent RISS.NET connectivity between the IISC, the NE HIDTA task forces, and Federal, state, and local law enforcement agencies enhance access to the agency site. The IISC consists of two operational components: Watch Center Section and Analytical Services Section.

## TASK FORCES OPERATING IN THE HIDTA REGION

The table below highlights the Federally-funded drug enforcement task forces operating in the HIDTA region. Multiple HIDTA task forces may make up an overarching HIDTA enforcement or investigative initiative.

| TASK FORCES | LOCATIONS |
|---|---|
| Central Massachusetts HIDTA Task Force | Worcester, MA |
| Financial Investigative Task Force (HIDTA) | Boston, MA |
| Fugitive Task Force (HIDTA) | Boston, MA |
| Greater Boston HIDTA Task Force | Boston, MA |
| Hartford County HIDTA Task Force | Windsor, CT |
| New Haven-Fairfield County HIDTA Task Force | Wilton, CT and Cheshire, CT |
| North Shore HIDTA Task Force | Methuen, MA |
| Northern Vermont HIDTA Task Force | Burlington, VT |
| Plymouth County HIDTA Initiative | Brockton, MA |
| Providence County HIDTA Task Force | Warwick, RI |

| TASK FORCES | LOCATIONS |
|---|---|
| Rhode Island HIDTA Task Force | Providence, RI |
| Southern Maine HIDTA Task Force | Portland, ME |
| Southern New Hampshire HIDTA Task Force | Manchester, NH |
| Southwestern Connecticut HIDTA Task Force | Bridgeport, CT |
| Western Massachusetts Task Force (HIDTA) | Springfield, MA |
| Maine Drug Enforcement Agency | Maine |
| New Hampshire Attorney General's Drug Task Force | New Hampshire |
| Vermont Drug Task Force | Vermont |
| Southern Vermont Drug Task Force | Vermont |
| Northwest Vermont Task Force | Vermont |
| Northeast Vermont | Vermont |
| Heroin Enforcement Action Team | Vermont |
| Essex County Drug Task Force | Essex County, MA |
| Northeast Merrimack Valley Drug Task Force | Essex County, MA |
| North Shore Drug Task Force | Essex County, MA |
| East Hampden County Narcotic Task Force | Hampden County, MA |
| Hampden County District Attorney's Narcotics Task Force | Hampden County, MA |
| Greater Boston Counter Crime Task Force | Middlesex County, MA |
| Suburban Middlesex County Drug Task Force | Middlesex County, MA |
| Southern Middlesex Drug Task Force | Middlesex County, MA |
| WEB Major Crimes Task Force | Plymouth County, MA |
| South Shore Drug Task Force | Plymouth County, MA |
| Boston Drug Task Force | Suffolk County, MA |
| North Suffolk Drug Task Force | Suffolk County, MA |
| Tactical Diversion Squad (DEA) | Boston, MA |
| North Worcester County Drug Task Force | Worcester County, MA |
| Community Narcotics Task Force | Worcester County, MA |
| Regional Drug and Crime Counter Crime Task Force | Worcester County, MA |
| Blackstone Valley Drug Task Force | Worcester County, MA |

## TASK FORCE COORDINATION

The mission of the Southern Maine HIDTA task force is to disrupt/dismantle core and secondary heroin, cocaine, and crack cocaine organizations, RPOTs, and other drug trafficking organizations operating in the Cumberland County, Maine area. The task force coordinates and shares intelligence with the Maine Drug Enforcement Agency, a state-sponsored agency with responsibility for the entire State of Maine, as necessary on cases of mutual interest.

The New Hampshire Attorney General's Drug Task Force (NH DTF) coordinates closely with the Southern New Hampshire Task Force, a NE HIDTA-supported initiative, administered and directed by the DEA in the Hillsborough County area, and in connection with the New

Hampshire State Police Narcotics Investigation Unit. In OCDETF cases, the NH DTF will often pool resources and play a supporting role for the HIDTA task force or NHSP/NIU.

The mission of the HIDTA-supported, DEA-led Northern Vermont HIDTA Task Force (NVTF) is to disrupt/dismantle heroin, cocaine, crack cocaine, synthetic opiate, and marijuana drug trafficking organizations, including those individuals and organizations operating along the Northern Vermont/Canadian border. The task force identifies, targets, arrests, and prosecutes illicit drug organizations, whose activities impact the Northern Vermont area, specifically the HIDTA-designated Chittenden County, and other regions of the country, thereby reducing the flow of drugs, illicit drug assets, and related violence. The NVTF coordinates and shares intelligence with the Vermont Drug Task Force, a state-sponsored task force responsible for the entire State of Vermont.

In the Commonwealth of Massachusetts, the Federally funded drug enforcement task forces are located within six different counties. Each of the task forces is comprised of Federal, state, and/or local law enforcement officers. In a review of all 15 NE HIDTA task forces conducted by the NE HIDTA Director and his Deputy Director, varying levels of coordination and cooperation between Federally funded task forces, HIDTA task forces and OCDETF investigations were revealed. To maintain areas where there is good coordination and enhance weak areas, the Director will continue to impress upon HIDTA task force commanders the need for cooperating and sharing information with all enforcement agencies. He will also meet with the leadership of non-HIDTA law enforcement agencies to further expand cooperation and coordination.

The NE HIDTA facilitates the sharing of intelligence among the many task forces situated throughout New England through the IISC. The IISC supports HIDTA enforcement initiatives, but the future may hold possibilities for coordination of services between the NE HIDTA, the New England State Police Information Network (NESPIN) and state fusion centers, which would include the JTTF.

The HIDTA task forces make every effort to share intelligence with other HIDTA task forces through the efforts of the IISC. Strategies are being developed to increase the level of two-way intelligence sharing.

The HIDTA coordinates with the JTTF when investigative information or intelligence reveals a nexus to terrorism-related activity.

### HIDTA EVALUATION

The New England HIDTA continues to seek innovative means to enhance its effectiveness. The decision to co-locate its IISC with the Massachusetts Commonwealth Fusion Center has provided a more seamless flow of information between local, state, and Federal agencies, and has become a template for other HIDTAs.

Additionally, the NE HIDTA remains an important part of the Domestic Highway Enforcement initiative and has been a focal point for operations along the I-95 Corridor.

During 2009, New England HIDTA task forces identified 390 DTOs and MLOs, a 26 percent increase from the previous year. Additionally, New England HIDTA task forces investigated 386 DTOs and MLOs and disrupted or dismantled 150.

# New York/New Jersey HIDTA – Designated in 1990
## Executive Director – Chauncey Parker

### PURPOSE AND GOALS

The mission of the New York/New Jersey (NY/NJ) HIDTA is to reduce domestic drug trafficking and measurably reduce illegal drug use and crime by enhancing and coordinating drug trafficking control efforts. Recognizing that there is no single solution, the NY/NJ HIDTA seeks to accomplish its mission through collaborative, measurable initiatives including enforcement, information sharing, training, and prevention.

### STRATEGY

The strategy of the NY/NJ HIDTA is to build partnerships to reduce crime, particularly drug-related crime, by enhancing and coordinating drug enforcement efforts. The NY/NJ HIDTA accomplishes this mission by promoting cooperation between agencies through the creation of co-located, commingled task forces, providing technological capabilities to enhance and expedite investigations, and leveraging resources to ensure they are used in the most efficient way possible.

### LOCATION

The NY/NJ HIDTA operates out of New York, NY. It encompasses 22 counties in 2 states:

- New York: New York City (Bronx, Kings, New York, Richmond, and Queens Counties), Albany, Clinton, Erie, Franklin, Monroe, Nassau, Onondaga, St. Lawrence, Suffolk, and Westchester Counties; and
- New Jersey: Bergen, Essex, Hudson, Mercer, Middlesex, Passaic, and Union Counties.

### INITIATIVES

The NY/NJ HIDTA has 14 initiatives, which include 1 management, 1 training, 1 intelligence, 1 technology, and 10 investigation/interdiction initiatives.

### SHORT-TERM OBJECTIVES

| YEAR | DTOs Expected to be Disrupted/ Dismantled | Target Return on Investment: Assets | Target Return on Investment: Drugs | Number of Deconflictions Expected to be Submitted | Number of Investigations Expected to be Provided Analytical Support | Number of Initiative Leads Expected to be Referred |
|------|------|------|------|------|------|------|
| 2010 | 105 | $5.57 | $18.09 | 103,000 | 887 | 1,698 |

## THREAT ASSESSMENT

The NY/NJ HIDTA region, specifically the New York City metropolitan area, is one of the largest drug markets in the United States and a major distribution center for cocaine, heroin, and marijuana. Colombian, Dominican, and Mexican drug trafficking organizations pose the greatest organizational drug threats to the NY/NJ HIDTA region. The St. Regis Mohawk Reservation, which straddles the United States/Canada border in northern New York, is the principal entry point for Canadian high-potency marijuana and ecstasy into the NY/NJ HIDTA region. Traffickers operating in the region launder and move hundreds of millions of dollars annually through money services businesses, structured deposits in traditional depository institutions, the Black Market Peso Exchange, and bulk cash smuggling.

The NY/NJ HIDTA region is one of the greatest strongholds for Colombian DTOs in the United States, and these organizations act as wholesale suppliers to other DTOs throughout the region and along the east coast. Dominican DTOs also are deeply entrenched in the region, distributing drugs at all levels, supplying markets throughout the HIDTA region, and expanding their operations, particularly in New Jersey. Mexican DTOs distribute a more diverse range of drugs than most Colombian and Dominican groups, and are supplying areas throughout the Northeast from the NY/NJ HIDTA region.

The threat from street gangs is increasing in many areas of the region as they have expanded their operations beyond traditional retail drug distribution in New York City and Newark to midlevel and wholesale level distribution in suburban areas, Upstate markets, and rural locations. The expansion of street gang drug distribution operations will likely occur at the expense of local independent dealers and small local criminal groups who are often intimidated by these gangs and cannot effectively compete with them in smaller drug markets. Drug distribution by street gangs in these smaller markets is expected to result in increased violent crime and property crime.

Cocaine availability and abuse are expected to remain relatively high and stable. The continued expansion of Mexican DTO distribution operations in the HIDTA region will supplement the availability of cocaine supplied by Colombian and Dominican traffickers.

Heroin availability is high and increasing as indicated by high purities, low prices, and increased milling operations in the NY/NJ HIDTA region. Heroin sold in New York City and Newark is among the highest purity and lowest priced heroin in the country. On Long Island, significant increases in heroin availability have led to a rise in heroin abuse, particularly among young people. In New Jersey, rising heroin demand has caused New York City-based DTOs to branch out to northern New Jersey, increasing heroin availability there.

Controlled prescription drugs (CPDs) —particularly opioid pain medications—are widely abused throughout the region and, in some areas, contribute to more overdose deaths than any other drug. Continued high levels of CPD abuse are expected to result in a rising number of overdoses and overdose deaths in the region.[11]

---

[11] National Drug Intelligence Center

## INTELLIGENCE INITIATIVES

Intelligence initiatives are a major pillar of the NY/NJ HIDTA strategy to more effectively target criminal organizations operating in the region. Through its intelligence subsystem, which is organized under the Regional Intelligence Center (RIC), the NY/NJ HIDTA provides law enforcement agencies in the region with better access to actionable intelligence, significantly improving their drug enforcement efforts. The RIC, which is led by the New York City Police Department (NYPD), provides event, case and subject deconfliction, analytical case support and strategic reporting, among other critical services. The RIC, which is staffed by 737 participants from numerous Federal, state and local law enforcement agencies, serves as the central conduit for criminal intelligence sharing among law enforcement agencies in the New NY/NJ HIDTA region.

The RIC is organized into several sections, including: the Watch Section; the NYPD Intelligence Section; the Narcotics Intelligence Unit; the High Intensity Financial Crime Area Money Laundering Intelligence Section; and the Firearms Section (Regional Crime Gun Center). Additional Intelligence Centers in New York and New Jersey include: New Jersey Intelligence Center, Westchester Intelligence Center, Nassau County Intelligence Center, Suffolk County Intelligence Center, Riker's Island Intelligence Center, Albany County Intelligence Center, Erie County Intelligence Center, Monroe County Intelligence Center, Onondaga County Intelligence Center, and the USSS Computer Forensics Lab.

The Watch, led by the NYPD, provides law enforcement with immediate access to a wide range of law enforcement and commercial databases 24 hours a day, seven days a week. Through information sharing agreements with Federal, state, and local law enforcement agencies in the New York metropolitan area, Watch analysts have access to virtually all law enforcement and commercial computer records. Inquiries can be run on persons, vehicles, business addresses, and telephone numbers, among other items. Federal, state, and local law enforcement use the Watch Section as a base of operations for intelligence sharing and coordination. Watch analysts provide participating agencies with critical, time-sensitive information and access to centralized law enforcement and commercial databases. Restricted use databases that cannot be located at the Watch are accessible through an agency representative.

The NYPD Intelligence Section is a collection of NYPD intelligence groups that collect, analyze, and disseminate intelligence via the NYPD's case management system. This is available to all HIDTA participants, either directly or through the Watch Section. The intelligence is collected through debriefings, confidential informants, technical surveillance, liaison with other domestic and international law enforcement agencies, and the investigation of leads from the Counter-Terrorism Hotline or other sources. This section also develops and refers cases, monitors trends and links across cases and source data (including the Internet), monitors precinct patterns to assists in crime strategies, and provides analytical support to ongoing cases.

The mission of the Narcotics Intelligence Unit (NIU) is to collect, analyze and distribute real-time tactical and strategic intelligence to law enforcement. The NIU is a collaborative effort between the DEA and NYPD. One of the most effective NIU initiatives, the Hidden Trafficker Program fills a key drug intelligence gap by notifying law enforcement personnel throughout New York and New Jersey when any individual from their jurisdiction is arrested elsewhere in the region for a drug felony or violent crime. In addition to providing local law enforcement with key information about the activities of individuals with criminal histories, the Hidden

Trafficker Program helps investigators identify patterns in narcotics movement within the region. The Hidden Trafficker Program generated over 5,300 notifications in 2009.

The NIU reviews all drug arrests in New York State on a daily basis. DEA analysts conduct checks on the Federal Narcotics and Dangerous Drug Information System (NADDIS). If arrestees appear in NADDIS they are considered "hits" and DEA case agents are then notified. The NIU prepares intelligence dossiers on particular drug arrests which are given to arresting officers and/or District Attorney's Offices on a real time basis.

In addition, the NIU prepares analytical reports on specific/exotic drug types as well as any new method of drug usage or distribution. It also tracks heroin stamp names from drug arrests and controlled buys. The NIU distributes intelligence alerts throughout the Intelligence Division for education and safety purposes. The unit also provides information and assistance to the DEA Domestic Monitoring Program (DMP), which is a program that provides data on the price, purity, and geographic source of heroin being sold at the retail level throughout the US. The NIU oversees the HIDTA Drug Intelligence Officers ("HIDTA DIOs") who are assigned to key locations throughout New York and New Jersey. The HIDTA DIOs serve as intelligence 'points of light' and collectively form a network for the sharing of timely and accurate drug intelligence in the region and beyond.

Another key component of the RIC is the High Intensity Financial Crime Area (HIFCA), a multi-agency financial intelligence, money laundering case support and financial institution outreach unit. It is comprised of approximately 33 investigators, analysts and support personnel from Federal, state, and local agencies who provide crucial intelligence support related to financial crimes investigations. HIFCA analysts initiate, develop and support high quality money laundering investigations at the local, state and Federal levels and assist HIDTA Task Forces in targeting the organizations and individuals responsible for laundering drug profits. The HIFCA undertakes extensive support activities for other NY/NJ HIDTA investigative components, such as the El Dorado Task Force and the NY OCDETF Strike Force. During 2009, the HIFCA provided analytical case support on over 700 occasions, with support ranging from simple database checks to complex, long-term financial record analysis. During this same period, the HIFCA conducted financial institution outreach and financial investigation training on 38 occasions, reaching over 1,900 attendees and students, and referred 133 investigative leads to other agencies.

The Firearms Section, led by ATF, provides a central location for all criminal firearm databases. The Firearms Section gathers and consolidates all aspects of intelligence on illegal firearms use and trafficking and makes that information available to law enforcement 24 hours a day, seven days a week. The mission of the Firearms Section is to centralize gun crime information throughout New York State and to target armed drug criminals (i.e., violent drug gangs) in the New York metropolitan area. The center also seeks to establish collaborative partnerships to centralize information on crime, guns and armed criminals and to fully utilize innovative technology to reduce violent crime. The Watch Section has 24/7 access to the Gun Center, and can query the Gun Center's databases to determine, among other things, if any target has been identified as a potential firearms trafficker. In 2007, the Firearms Intelligence Unit was created within the Regional Crime Gun Center to collect and analyze intelligence related to the identification of individuals committing illegal sale, use, and possession of firearms within New York City and the trafficking of firearms into New York City.

In addition to the sections identified above, the HIDTA has established the following intelligence centers throughout the region, which are connected to the RIC by email via the HIDTANET.

The Westchester Intelligence Center (WIC) is located in White Plains, NY, and has established a central point of contact for information sharing within Westchester County. The WIC provides analytical and strategic case support to Federal, state, and local law enforcement agencies operating in Westchester County. The WIC also provides case/subject deconfliction services through SAFETNet, as well as intelligence profiles on gangs. The goal of the WIC is to assist law enforcement agencies through case support services to disrupt and/or dismantle DTOs operating in Westchester County.

The New Jersey Intelligence Center is co-located with the NJ Drug Trafficking Organization Task Force at the DEA office in Newark, New Jersey. The NJIC, which is linked to the RIC, provides strategic and analytical case support to law enforcement agencies in the seven HIDTA counties in northeastern New Jersey, and outside the HIDTA area on a selected case basis. The NJIC is developing secure electronic connectivity among Federal, state, and local law enforcement agencies in the seven county area, providing them with access to pre-existing Federal, state, and local law enforcement automated databases. The NJIC has also coordinated the implementation of the Photo Imaging Mugshot System (PIMS) in the HIDTA counties in New Jersey. PIMS enables agencies to share arrest photographs and biographic data for arrestees. It is expected that the PIMS network will eventually be implemented throughout the state.

The Suffolk County Intelligence Center is located at the Suffolk County Police Department in Yaphank, NY. The SCIC is linked to the RIC and provides strategic and analytical case support to all law enforcement agencies in Suffolk County.

The Nassau County Intelligence Center is located at the Nassau County Police Academy in Massapequa Park, NY. It is linked to the RIC and provides strategic and analytical case support to all law enforcement agencies in Nassau County.

The primary function of the Intelligence Center at Riker's Island is to collect intelligence on index crime, narcotics, gangs and terrorism. All intelligence collected by participating agencies is entered into IDS. When applicable, case referrals are distributed to appropriate investigative units.

The USSS Computer Forensics Lab is staffed by representatives from the U.S Secret Service, New York State Police, Rockland County Sheriff's Department, ICE, DEA, U.S. Postal Service, Department of Commerce, and ATF. The primary capabilities of the lab include forensic examinations of computers, cellular phones or any global telecommunication device, skimmer devices and all other digital electronic media storage, mobile wireless tracking, live computer forensic analysis and capture, trial preparation and expert testimony, and field-based technical assistance. The Computer Forensics Lab has recently been expanded and is available to both assist and provide access to all law enforcement agencies in the NY/NJ HIDTA region.

The Intelligence Centers in Albany, Erie, Monroe and Onondaga Counties work closely with the HIDTA Regional Intelligence Center in New York City, and other intelligence centers in New York State to provide a comprehensive picture of drug trafficking and drug-related crime throughout the state.

## TASK FORCES OPERATING IN THE HIDTA REGION

The table below highlights the Federally-funded drug enforcement task forces operating in the HIDTA region. Multiple HIDTA task forces may make up an overarching HIDTA enforcement or investigative initiative.

| TASK FORCES | LOCATIONS |
|---|---|
| New York OCDETF Strike Force (HIDTA) | New York, NY |
| New Jersey Drug Trafficking Organization Task Force (HIDTA) | Newark, NY |
| El Dorado Money Laundering Task Force (HIDTA) | New York, NY |
| Regional Fugitive Task Force (HIDTA) | New York, NY |
| New York HIDTA Intelligence and Investigative Support Center (HIDTA) | New York, NY |
| Tactical Diversion Squad (DEA) | New York, NY |
| Tactical Diversion Squad (DEA) | Albany, NY |
| Buffalo Drug Enforcement Task Force (HIDTA) | Buffalo, NY |
| Central New York Drug Enforcement Task Force (HIDTA) | Syracuse, NY |
| Capital District Drug Enforcement Task Force (HIDTA) | Albany, NY |
| Rochester Drug Enforcement Task Force (HIDTA) | Rochester, NY |
| Franklin County Drug Enforcement Task Force (HIDTA) | Franklin County, NY |
| Adirondack Drug Enforcement Task Force (HIDTA) | Plattsburgh, NY |
| DEA New York Drug Enforcement Task Force (DOJ) | New York, NY |
| ATF Firearms Trafficking Task Force (DOJ) | Brooklyn, NY |
| ICE Airport Drug Enforcement Task Force (DHS) | Queens, NY |
| Westchester County Drug Enforcement Task Force (DOJ) | Westchester County, NY |
| FBI Westchester Violent Gang Task Force (DOJ) | Westchester County, NY |
| Long Island Drug Enforcement Task Force (DOJ) | Long Island, NY |
| Long Island Violent Gang Task Force (DOJ) | Long Island, NY |
| FBI Capital District Violent Gang Task Force (DOJ) | Albany, NY |
| ICE Erie County Drug Task Force (DHS) | Buffalo, NY |
| ICE Clinton County Drug Task Force (DHS) | Clinton County, NY |
| New York State Police Counter Narcotics Enforcement Teams (DOJ) | Albany, NY |
| FBI Violent Gang Task Force (DOJ) | Newark, NJ |

## TASK FORCE COORDINATION

There are a number of established avenues of communication, coordination, and collaboration between these HIDTA-funded task forces. All are required to submit case, subject, and event information through the SAFETNet deconfliction system at the Regional Intelligence Center (RIC).

NY/NJ HIDTA task forces share information through various components of the RIC. The Watch provides a one-stop shopping source for critical, time-sensitive information, such as criminal profile and database checks, 24 hours-a-day, seven days a week. The Narcotics Intelligence Unit (NIU) provides strategic analysis and case support for drug-related investigations, thereby facilitating cooperation and intelligence sharing. This includes a network of drug intelligence officers, strategically located throughout the NY/NJ HIDTA region to help ensure the efficient collection, analysis, and dissemination of criminal intelligence to area law enforcement entities. Additionally, through the NIU's Hidden Trafficker program, law enforcement personnel are notified when any individual from their region is arrested for a drug felony or violent crime in the New York metropolitan area. The Regional Gun Center gathers and consolidates intelligence on illegal firearms use and trafficking and makes that information available to law enforcement at all hours of the day.

Additionally, there are various informal coordination mechanisms among all of the task forces within the NY/NJ HIDTA. Participants interact through active cases, operational contacts, periodic meetings, coordinating committees, trainings, and conferences.

The NY/NJ HIDTA plays a central role in providing training to the task forces to ensure the latest information and enforcement techniques are shared and coordinated. Every year, thousands of law enforcement personnel from the region participate in courses through the NY/NJ HIDTA Training Initiative.

Leaders, or their representatives, from the Federal, state, and local law enforcement agencies who participate in the task forces serve on the HIDTA Executive Board, thereby promoting information exchange and coordination. Task forces also participate in the preparation of the annual Threat Assessment and Strategy reports. The information they provide is shared with their agencies and with the Executive Board for review and approval.

### *HIDTA EVALUATION*

The NY/NJ HIDTA continues to effectively engage drug trafficking and money laundering organizations within its area of responsibility. The HIDTA recognizes the drug trafficking threat along the Northern border and is taking steps to gather intelligence in order to effectively address the threat.

In 2009, 910 DTOs/MLOs were identified of which the HIDTA expected to dismantle or disrupt 133. The HIDTA disrupted or dismantled 83 DTOs, compared to 78 the prior year. HIDTA Task Forces removed $179 million of illegal drugs from the marketplace and $89 million in related assets for a combined return on investment of $34.

# North Florida HIDTA – Designated in 2001
# Executive Director – Edward Williams

## PURPOSE AND GOALS

The mission of the North Florida HIDTA (NFHIDTA) is to measurably reduce drug trafficking, related money laundering, and violent crime through a balanced partnership of Federal, state, and local law enforcement leaders directing intelligence-driven initiatives that are performance-oriented and aimed at eliminating or reducing drug trafficking and its harmful consequences in North Florida and the United States.

## STRATEGY

The NFHIDTA will continue to foster cooperative and effective working relationships among the 9 Federal, 9 state, and 18 local agencies in an effort pursue the 2 HIDTA program Goals. Goal one is to disrupt the market for illegal drugs by dismantling or disrupting drug trafficking and/or money laundering organizations. Goal two is to improve the efficiency and effectiveness of the HIDTA initiatives.

## LOCATION

The NFHIDTA operates out of Jacksonville, Florida. It encompasses 10 counties: Alachua, Baker, Clay, Columbia, Duval, Flagler, Marion, Nassau, Putnam, and St. Johns.

## INITIATIVES

The NFHIDTA has 15 initiatives, which include 1 management, 1 training, 1 prevention, 1 intelligence, 1 prosecution, and 10 investigation/interdiction initiatives.

## SHORT-TERM OBJECTIVES

| YEAR | DTOs Expected to be Disrupted/ Dismantled | Target Return on Investment: Assets | Target Return on Investment: Drugs | Number of Deconflictions Expected to be Submitted | Number of Investigations Expected to be Provided Analytical Support | Number of Initiative Leads Expected to be Referred |
|------|------|------|------|------|------|------|
| 2010 | 48 | $3 | $12 | 1,750 | 739 | 70 |

## THREAT ASSESSMENT

For the year 2009, law enforcement officials in the North Florida region almost unanimously reported that transportation and distribution of diverted pharmaceuticals have surpassed the threat posed by traditional street drugs.

Production of crack cocaine, marijuana, and methamphetamine continues to some extent in almost all areas of North Florida. Most of the available crack in the region is produced locally. Marijuana cultivation occurs in the region with a continuing shift toward high quality indoor grow operations, both hydroponic and soil. The Florida housing market continues to struggle, offering ample opportunities for marijuana growers to purchase cheap houses that can be transformed into grow houses. Methamphetamine production continues in various areas in the region. Some agencies have reported seeing more red phosphorous labs than in previous years. The "one pot" production method continues to increase in popularity among methamphetamine producers.

Transportation of illicit drugs continues through the region's seaports, airports, railways, interstate highways and local roads. The variety of transportation methods in the NFHIDTA remains the greatest threat from the NFHIDTA to the rest of the United States. Personal, rental, and commercial vehicles, including tractor trailers, remain the most common method of transportation of illegal drugs and proceeds. Upper and mid-level drug distribution organizations transport large quantities of illegal drugs from source areas such as California, Texas, Arizona, Georgia, and South Florida through the highway system to local markets. The amount of drugs passing through the region en route to other national markets remains difficult to quantify. Large shipments are frequently disguised among shipments of legitimate goods. Package delivery services are frequently used by drug trafficking organizations and criminal groups to transport significant quantities of marijuana, and to a lesser extent cocaine, methamphetamine, MDMA, and diverted pharmaceuticals, into the region from distribution hubs, such as Georgia, Mexico, South Florida, Canada, California, and Texas. Vessels, including fishing boats and pleasure crafts, are used in the transportation of illegal drugs along coastal and intercoastal waterways. Drugs are concealed aboard the vessels and transported within and outside the region. Through the Port of Jacksonville, drugs are transported directly from international markets into the United States. Intelligence indicates the transit route from Puerto Rico to the Port of Jacksonville may be a primary conduit for illegal drugs concealed within containers. Business agreements continue to expand the port, but there has been no noticeable increase in drugs trafficked through the port as a result.

Distribution of drugs, on both the wholesale and retail levels, continues out of private residences, on street corners, and a variety of other sites. The unlawful distribution of diverted pharmaceuticals has become an enormous problem for the NFHIDTA. The organizations and groups responsible for distribution are predominantly local or regional. Retail-level distribution is most prevalent. However, some medical professionals have been involved in the wholesale diversion of prescription pharmaceuticals. Additionally, street-level groups continue to distribute diverted pharmaceuticals in conjunction with other street level drugs, such as powder and crack cocaine. Marijuana is distributed in retail to wholesale amounts in rural, suburban, and urban areas of the region. Sales take place anywhere from private residences, to parking lots, and other public places. Cocaine is distributed in both wholesale and retail amounts in the region, while crack cocaine is usually converted from wholesale amounts of powder cocaine by retail dealers. Local, multi-state, and international groups all participate in the distribution of these drugs. Both of these drugs are found in all areas of the NFHIDTA, but crack cocaine is generally more popular among lower income urban residents. Methamphetamine is distributed in retail quantities throughout the area by a variety of groups. Most distribution in 2009 continued to be facilitated by local individuals who often distributed only to personally known groups of users. Authorities advised that some Mexican-based groups continue to distribute wholesale amounts of methamphetamine brought in from Mexico. Methamphetamine is primarily sold from private residences and often advertised by word of mouth. MDMA is distributed on the wholesale and retail levels in the region by local, multi-state, and international organizations and groups. MDMA has steadily continued to migrate from the distribution markets of clubs and nightlife districts into street-level markets and is often distributed with other traditional street drugs. The availability of heroin continues to decline in the region; however, the drug is still available in limited retail quantities.

DTOs in North Florida utilize a variety of illicit financial techniques to fund their illegal operations and to launder drug proceeds. According to numerous local, state, and Federal law enforcement agencies and task forces surveyed in the NFHIDTA, DTOs in the region typically utilize wire transfers, parcel delivery services, and bulk currency concealed in private and commercial vehicles to move currency and drug proceeds throughout the NFHIDTA. Furthermore, several organizations in the region have been identified as laundering drug proceeds through local business fronts, often commingling drug proceeds with legitimate business ventures. Money launderers also structure bank deposits in attempts to avoid law enforcement attention. Unlicensed money remitters and other deceptive money service businesses also have been known to work with drug traffickers.

Drug-related violent crimes, such as burglaries, robberies, home invasions, and murders occur in the region, particularly in Jacksonville's northwest neighborhoods. The rates of these crimes remain higher than many other areas of the state. For 2009, law enforcement agencies within the North Florida region have noted a continued gang presence—most of which are local, loose knit gangs with tenuous national affiliations. However, some groups claim affiliation with nationally recognized gangs, such as Bloods, Crips, Latin Kings, or Mara Salvatrucha (MS 13). While in most cases the affiliation is based more on local gangs' imitation of national gangs, several documented national gang members have been sighted in the area. These bona fide national gang members have been known to recruit in the area, but usually with only limited success compared to the numbers recruited by the local gangs.

## INTELLIGENCE INITIATIVES

The NFHIDTA IISC is the sole intelligence component of the NFHIDTA. The NFHIDTA IISC's mission is to continue to support the NFHIDTA initiatives and other non-HIDTA law enforcement agencies with investigations that have a drug nexus, providing tactical and strategic analysis.

## TASK FORCES OPERATING IN THE HIDTA REGION

The table below highlights the Federally-funded drug enforcement task forces operating in the HIDTA region. Multiple HIDTA task forces may make up an overarching HIDTA enforcement or investigative initiative.

| TASK FORCES | LOCATIONS |
|---|---|
| Clay County Drug Task Force (JAG) | Clay County |
| Jacksonville Criminal Enterprise Investigative Task Force (FBI) | Duval County |
| Multi-Agency Drug Enforcement Team | Marion County |
| Gainesville-Alachua County Drug Task Force | Alachua County |
| Combined Alachua Drug Enforcement Team (HIDTA) | Alachua County |
| Cash and Asset Seizure Team (HIDTA) | Duval County |
| Fugitive Apprehension Strike Team (HIDTA) | Duval County |
| Gateway (HIDTA) | Columbia County |
| Maritime & Land Investigation and Interdiction Initiative (HIDTA) | Duval County |
| North Florida HIDTA Task Force (HIDTA) | Duval County |
| Prescription Drug Squad (HIDTA) | Duval County |
| Tri-County (HIDTA) | St. Augustine |
| Unified Drug Enforcement Strike Team (HIDTA) | Marion County |
| Violent Crime and Narcotics Task Force (HIDTA) | Duval County |

## *TASK FORCE COORDINATION*

The NFHIDTA plays an integral role in facilitating the sharing of information and intelligence among various law enforcement agencies and task forces, including HIDTA and non-HIDTA participants. The Clay County Drug Task Force and the Jacksonville Criminal Enterprise Investigative Task Force were identified as non-HIDTA Federally funded task forces operating within the NFHIDTA region. Both task forces share information across all platforms of government – Federal, state, and local – to increase productivity and avoid duplication of investigative efforts. As the FBI's Jacksonville Criminal Enterprise Investigative Task Force primarily focuses on the dismantlement and disruption of violent criminal gangs, the drug investigative portions of their cases are referred to the NFHIDTA's Violent Crime Narcotics Task Force. There is a free exchange of information between the two task forces during routine and ad hoc meetings and via ongoing deconfliction processes. In addition, the Multi-Agency Drug Enforcement Team (MADET) out of Marion County and the Gainesville-Alachua County Drug Task Force share their information with the HIDTA initiatives within their respective counties, as well as with the NFHIDTA IISC to enhance coordination and reduce duplication.

Routinely, current and potential drug trafficking trends and officer safety issues are disseminated by the NFHIDTA IISC through intelligence briefs to law enforcement agencies within the HIDTA and made accessible to a larger population of law enforcement personnel via the NFHIDTA webpage. Additionally, on an annual basis, analysts from the HIDTA IISC solicit current drug trends and related information from regional law enforcement drug units for analysis and synthesis into the NFHIDTA's Annual Drug Threat Assessment, which is disseminated to a wide-reaching law enforcement community, NDIC and ONDCP.

NFHIDTA task forces are mandated to submit case/subject and event information for deconfliction through the HIDTA Intranet Based Information System (HIBIS) and its subcomponent, National Information Narcotics Joint Agencies System (NINJAS). Non-HIDTA agencies operating within the NFHIDTA are encouraged to share their case/subject and event deconfliction information with the HIDTA IISC for inclusion in HIBIS and NINJAS, in an effort to expand the deconfliction platform. The NFHIDTA provides deconfliction services to a total of 59 Federal, state, and local law enforcement agencies.

North Florida law enforcement and intelligence resources operate under a mutually agreed upon "Information and Intelligence Sharing Plan". This plan is the architecture for a regional "fusion system" that directs the sharing of information. This fusion system is entitled the Northeast Florida Fusion System Cell (NF-FSC) and is co-located in the NFHIDTA IISC. The IISC and the JTTF are two of the six "nodes" in the fusion system. The information is shared by way of personnel who routinely staff the NFHIDTA IISC and the FBI's JTTF, as well as members of other participating NFHIDTA law enforcement agencies.

### *HIDTA EVALUATION*

The NFHIDTA is meeting or exceeding its performance objectives and targeting the regional threat in a cost-effective manner. The NFHIDTA fosters a neutral environment and brings all levels of government together, enhancing cooperative law enforcement efforts. In addition, the HIDTA continues to play a fundamental role in promoting and assisting law enforcement and investigative support initiatives with information sharing and training needs.

In 2009, NFHIDTA initiatives identified 155 DTOs, 45 were disrupted or dismantled. Based on the expected output of 48 DTOs to be disrupted or dismantled, the NFHIDTA achieved 94 percent of its goal. The NFHIDTA strives to identify and subsequently disrupt or dismantle mid-and wholesale level multi-state and international DTOs. Disrupting or dismantling such DTOs is an onerous and complex task, which generally leads to the expenditure of more time and resources than eliminating a local street level DTO. Of the 155 DTOs identified by the NFHIDTA initiatives, in CY 2009 43 percent, or 67, were multi-state or international in scope. In addition, four cases received OCDETF designation in CY 2009, bringing the total active OCDETF cases in the NFHIDTA to 20.

## North Texas HIDTA – Designated in 1998
## Executive Director – Lance Sumpter

### PURPOSE AND GOALS

The mission of the North Texas HIDTA (NT HIDTA) is to coordinate Federal, state, and local law enforcement resources to reduce the availability of illicit drugs and related violence by:

- Effectively using intelligence to detect, disrupt, and dismantle drug trafficking organizations (DTOs) and money laundering organizations (MLOs), and
- supporting effective demand reduction strategies and programs.

The Vision of the NT HIDTA is to support the National Drug Control Strategy by ridding communities in the North Texas HIDTA region of the dangers of illicit drugs.

### STRATEGY

The NT HIDTA Executive Board oversees the HIDTA Director, who implements the HIDTA strategy in cooperation with the NT HIDTA staff, participating Federal, state, and local officers, and support personnel. The Board extends its oversight by governing four subcommittees: Intelligence, Budget, Domestic Highway Enforcement, and Initiative Review. The Executive Board evaluates the initiatives through the Initiative Subcommittee. This subcommittee ensures that the initiatives adhere to ONDCP and NT HIDTA goals. The Executive Board also determines if new initiatives should be implemented to address identified emerging drug threats.

NT HIDTA initiatives are designed and implemented to identify, investigate, and dismantle or disrupt the area's most dangerous DTOs and MLOs. Each investigative initiative is anchored by a Federal agency and addresses a primary aspect of the HIDTA strategy. Five initiatives focus on large scale DTOs operating in their respective geographical areas. Two initiatives were formed to address narcotics organizations that use violence as a means to advance their drug trafficking activities. An initiative in central Oklahoma was established to reduce violent crime in that region. A commercial smuggling initiative focuses on international DTOs. And, a new money laundering initiative was established in 2009 to address money laundering organizations operating in the region. Additionally, in 2010 the NT HIDTA will collaborate with three drug demand reduction programs within the region to provide added value as law enforcement and expand information sharing.

The NT HIDTA Intelligence Subcommittee reviews the HIDTA intelligence plan and collaborates with the regional intelligence community to ensure that the HIDTA intelligence initiative stays in the forefront on intelligence developments. This subcommittee is comprised of members of the HIDTA Executive Board. However, representatives from the North Central Texas Fusion Center, Metro Operations Support Analysis and Intelligence Center are included in the subcommittee to increase collaboration and engagement with the state fusion centers.

### LOCATION

The NT HIDTA's main office is located in Irving, Texas. The NT HIDTA encompasses 21 counties in 2 states.

- Texas: Collin, Dallas, Denton, Ellis, Henderson, Hood, Hunt, Johnson, Kaufman, Lubbock, Navarro, Parker, Rockwall, Smith, and Tarrant, (Included within the designation are the cities of Dallas and Ft. Worth); and
- Oklahoma: Cleveland, Comanche, Muskogee, Oklahoma, Sequoyah, and Tulsa counties.

## *INITIATIVES*

The NT HIDTA has 16 initiatives, which include 1 management, 1 training, 3 intelligence, and 11 investigation/interdiction initiatives.

## *SHORT-TERM OBJECTIVES*

| YEAR | DTOs Expected to be Disrupted/ Dismantled | Target Return on Investment: Assets | Target Return on Investment: Drugs | Number of Deconflictions Expected to be Submitted | Number of Investigations Expected to be Provided Analytical Support | Number of Initiative Leads Expected to be Referred |
|---|---|---|---|---|---|---|
| 2010 | 33 | $6 | $17 | 22,072 | 543 | 72 |

## *THREAT ASSESSMENT*

The Dallas/Fort Worth metropolitan area is the core of the NT HIDTA, a region recognized as a national distribution center for illicit drugs, due to its proximity to the United States/Mexico border and its multifaceted transportation and financial infrastructures. Law enforcement investigations reveal that Mexican DTOs are the primary suppliers of wholesale quantities of methamphetamine, powder cocaine, commercial grade marijuana, and black tar heroin in the NT HIDTA. These DTOs use "cell heads" in Dallas and Oklahoma City to manage the wholesale narcotic distribution within individual markets. Mexico is the primary source of ice methamphetamine, a principal drug threat in the area.

The NT HIDTA region is a transportation hub for both licit and illicit commerce, due to its proximity to the United States/Mexico border and its major airport. The NDIC reports significant drug activity flowing through the region to northern, northeastern, and southeastern areas of the United States.

## *INTELLIGENCE INITIATIVES*

The NT HIDTA Regional Intelligence Support Center (RISC) is a co-located, multi-agency initiative that provides full intelligence analysis and support to the NT HIDTA investigative initiatives from case targeting through prosecution. The RISC, operational since 1998, is located in Irving, Texas and co-managed by the DEA and the Dallas Police Department. The RISC electronically links the Oklahoma Intelligence Center, Texas Narcotics Intelligence Center and remote sites to support a coalition of Federal, State, and local agencies in Oklahoma and Texas.

Intelligence sharing and deconfliction support services are provided by the RISC, the Oklahoma Intelligence Center (OIC) and the Texas Department of Public Safety (DPS) Texas Narcotics Information System (TNIS). The NT HIDTA RISC and OIC Initiatives provide deconfliction services to the initiatives and law enforcement agencies with their respective states. The deconfliction is an automated system that improves the safety of enforcement operations and the efficiency of investigations. Without exception, deconfliction is viewed as a critical officer safety tool which makes the HIDTA program unique from any other task force program. The RISC collects and analyzes information from all NT HIDTA task forces, as well as other participating task forces and agencies, provides event and subject deconfliction services, multi-source name checks, investigative case support, toll analysis, charting and graphic work, as well as post-seizure and trend/predictive analysis. The RISC also provides continual evaluation of drug threats to the region to identify changes in smuggling patterns and trends. This support helps regional initiatives identify, investigate and dismantle or disrupt the area's most dangerous and prolific DTOs, drug dealers, MLOs, weapons traffickers, and violent criminals. The Watch Center is currently manned by officers from Southlake Department of Public Safety, University Park Police Department, Fort Worth Police Department, Tarrant County Sheriff's Office, an IRS Intelligence Analyst and two HIDTA Analysts. After-hour and weekend Watch Center requests are automatically routed to the Irving Police Department for processing.

The OIC provides intelligence support to the NT HIDTA enforcement initiatives in Oklahoma and deconfliction services to all law enforcement agencies in Oklahoma. The OIC is manned by intelligence analysts from the Oklahoma Bureau of Narcotics (OBN). These analysts collect and disseminate intelligence with regard to the identification and investigation of DTOs and MLOs in Oklahoma. By improving the exchange of intelligence and information through more efficient coordination and communications, the RISC improves the abilities of Federal, State, and local law enforcement agencies to identify, arrest, and prosecute key members of DTOs and MLOs. Trend and predictive analysis developed by the RISC assists the NT HIDTA Executive Board in utilizing its limited resources more efficiently.

## TASK FORCES OPERATING IN THE HIDTA REGION

The table below highlights the Federally-funded drug enforcement task forces operating in the HIDTA region. Multiple HIDTA task forces may make up an overarching HIDTA enforcement or investigative initiative.

| TASK FORCES | LOCATIONS |
|---|---|
| Central Oklahoma Task Force (HIDTA) | Oklahoma City, OK |
| Central Oklahoma Metro Fugitive Task Force (HIDTA) | Oklahoma City, OK |
| Tulsa Regional Drug Task Force (HIDTA) | Oklahoma City, OK |
| Commercial Smuggling Initiative (HIDTA) | Irving, TX |
| Eastern Drug Initiative (HIDTA) | Irving, TX |
| East Texas Violent Crime Initiative (HIDTA) | Irving, TX |
| Northern Drug Initiative (HIDTA) | Irving, TX |
| North Texas DHE Initiative (HIDTA) | Irving, TX |
| Southern Money Laundering Initiative (HIDTA) | Irving, TX |
| Violent Crime Initiative (HIDTA) | Irving, TX |
| Western Drug Initiative (HIDTA) | Irving, TX |
| Tulsa County Sheriff's Office | Tulsa County, OK |

| TASK FORCES | LOCATIONS |
|---|---|
| District 27 Drug Task Force | Sequoyah County, OK |
| District 5 Drug Task Force | Comanche County, OK |
| Tactical Diversion Squad (DEA) | Dallas, TX |
| DEA Dallas Division Task Forces (DEA) | Dallas, TX |
| DEA Dallas Division Task Forces (DEA) | Fort Worth, TX |
| DEA Dallas Division Task Forces (DEA) | Tyler, TX |
| DEA Dallas Division Task Forces (DEA) | Lubbock, TX |
| DEA Dallas Division Task Forces (DEA) | Oklahoma City, OK |

## TASK FORCE COORDINATION

The NT HIDTA facilitates cooperation and joint efforts among 63 Federal, state, and local law enforcement agencies. The HIDTA plays a leading role in coordinating the activities of multiple interagency task forces, drug units and investigative support initiatives, including information sharing, training, and more importantly their deconfliction efforts, which is provided by the NT HIDTA RISC and the OIC. Currently no other regional intelligence center or fusion center in the NT HIDTA region provides deconfliction for officer safety and investigative efficiency. In 2009, the NT HIDTA saw a 22 percent increase in case and subject deconfliction requests compared to 2008. Current users of deconfliction services include all HIDTA initiatives, member agencies and non-HIDTA agencies. The NT HIDTA also provides numerous free training courses that are attended by officers in the area and out-of-state to encourage intelligence sharing. Efforts are being made to increase collaboration with local and State fusion/intelligence centers.

The NT HIDTA Executive Board requires all regional HIDTA task forces to use SAFETNet, as well as the NVPS, for target deconfliction activities. The HIDTA encourages all other enforcement task forces, whether Federally funded or not, to use SAFETNet for deconfliction purposes.

In Texas and Oklahoma, all drug task forces coordinate and share information with the HIDTA RISC, the Texas Narcotic Information System (TNIS), the OIC, and other Federal, state, and local agencies. Intelligence analysts from participating Federal, state, and local agencies also share information through intelligence meetings hosted by their agencies, NT HIDTA, or through informal networking. The NDIC field specialists provide support on a regular, informal, and formal basis by assisting with an annual Drug Market Analysis and Threat Assessment.

## HIDTA EVALUATION

The NT HIDTA program is achieving its stated mission and long-term goals. The HIDTA's short-term goals and many of its performance targets are being met or exceeded.

The strategic location of the NT HIDTA serves as a distribution area for national and transnational drug trafficking organizations as identified in previous years. The program reported that the Dallas/Fort Worth area was being used as a staging area for illicit drugs and a consolidation point for bulk currency and monetary instruments. ONDCP has encouraged the HIDTA's management to increase its interaction and collaboration with other HIDTAs and agencies. As a result of this increased emphasis on collaboration by the HIDTA's management, the number of investigative leads provided by the NT HIDTA to other HIDTAs and other agencies grew by more than 150 percent, from 79 in 2008 to 120 during 2010.

In 2009, the NT HIDTA disrupted or dismantled 25 DTOs. The HIDTA focused most of its investigative efforts on international and multi-state DTOs. Due to increased intelligence and investigative connectivity, the HIDTA successfully met the goals in working on complex cases. The NT HIDTA identified 72 DTOs, 35 percent of which were either dismantled or disrupted.

# Northern California HIDTA – Designated in 1997
## Executive Director – Ron Brooks

### PURPOSE AND GOALS

The Northern California HIDTA (NC HIDTA)'s mission is to measurably reduce the availability of illicit drugs and drug-related crime and violence in support of the National Drug Control Strategy by encouraging: balanced governance of the HIDTA, interagency cooperation, the sharing of information, and use of strategic and tactical intelligence in the planning, budgeting, and investigative processes.

### STRATEGY

The NC HIDTA fosters a comprehensive response in combating illicit drug activity by bringing together all available law enforcement resources in a cohesive strategy to address the problem. NC HIDTA law enforcement initiatives focus on DTOs, money laundering groups, violent drug offenders, open-air drug markets, and domestic drug movement. Newly emerging narco-terrorism trends are also carefully monitored, and information is shared with the Northern California Regional Intelligence Center (NCRIC), the FBI's JTTF, the California State Terrorism Threat Assessment Center (STTAC), the California Department of Justice Bureau of Investigation and Intelligence (BII), and local law enforcement agencies.

### LOCATION

The NC HIDTA operates out of San Francisco, California. The 10 counties that comprise the NCHIDTA include: Alameda, Contra Costa, Lake, Marin, Monterey, San Francisco, San Mateo, Santa Clara, Santa Cruz, and Sonoma.

### INITIATIVES

The NC HIDTA has eight initiatives: one management initiative, one training initiative, one intelligence initiative, and five investigation initiatives.

### SHORT-TERM OBJECTIVES

| YEAR | DTO/MLOs Expected to be Disrupted/ Dismantled | Target Return on Investment: Assets | Target Return on Investment: Drugs | Number of Deconflictions Expected to be Submitted | Number of Investigations Expected to be Provided Analytical Support | Number of Initiative Leads Expected to be Referred |
|------|------|------|------|------|------|------|
| 2010 | 34 | $9.17 | $551.71 | 16,500 | 125 | 113 |

## THREAT ASSESSMENT

Ice methamphetamine trafficking and abuse are the most significant drug threats to the NC HIDTA region. Mexican DTOs are the primary transporters and distributors of the drug. They typically smuggle the drug to the region through ports of entry (POEs) along the United States/Mexico border. Methamphetamine production, which declined significantly in previous years because of enforcement operations and legislation regulating the sale of precursor chemicals, appears to be on the rise again. Methamphetamine laboratory seizures in the NC HIDTA region have declined significantly from 45 in 2005 to 19 in 2009. Large-scale pseudoephedrine "smurfing" operations by Mexican DTOs and criminal groups that employ numerous individuals to purchase cold medications from local retailers are the likely sources of precursor chemical supplies for these super-labs.[12] More drug-related crimes, including violent crimes and property crimes, are attributed to methamphetamine trafficking and abuse than to any other illicit drug.

Marijuana is the most widely available and commonly abused illicit drug in the region. Cannabis cultivation has increased dramatically in the NC HIDTA region over the last five years, making the region one of the most prominent marijuana production areas in the Nation. Moreover, California is the leading cannabis cultivation state in the United States. According to statistics provided by the DEA through its San Francisco Field Division's Domestic Cannabis Eradication Suppression Program (DCESP), approximately 7.5 million marijuana plants were seized in California during Calendar Year 2009.

## INTELLIGENCE INITIATIVES

The mission of the NC HIDTA Bay Area Narcotics Information Network (BAYNIN), including its IISC, is to provide narcotic related intelligence sharing, enhance officer safety, provide analytical case support, make available high tech surveillance and telephone intercept equipment, and provide narcotics training to all law enforcement agencies in the ten-county NC HIDTA region.

In November 2007, the NC HIDTA Executive Board established the Northern California Regional Intelligence Center (NCRIC). The NCRIC is comprised of the personnel, intelligence and investigative equipment resources of the NCHIDTA and the Homeland Security Programs of the former Northern California Regional Terrorism Threat Assessment Center (NCRTTAC) and former Bay Area Terrorism Early Warning Groups (TEWG)'s. The NCRIC serves as the Regional "All Crimes" Intelligence Fusion Center for the Federal Northern District of California. The NCRIC is a cooperative Federal, state, and local public safety effort to centralize the intake, analysis, fusion, synthesis, and appropriate dissemination of criminal and homeland security intelligence in the greater San Francisco Bay Area and the Northern Coastal Counties of California.

The BAYNIN Initiative is a multi-agency coalition of Federal, state, and local agencies in the San Francisco Bay Area that have co-located to serve as a regional narcotic information center. BAYNIN is designed to enhance the ability of NC HIDTA initiatives and agencies to

---

[12] "Smurfing" refers to the action of going from store to store purchasing the maximum limit allowable under the law of pseudoephedrine and ephedrine products at each store and then pooling these products which will then be provided to a cook.

identify, target, arrest, and prosecute key members of criminal organizations by facilitating the exchange of information through enhanced coordination and support.

NC HIDTA's Deputy Director, assigned by the California Department of Justice Bureau of Narcotic Enforcement, provides overall management of the BAYNIN Initiative. A DEA group supervisor provides direct supervision of the analytical support staff. Analytical support is provided by SMCSO, CA DOJ and the California National Guard. BAYNIN provides four primary services:

- Event and investigation deconfliction;
- Investigative support;
- Wire intercepts; and
- Specialized equipment.

BAYNIN provides NC HIDTA's task force personnel, through the Western States Information Network (WSIN), a 24 hours a day, seven days a week deconfliction service that consists of an event deconfliction system to coordinate critical law enforcement investigative or enforcement events, such as search and arrest warrants, undercover drug buy operations, and surveillance. The primary purpose of the deconfliction system is officer safety.

BAYNIN provides essential investigative support services to the entire NC HIDTA region. The IISC provides analytical services to all initiatives to ensure as many violators as possible are identified and relationships to other violators are discovered and then appropriately exploited. BAYNIN's event deconfliction services provide essential officer safety, while ensuring agencies have the opportunity to share their information to enable them to work together and to more efficiently attack DTOs that cross jurisdictional boundaries.

In addition, BAYNIN gives investigators instant access to a wide range of intelligence database and officer safety information through its connectivity with the Statewide Investigative Network System (SINS), which electronically links the SWB HIDTA/CA Region, Los Angeles, Northwest, Hawaii, and Central Valley HIDTAs with NC HIDTA. BAYNIN also offers all participating agencies connectivity with commercial databases, various financial databases, allied agency databases, NADDIS, Firebird, Cal Photo, Cal Gang, the California Law Enforcement Telecommunications System (CLETS), EPIC, and, most recently, the DEA Internet Connectivity Endeavor System (DICE).

Tactical case support, including toll analysis, link analysis, charts and graphs, and "one-stop record checks," is currently offered to participating agencies by BAYNIN's IISC. IISC analysts use software such as Analyst's Notebook, i-Base, PenLink, and other recognized analytical tools to support counterdrug investigations in the NC HIDTA region. Priority is given to supporting investigations that have been accepted by the OCDETF and those targeting documented DTOs. BAYNIN also hosts a money-laundering enforcement and analytical unit for participating agencies. In addition, BAYNIN provides strategic planning for HIDTA initiatives via its annual Threat Assessment.

Wire intercept services are provided by BAYNIN through a fully equipped and staffed Wire Intercept facility available at no cost to Federal, state, or local law enforcement agencies in the region to support drug investigations. This centrally located facility is in the San Francisco office of the California Department of Justice's Bureau of Narcotics Enforcement and serves as a platform to support Federal or state court-authorized wire intercepts (Title III cases), and remote surveillance monitors. This 12-station facility is state-of-the-art and capable of receiving all existing voice and most data transmissions, including Nextel push-to-talk. NC HIDTA IISC support is available for any investigation utilizing the Wire Intercept facilities.

NC HIDTA currently communicates with other HIDTAs and other law enforcement agencies using the secure Regional Information Sharing System email service (RISS.NET). The IISC uses RISS Leads, Law Enforcement Online (LEO), and other services available through RISS and LEO to share information and best practices with other law enforcement and counterdrug agencies.

## *TASK FORCES OPERATING IN THE HIDTA REGION*

The table below highlights the Federally-funded drug enforcement task forces operating in the HIDTA region. Multiple HIDTA task forces may make up an overarching HIDTA enforcement or investigative initiative.

| TASK FORCES | LOCATIONS |
|---|---|
| Alameda County Narcotics Task Force | Alameda County |
| Southern Alameda Narcotics Enforcement Team | Alameda County |
| The Southern Alameda County Gang Violence Suppression Task Force | Alameda County |
| East Bay PTO Task Force (HIDTA) | Alameda County |
| Central Contra Costa Narcotic Enforcement Team | Contra Costa County |
| West County Narcotic Enforcement Team | Contra Costa County |
| Marin County Narcotics Task Force | Marin County |
| Narcotics Enforcement Unit County of Monterey | Monterey County |
| Monterey County Multi-Jurisdictional Meth Enforcement Team | Monterey County |
| County of Monterey Marijuana Eradication Team | Monterey County |
| Tactical Diversion Squad (DEA) | Oakland |
| San Francisco Metro (HIDTA) | San Francisco |
| Santa Clara County Specialized Enforcement Team | Santa Clara County |
| San Jose Police Department's Narcotics and Covert Investigation | San Jose |
| South Bay Metro Task Force (HIDTA) | San Jose |
| Santa Clara County Sheriff's Marijuana Eradication Team | Santa Clara County |
| Santa Clara County Sheriff's Office | Santa Clara County |
| Santa Cruz County Narcotics Enforcement Team | Santa Cruz County |
| San Mateo Narcotic Task Force (HIDTA) | San Mateo County |
| North County PTO Task Force (HIDTA) | Sonoma County |
| Sonoma County Narcotics Task Force | Sonoma County |

## *TASK FORCE COORDINATION*

Each task force is mandated by MOU or memorandum of agreement (MOA) to deconflict and share information as a prerequisite to accepting Federal funds. Furthermore, the NC HIDTA outreaches to the OCDETF Pacific Region program by attendance and active participation at its weekly board meetings and annual conference. The NC HIDTA provides the OCDETF Pacific Region a copy of its annual Threat Assessment and Annual Report.

Each task force deconflicts through WSIN. That is accomplished by identifying a target, location, vehicle, boat, or telephone number and submitting the data via telephone, computer (direct data link or e-mail), or fax to WSIN for subject deconfliction. In the event of a search warrant or surveillance of some other type of law enforcement activity, the event is similarly entered into WSIN for event deconfliction. Depending on the results of the inquiry, the submitter is advised that there is no "hit" and can proceed, or advised that there is a "hit" and informed the source of the information and contact number.

Task Forces further share information through regularly scheduled area meetings, the annual Task Force Commanders Meeting, the California Narcotics Officers Association Conference, and the annual Threat Assessment input.

The NC HIDTA facilitates cooperation, information sharing, and joint efforts among more than 50 Federal, state, and local law enforcement agencies, involving over 199 personnel participating in the NC HIDTA task force and intelligence initiatives. The NC HIDTA's IISC brings an enhanced level of intelligence resources to the NC HIDTA law enforcement community by supporting lines of communication and by providing and coordinating a secure exchange of data and intelligence. It does this by distributing intelligence products, attending Federal, state, and local intelligence meetings, providing investigative support and training, and by hosting narcotics related symposiums and conferences.

Within the investigative realm, the IISC focuses on defining viable targets and providing meaningful case support based upon major drug trafficking intelligence information that has been gathered by both the IISC and various law enforcement elements within the region. This results in an intelligence product that supports the original investigation, documents trends, and identifies future resource and training needs.

The NC HIDTA task forces then apply all necessary investigative resources to identify, prioritize, target, and dismantle the major poly-DTOs found operating in the HIDTA on regional, national, and international levels. Case, subject, and event deconfliction are required components of these efforts.

Cooperation by each Federal, state, and local participant with the NC HIDTA is fluid and seamless. The HIDTA actively provides support to each Federal, state, and local participant and, because of this support, enjoys unfettered access to investigative data. Furthermore, each analyst has either obtained or is in the process of obtaining Secret or Top Secret security clearance to further support access to sensitive data and information sharing.

To facilitate information-sharing and enforcement activities, NCRIC intelligence analysts are embedded in the FBI JTTF. They attend weekly staff meetings at the NCRIC to provide available information for case deconfliction and case support between the JTTF, HSP, and the NC HIDTA.

To share secure communications, analysts and managers assigned to the NCRIC have access to the California Joint Regional Information Exchange System (Cal JRIES) as well as FBI's LEO system. Additionally, appropriate law enforcement intelligence bulletins are passed between NC HIDTA IISCs to the NCRIC and FBI.

All law enforcement agencies, task forces (to include all JTTFs), and intelligence centers within the NC HIDTA, as well as all HIDTA task force teams, are required to utilize the WSIN to perform all case deconfliction and event deconfliction.

The NC HIDTA is an essential element of information sharing among task forces. With sponsored training courses, meetings, and acting as a broker for multi-jurisdictional/multi-agency investigations, the HIDTA's contribution is significant. The intelligence analysts of the NC HIDTA are crucial to the success of many investigations.

The NC HIDTA and the Department of Homeland Security fusion center are co-located through the NCRIC in order to share information, deconflict, and communicate securely regarding public safety and violence. Whereas the NC HIDTA's mission is directed at narcotic enforcement, and the Department of Homeland Security fusion center's mission is terrorism related, they share the common responsibility and noble cause of securing the safety of our communities, states, and Nation.

## HIDTA EVALUATION

The NCHIDTA has continued to grow into the core component of an "All Crimes, All Threats, and All Hazards" Fusion Center by collocating as a full member of the Northern California Regional Intelligence Center (NCRIC). The sharing of resources, training, and databases has elevated communications to real-time response capabilities between the NCHIDTA and its law enforcement partners. The co-location of the NCHIDTA with Homeland Security and JTTF personnel at the NCRIC has resulted in robust cross training and intelligence sharing between personnel investigating drug trafficking organizations to the global threat of domestic and international terrorism.

At the beginning of 2009 the HIDTA's initiatives had identified 74 DTOs operating in Northern California. In 2009, the NC HIDTA disrupted or dismantled 24 DTOs. The remaining DTO's/MLOs are long-term cases still being investigated by NCHIDTA initiatives.

## Northwest HIDTA – Designated in 1997
## Executive Director – Dave Rodriguez

### PURPOSE AND GOALS

The Northwest HIDTA mission is to measurably reduce drug trafficking, money laundering, and drug related violent crimes through intelligence driven targeting of drug trafficking organizations and to reduce demand by supporting treatment and effective demand reduction programs. The Northwest HIDTA program focuses on high-value trafficking targets and financial infrastructures.

### STRATEGY

Northwest HIDTA law enforcement initiatives have established priorities that focus on immobilizing DTOs, especially those involved with drug-related violent crime, and targeting those DTOs that have the greatest adverse impact on the quality of life in neighborhoods and communities. A concentration on firearm seizures and use to perpetrate crime is another substantial commitment by all Northwest HIDTA investigative initiatives. There is a determined effort to counter drug movement into and through the region and to arrest those who conceal the proceeds from illegal drug sales within the region. This is exemplified by the continuing enhancements to regional interdiction initiatives.

### LOCATION

The Northwest HIDTA operates out of Seattle, Washington. The 14 counties that comprise the Northwest HIDTA region include Benton, Clark, Cowlitz, Franklin, King, Kitsap, Lewis, Pierce, Skagit, Snohomish, Spokane, Thurston, Whatcom, and Yakima.

### INITIATIVES

The Northwest HIDTA has 15 initiatives, which include 1 management, 1 training, 1 prevention/treatment, 1 intelligence, 2 interdiction, and 9 investigation initiatives.

### SHORT-TERM OBJECTIVES

| YEAR | DTOs Expected to be Disrupted/ Dismantled | Target Return on Investment: Assets | Target Return on Investment: Drugs | Number of Deconflictions Expected to be Submitted | Number of Investigations Expected to be Provided Analytical Support | Number of Initiative Leads Expected to be Referred |
|------|------|------|------|------|------|------|
| 2010 | 54 | $7 | $265 | 29,000 | 550 | 546 |

### THREAT ASSESSMENT

Methamphetamine and marijuana are identified as the greatest illicit drug threats to Washington State. Methamphetamine production, distribution, and use contribute to a wide range of criminal activities. According to law enforcement officials, ice methamphetamine contributes more than any other drug to both violent and property crimes in the state. Marijuana is the most prevalent drug of abuse in Washington, according to the 2010 Northwest HIDTA Threat Assessment Survey. Cannabis cultivated in both indoor and outdoor grows throughout Washington and, to a lesser extent, Canada-produced marijuana, commonly known as British Columbia (BC) Bud, supply the drug market. Cocaine is a significant threat and among the most common drugs identified in emergency room reports. Use and addiction are widespread throughout the region. Heroin, produced in Mexico, is a significant and increasing threat. It has become readily available in the urban areas of the state, and seizures have increased significantly over the last year. MDMA (3,4-methylenedioxy-methamphetamine, commonly known as ecstasy) is also a significant problem, although most seizures appear destined for other markets. The Washington/Canada border is a transshipment point for MDMA to be transported to the rest of the United States. MDMA mimic tablets, containing Benzylpiperazine (BZP) and/or Trifluoromethylphenylpiperazine (TFMPP), are an increasing threat. Other synthetic drugs like lysergic acid diethylamide (LSD) and gamma hydroxybutyric acid (GHB) are a low threat.

## INTELLIGENCE INITIATIVES

The mission of the IISC is to provide HIDTA-wide intelligence and information sharing to the Northwest HIDTA initiatives. First funded by HIDTA in 1997, the key initiative of the Northwest HIDTA is the IISC. The primary task of the IISC is to provide analytical support and intelligence information services to the HIDTA task forces and participating agencies in the HIDTA region. The Northwest HIDTA IISC also provides intelligence data to other task forces and drug law enforcement agencies in the State. The goal is to coordinate efforts and improve investigative performance to disrupt the drug markets in HIDTA counties, thereby achieving a reduction in the availability and use of drugs among youth and adults. The Northwest HIDTA IISC focuses on high-value trafficking targets and financial infrastructure, while also supporting all HIDTA initiatives. The IISC has one Criminal Intelligence Specialist (CIS) co-located at the Spokane County HIDTA Task Force. The Northwest HIDTA IISC also coordinates activities and shares intelligence with the Pacific Integrated Border Intelligence Team (IBIT), which is an intelligence unit of the Northwest HIDTA Border Task Force in Blaine, Washington.

## TASK FORCES OPERATING IN THE HIDTA REGION

The table below highlights the Federally-funded drug enforcement task forces operating in the HIDTA region. Multiple HIDTA task forces may make up an overarching HIDTA enforcement or investigative initiative.

| TASK FORCES | LOCATIONS |
|---|---|
| Clark-Skamania Drug Task Force (HIDTA) | Vancouver |
| Cowlitz-Wahkiakum Narcotics Task Force (HIDTA) | Kelso |
| Northwest HIDTA Border Task Force (HIDTA) | Blaine |
| Northwest HIDTA Integrated Task Force (HIDTA) | Seattle |
| Snohomish Regional Drug Task Force (HIDTA) | Marysville |
| Spokane County HIDTA Task Force (HIDTA) | Spokane |
| Tacoma Regional HIDTA Task Force (HIDTA) | Tacoma |
| Thurston County Narcotics Task Force (HIDTA) | Tumwater |

| TASK FORCES | LOCATIONS |
|---|---|
| Yakima County HIDTA Task Force (HIDTA) | Yakima |
| Washington State Patrol Investigative Assistance Initiative (HIDTA) | Olympia |
| Northwest HIDTA International Money Laundering TF (HIDTA) | Seattle |
| Pacific Northwest Fugitive Apprehension Task Force (HIDTA) | Seattle |
| Tactical Diversion Squad (DEA) | Seattle |
| Puget Sound Violent Crimes Task Force (HIDTA) | Seattle |
| Eastside Narcotics Task Force (BYRNE) | Bellevue |
| Northwest Regional Drug Task Force (BYRNE) | Bellingham |
| Skagit County Interlocal Drug Enforcement Unit (BYRNE) | Mount Vernon |
| South Snohomish County Narcotics Task Force (BYRNE) | Lynnwood |
| Tri-City Metro Drug Task Force (BYRNE) | Pasco |
| West Sound Narcotics Enforcement Team (BYRNE) | Port Orchard |

## *TASK FORCE COORDINATION*

All drug task forces receiving HIDTA funding and operating in Washington State are mandated to use the Northwest HIDTA IISC deconfliction system. All task forces receiving other Federal funding are also required by the Washington State Administrating Agency to utilize the Northwest HIDTA deconfliction services. Additionally, all of the DOJ investigative agencies in Washington State have agreed to use the Northwest HIDTA Watch Center for deconfliction purposes. The Northwest HIDTA Watch Center uses the WSIN as the primary information source, with access to the national RISS database. This database supplies law enforcement with drug intelligence information from Federal, state, and local agencies. Through this connection with the WSIN/RISS database, Northwest HIDTA is also now connected to the National Virtual Pointer System (NVPS). The NVPS provides participating agencies the capability to exchange target pointer information through a single point of entry using a sensitive but unclassified secure network.

The task forces often work together on overlapping investigations or resource sharing. All drug task forces share information with the Northwest HIDTA IISC and the NDIC field specialist on a regular, informal basis, and formally by a mandated report and Threat Assessment survey. This annual Northwest HIDTA Threat Assessment survey is a requirement for all HIDTA task forces, and has been mandated for completion by all other task forces by the State Administrating Agency. The Washington Narcotics Investigators Association brings together the narcotics investigators in the State of Washington to facilitate and encourage active communication among education, treatment, and law enforcement personnel. Additionally, the Washington State Patrol sponsors semi-annual task force commanders' conferences for all drug units and task forces throughout the State of Washington to exchange information and address issues of mutual concern. Each year, both of these organizations combine their individual conferences with similar organizations in the State of Oregon.

The Northwest HIDTA plays a central role in assuring coordination and cooperation as well as information sharing exists among all drug task forces. Through initiatives such as the DMEIP and the DHE, the Northwest HIDTA coordinates activities and promotes information sharing among task forces and agencies throughout Washington State that may be outside the HIDTA umbrella. Northwest HIDTA-sponsored training programs are available to all law enforcement personnel, not only to HIDTA task forces. In 2009, 57 training programs, many at no cost, were coordinated by the Northwest HIDTA and presented to 1,165 law enforcement personnel throughout the area. The State WSIN representatives routinely coordinate with Northwest HIDTA trainers to present RISSIntel/RISSafe training of law enforcement agencies throughout the State. This has been a well-received opportunity to present a combined WSIN/HIDTA training and education program. The demands for Northwest HIDTA-loaned surveillance equipment continued through the year, and the HIDTA electronics technician worked in support of many agencies throughout the State.

## HIDTA EVALUATION

The Northwest HIDTA is meeting or exceeding its performance objectives and targeting the regional threat in a cost-effective manner. The Northwest HIDTA fosters a neutral environment and brings all levels of government together, enhancing cooperative law enforcement efforts. In addition, the HIDTA continues to play a fundamental role in promoting and assisting law enforcement and investigative support initiatives with information sharing and training needs.

The Northwest HIDTA has implemented its second Native American Project in conjunction with the Snohomish Regional Drug Task Force and the following Tribes: Tulalip, Stillaquamish, Swinomish, and the Sauk Suiattle. The purpose of this project is to fund intelligence-driven operations to detect, deter, interdict, disrupt, and/or dismantle organizations involved in drug trafficking in general on tribal lands, specifically the Yakima Reservation.

During CY 2009, Northwest HIDTA initiatives identified 133 DTOs and MLOs. By the end of the year, 25 percent of these DTOs and MLOs were disrupted, and another 20 percent were dismantled. In total, 60 DTOs or MLOs, 45 percent of those identified, were either disrupted or dismantled.

# Ohio HIDTA – Designated in 1999
## Executive Director – Derek Siegle

## *PURPOSE AND GOALS*

The mission of the Ohio HIDTA is to reduce drug availability by creating intelligence-driven task forces aimed at eliminating or reducing drug trafficking and its harmful consequences through enhancing and helping to coordinate drug trafficking control efforts among Federal, state, and local law enforcement agencies.

## *STRATEGY*

The Ohio HIDTA will continue to coordinate Federal, state, and local law enforcement activities to target DTOs involved in illegal drug production, transportation, and distribution. By commingling and collocating full-time and part-time Federal, state, and local law enforcement investigators, analysts, and officers, Ohio HIDTA-funded task forces achieve a balanced and effective attack on all aspects of the illicit drug market. To maximize results, the Ohio HIDTA facilitates cooperation and joint efforts among more than 169 Federal, state, and local law enforcement agencies, involving over 709 personnel participating in the Ohio HIDTA regional initiatives. These partnerships, developed over time, have become the foundation of the Ohio HIDTA program and are the key to its success.

## *LOCATION*

The Ohio HIDTA operates out of Brooklyn Heights, Ohio which is a suburb of Cleveland. The 11 designated counties that comprise the Ohio HIDTA region are Cuyahoga, Fairfield, Franklin, Greene, Hamilton, Lucas, Mahoning, Montgomery, Stark, Summit, and Warren.

## *INITIATIVES*

The Ohio HIDTA has 16 initiatives, which include 1 management, 1 training, 3 intelligence and 11 investigation/interdiction initiatives.

## *SHORT-TERM OBJECTIVES*

| YEAR | DTOs Expected to be Disrupted/ Dismantled | Target Return on Investment: Assets | Target Return on Investment: Drugs | Number of Deconflictions Expected to be Submitted | Number of Investigations Expected to be Provided Analytical Support | Number of Initiative Leads Expected to be Referred |
|------|------|------|------|------|------|------|
| 2010 | 36 | $4.41 | $10.85 | 7,300 | 82 | 313 |

## THREAT ASSESSMENT

The counties that comprise the Ohio HIDTA contain more than half of Ohio's population and encompass the nine largest cities in the state. The numerous interstate highways that link the HIDTA region to major drug source areas, including the Southwest Border, Chicago, Detroit, New York City, and Canada, are used by traffickers to smuggle illicit drugs into and through the region. Significant amounts of the illicit drugs transported into the area are abused locally, while some are transshipped to drug markets in neighboring states. The distribution and abuse of cocaine pose the greatest drug threat to the Ohio HIDTA region; however, heroin is expected to surpass cocaine as the greatest drug threat in the near term, as the availability of cocaine has decreased in some areas of the region, resulting in higher wholesale prices. The availability of Mexican black tar heroin and brown powder heroin has increased throughout much of the HIDTA region. Consequently, the price of heroin has decreased in some areas. Indoor marijuana production is increasing in some areas of the HIDTA region. Most of the marijuana available and abused in the HIDTA region is commercial-grade Mexican marijuana. Locally produced marijuana also is readily available throughout the HIDTA region, and Canadian high-potency marijuana is primarily available in northern Ohio. Controlled prescription drugs are widely abused throughout the Ohio HIDTA region, and prescription opioid abuse has contributed to increased overdose deaths throughout the state. This problem has been exacerbated by the opening of rogue pain clinics in Southern Ohio. The availability and abuse of other drugs, including MDMA, methamphetamine, PCP, and khat vary throughout the state.[13]

## INTELLIGENCE INITIATIVES

The IISC provides tactical, operational, and strategic intelligence support to the Ohio HIDTA investigative and interdiction initiatives, as well as to other participating agencies. The Deconfliction Center within the IISC handles all event and subject deconflictions and performs numerous law enforcement and public database checks. The Analytical Unit within the IISC provides operational case support primarily in the form of telephone toll analysis, link analysis, biographical research, and post-seizure analysis. The Analytical Unit also provides strategic support in the form of the annual Threat Assessment and Intelligence Bulletins. The Analytical Unit is also responsible for drafting the Annual Report, the Initiative Budgets and Descriptions, and the annual Strategy. The IISC Coordinator is responsible for the management of the IISC and is assisted by an FBI Special Agent and a Cleveland Police Department Lieutenant in the everyday supervision of the analysts and personnel assigned to the IISC. The IISC's structure and design are ever-changing, as are the personnel assigned from the participating agencies.

## TASK FORCES OPERATING IN THE HIDTA REGION

The table below highlights the Federally-funded drug enforcement task forces operating in the HIDTA region. Multiple HIDTA task forces may make up an overarching HIDTA enforcement or investigative initiative.

---

[13] Ohio High Intensity Drug Trafficking Area Drug Market Analysis 2010

| TASK FORCES | LOCATIONS |
|---|---|
| Akron/Summit County HIDTA Drug Task Force (HIDTA) | Akron |
| Commercial Vehicle Intelligence Initiative (HIDTA) | Cleveland |
| DEA Youngstown Drug Task Force (HIDTA) | Youngstown |
| Hotel Interdiction Team (HIDTA) | Cleveland |
| Mahoning Valley Law Enforcement Task Force (HIDTA) | Youngstown |
| Miami Valley Drug Task Force (HIDTA) | Miamisburg |
| Northeast Ohio Drug Task Force (HIDTA) | Cleveland |
| Northern Ohio Law Enforcement Task Force (HIDTA) | Cleveland |
| Northwest Ohio Drug Task Force (HIDTA) | Toledo |
| Ohio Violent Fugitive Task Force (HIDTA) | Ohio |
| South Central Drug Task Force (HIDTA) | Columbus |
| Southwest Ohio Regional Drug Task Force (HIDTA) | Lebanon |
| Stark County Violent Crimes Task Force (HIDTA) | Canton |
| Toledo Metro Drug Task Force (HIDTA) | Toledo |
| Central Ohio Drug Enforcement Task Force | Newark |
| Clermont County Drug Unit | Batavia |
| Columbiana County Drug Task Force | Lisbon |
| Northeast Hamilton County Drug Task Force | Cincinnati |
| Grand Lakes Task Force | Wapakoneta |
| Greene County Agencies for Combined Enforcement (ACE) | Beavercreek |
| Lawrence Drug and Major Crimes Task Force | Ironton |
| Law Enforcement Against Pushers Drug Task Force (LEAP) | Delaware |
| Medina County Drug Task Force | Medina |
| Medway Drug Enforcement Agency | Wooster |
| METRICH Enforcement Unit | Mansfield |
| Multi-Area Narcotics Unit | Defiance |
| Ottawa County Drug Task Force | Port Clinton |
| Southeastern Narcotics Team Task Force | Cambridge |
| Southeast Area Law Enforcement Task Force | Garfield Heights |
| Trumbull, Ashtabula, Geauga Task Force | Middlefield |
| U.S. 23 Pipeline Major Crimes Task Force | Chillicothe |
| West Central Ohio Crime Task Force | Lima |
| Westshore Enforcement Bureau | Bay Village |
| Fairfield-Hocking Major Crimes Unit | Lancaster |
| Greater Warren County Drug Task Force | Lebanon |
| Lake County Narcotics Agency | Painesville |
| Lorain County Drug Task Force | Elyria |
| Mahoning Valley Law Enforcement Task Force | Youngstown |

| TASK FORCES | LOCATIONS |
|---|---|
| Stark County Drug Unit | Canton |
| Summit County Drug Unit | Akron |
| Hamilton County RENEW | Cincinnati |
| Franklin County Drug Task Force | Columbus |

## TASK FORCE COORDINATION

Task forces in Ohio coordinate with each other, with Ohio HIDTA task forces, and with OCDETF task forces. All task forces can use the Ohio HIDTA deconfliction program for both subject and event deconfliction. Ohio HIDTA task force commanders meet regularly with participating law enforcement agencies in their respective areas to share investigative information on drug traffickers, DTOs, and drug trends. Since many of the Ohio HIDTA task forces contain personnel from the Office of Criminal Justice Byrne Grant task forces, the commanders from both groups attend and share information through the Office of Criminal Justice Services (OCJS), the Ohio Task Force Commanders Associations, OCJS quarterly meetings, and quarterly HIDTA Task Force Commanders meetings with the Executive Director of the Ohio HIDTA. All non-HIDTA drug task forces receiving Federal funding are funded out of OCJS via the Byrne Grant. Any law enforcement agency can attend the quarterly HIDTA meetings to learn of opportunities to increase their unit's investigative abilities. In addition, the U.S. Attorneys' Offices meet regularly with the heads of Federal agencies involved in the Ohio HIDTA program, as well as task force commanders, to share information and set investigative goals on both HIDTA and OCDETF cases. The Ohio HIDTA's training programs are also available to officers and agents statewide.

The nature and extent of cooperation by each Federal, state, and local participant is made certain by the Ohio HIDTA. A deconfliction report is prepared monthly by the IISC. The report shows those agencies that are following the guidelines for subject and event deconfliction. The HIDTA Executive Director and Program Manager visit Ohio HIDTA task forces to ensure commanders are holding regularly scheduled briefings with participating Federal, state, and local agencies. Finally, the U.S. Attorneys' Office ensures information is exchanged between investigators and agencies to enhance case investigations and prevent duplication of effort.

The nature and extent to which information-sharing and enforcement activities are coordinated with JTTFs is also ensured by the Ohio HIDTA through the Ohio HIDTA Director's attendance to JTTF Executive Board meetings.

## HIDTA EVALUATION

The Ohio HIDTA facilitates cooperation and joint investigative efforts between numerous law enforcement organizations throughout the region. In Calendar Year (CY) 2009, there were 709 personnel representing 169 Federal, state, and local law enforcement agencies participating in the Ohio HIDTA Initiatives. The Ohio HIDTA Initiatives and Investigative Support Center combine and coordinate their efforts to make significant progress in identifying, investigating, and dismantling or disrupting the area's most dangerous and prolific DTOs, drug dealers, money launderers, street gangs and violent criminals.

During CY 2009, Ohio HIDTA Initiatives accounted for drug seizures worth more than $47 million in illicit wholesale drug proceeds were confiscated from regional DTOs, having a lasting effect on their ability to continue to operate. These seizures represent a substantial reduction in illicit drug availability.

Every Ohio HIDTA budget dollar spent on law enforcement and intelligence initiatives contributed to the removal of $17.69 in illicit drugs from the market, and to the seizure of $7.78 of drug-related assets. Ohio HIDTA law enforcement and intelligence initiatives achieved a notable combined ROI of $25.46 for every $1.00 of Ohio HIDTA funds expended.

During 2009, Ohio HIDTA Initiatives had 171 DTOs under investigation. Of the 171 DTOs, 39 were disrupted and 19 of the targeted DTOs were totally dismantled. In total, Ohio HIDTA Initiatives disrupted or dismantled 58 DTOs in CY 2009.

During CY 2009, Ohio HIDTA Initiatives targeted numerous complex cases involving larger DTOs.  In addition, Ohio HIDTA Initiatives developed enough information to identify five of these more complex investigations as CPOT-linked cases and an additional nine have been identified as RPOT-linked cases.

The Ohio HIDTA plays an integral part in the nationwide Domestic Highway Enforcement Corridor Projects and is participating to the fullest extent in the Priority Drug Investigations Project, a multi-HIDTA and multi-agency effort targeting Dominican DTOs.

# Oregon HIDTA – Designated in 1999
## Executive Director – Chris Gibson

## PURPOSE AND GOALS

In conjunction with the national program goals, the Oregon HIDTA mission is to facilitate, support and enhance collaborative drug control efforts among law enforcement agencies and community-based organizations, thus significantly reducing the impact of illegal trafficking and use of drugs throughout Oregon.

## STRATEGY

The Oregon HIDTA will continue to foster cooperative and effective working relationships among the 8 Federal agencies, 3 state agencies, 40 local agencies and the U.S. Attorneys' Office in the District of Oregon to achieve the common goals of disrupting and dismantling drug trafficking and money laundering organizations, and reducing the demand for, and availability of, drugs.

## LOCATION

The Oregon HIDTA operates out of Salem, Oregon. The Oregon HIDTA region includes the counties of Clackamas, Deschutes, Douglas, Jackson, Lane, Marion, Multnomah, Umatilla, and Washington, and the Warm Springs Indian Reservation.

## INITIATIVES

The Oregon HIDTA has 15 initiatives, which include 1 management, 1 training, 1 prevention, 1 intelligence, 1 drug fugitive, 1 interdiction, 1 investigation/prosecution, and 8 investigation initiatives.

## SHORT-TERM OBJECTIVES

| YEAR | DTOs Expected to be Disrupted/ Dismantled | Target Return on Investment: Assets | Target Return on Investment: Drugs | Number of Deconflictions Expected to be Submitted | Number of Investigations Expected to be Provided Analytical Support | Number of Initiative Leads Expected to be Referred |
|------|------|------|------|------|------|------|
| 2010 | 49 | $2 | $55 | 32,000 | 405 | 262 |

## THREAT ASSESSMENT

Illicit substance use in Oregon exceeds the national per capita average. From 2006 through 2007, Oregon ranked in the top one-fifth of states with reported rates of past-month substance use by people aged 18 and older. A 2008 study conducted by ECONorthwest estimated the total direct economic costs from illicit drug use in Oregon at nearly $2.7 billion in 2006. Of the estimated $2.7 billion in costs, 70 percent was attributed to lost earnings from victims of crime and illicit drug users who perpetrate crime, 20 percent was tied to drug enforcement and the criminal justice system, and 10 percent was connected to healthcare costs.

131

The problem is compounded as drug users and distributors often engage in illegal activities such as money laundering, identity theft, burglaries, property theft, fraud, and other crimes to support drug addictions and finance trafficking and distribution operations.

Drug-related deaths decreased seven percent statewide in 2009, with fatalities dropping from 229 in 2008 to 213 in 2009. Deaths related to heroin use comprised the highest number of deaths, increasing seven percent from 2008 (119) to 2009 (127), the highest number since 2000. The second-highest number of deaths was related to methamphetamine, which declined 18 percent between 2008 (106) and 2009 (87). Cocaine-related deaths dropped 37 percent to 32 deaths in 2009 from 51 reported in 2008. Multnomah County, the most populous county in Oregon, reported the highest number of drug-related deaths statewide, with 94 deaths in 2009. Lane County ranked second with 33 fatalities in 2009, followed by Clackamas (15), Washington (15), and Marion (13) counties. Heroin accounted for the most deaths in Multnomah, Clackamas, Washington, and Marion Counties.

Methamphetamine continues to be widely used and trafficked throughout the HIDTA region. However, reported local methamphetamine lab seizures remain at low levels. From 2004 to 2009, labs reported by law enforcement declined by 97 percent due largely to strict pseudoephedrine control legislation enacted by the Oregon legislature, as well as the enactment of the Federal Combat Methamphetamine Epidemic Act of 2005.

During the last six years, the form of methamphetamine being seized by law enforcement has switched from powder to a more addictive form called "ice" or "crystal meth." Oregon legislation to restrict the availability of pseudoephedrine appears to have reduced the number of methamphetamine labs reported to be operating in the State. While reported methamphetamine labs have hit an historic low in Oregon during 2009 (13), crystal meth continued to be available as Mexican drug traffickers imported the finished product from labs outside the state and from Mexico.

In addition to methamphetamine use, marijuana use, cultivation, and trafficking are also expanding. Law enforcement officers report that the size of outdoor marijuana cultivation sites discovered on public and private lands in Oregon has increased over the past several years primarily due to the expansion of operations by Mexican DTOs. The number of plants seized from outdoor cultivation operations in Oregon in 2009 was more than five times the number seized in 2005. The discovered plants number in the thousands per grow, as opposed to hundreds seized in previous years. The harvested product is distributed both locally and nationally. Additionally, Federal law enforcement report that Asian crime groups are increasingly involved in marijuana trafficking and have established large coordinated indoor grow operations in Oregon, Washington, and Northern California.

### INTELLIGENCE INITIATIVES

The Mission of the Oregon HIDTA IISC is to provide accurate, detailed, and timely tactical, investigative and strategic drug intelligence to HIDTA initiatives, HIDTA participating agencies, and other law enforcement agencies as appropriate, enabling a more effective and efficient utilization of drug investigative resources. The Oregon HIDTA IISC serves as a hub for the sharing and case deconfliction of drug intelligence among local, state, and Federal law enforcement agencies in the region. The initiative is operated in conjunction with the Oregon State Department of Justice's Criminal Intelligence Unit (OCIU). The Oregon State Department of Justice is the sponsoring law enforcement agency for this initiative, and the HIDTA IISC staff is comprised of ODOJ employees and members from participating law enforcement agencies. The Oregon Department of Justice is also the fiscal agent for the Oregon HIDTA.

The Oregon HIDTA IISC is the centerpiece of a successful intelligence network created by the Oregon Department of Justice, and significantly enhanced by the HIDTA program in 1999. Services provided by the IISC continue to be in great demand, as law enforcement agencies discover the advantages of intelligence-lead investigations. A major enhancement to the IISC occurred in 2003. Funds allocated from the National HIDTA program allowed the Oregon HIDTA IISC to convert the original Oregon Department of Justice intelligence database to a web-enabled system allowing investigators to access the system from their desktop computer. This essentially put a direct connection for investigators to the IISC in their office, and therefore put the IISC on these investigators' minds. This built-in advertisement increased demand for analytical assistance, intelligence submissions, and inquiries significantly.

The initiative is coupled with a statewide intelligence system that coordinates intelligence and provides case and event deconfliction support to all participating agencies. The initiative is a designated RISS.Net Node which connects the Oregon HIDTA and the OSIN system to the other national RISS.Net Projects and architecture. The initiative also provides and manages encrypted sensitive but unclassified email for all HIDTA task forces and law enforcement agencies in Oregon.

Another major enhancement occurred in 2007 with the establishment of the Oregon TITAN Fusion Center. The center is comprised of analysts and investigators from the FBI, ATF, IRS, Oregon National Guard, the Oregon State Police, the Salem Police Department, the U.S. Department of Homeland Security, and the Oregon Department of Justice. A decision was made to house the group within the existing HIDTA Watch Center to better integrate and streamline intelligence flowing into both intelligence operations. All cases are deconflicted by both groups for greater investigative efficiency. This initiative receives administrative oversight and direction from the Oregon HIDTA Executive Board, the HIDTA Director, and the Intelligence Subcommittee. The initiative has completed its electronic infrastructure, and has met all General Counter-drug Intelligence Plan (GCIP) goals and requirements for HIDTA IISCs.

The Oregon HIDTA hosts and operates a remote criminal intelligence database. This system is called the Oregon State Intelligence Network (OSIN) and provides all Oregon drug task forces, HIDTA drug task forces, state and local law enforcement agencies, and Federal law enforcement agencies, remote access to the intelligence database and geo-event deconfliction services. Using RISS.Net access via a secure intranet, law enforcement agencies are able to make direct, real-time intelligence submissions and inquires directly into the OSIN system. A query of the system gives law enforcement personnel access to not only drug crime-related intelligence, but all crimes, gang, and criminal organization intelligence. This integration of intelligence resources enables personnel to recognize the connection drug crime suspects have with other major crimes, such as weapons-related offenses, identity theft, financial fraud, auto theft, and gang-related violence.

The OSIN website operates on the RISS.Net system and is now directly connected to the WSIN system. A query of either the OSIN database, or the WSIN system, automatically queries the other system. This system provides the initiative and its users with a secure and encrypted means of networking classified and confidential information. This includes e-mail communications, which are now integrated with the FBI sponsored LEO communication system.

In addition to the OSIN system, the HIDTA IISC also hosts an "outward facing" website called OSIN.info. The website is used to post important news stories, links to investigative websites, and all publications written by the IISC and the Oregon DOJ legal staff. Each analyst in this initiative currently has the ability to access a common case management system, and a wide variety of law enforcement, government, and commercial database resources from his/her workstation computer. This enables the analyst to conduct a significant amount of research from one location and provides another level of case/subject deconfliction through the networked case management system. Analysts also access the Internet and FinCEN from their workstations. They also have the capability, through the RISS.Net system, to electronically share analytical products with case investigators in a secure law enforcement environment.

## TASK FORCES OPERATING IN THE HIDTA REGION

The table below highlights the Federally-funded drug enforcement task forces operating in the HIDTA region. Multiple HIDTA task forces may make up an overarching HIDTA enforcement or investigative initiative.

| TASK FORCES | LOCATIONS |
|---|---|
| Blue Mountain Narcotics Team (HIDTA) | Pendleton |
| Central Oregon Drug Enforcement (HIDTA) | Bend |
| Clackamas County Interagency Task Force (HIDTA) | Oregon City |
| Cops Mentoring Youth – Oregon Partnership (HIDTA) | Portland |
| Douglas County Interagency Narcotics Team (HIDTA) | Roseburg |
| HIDTA Interdiction Team (HIDTA) | Portland |
| Oregon HIDTA DEA (DEA) | Portland, Salem, Eugene, Medford |
| Intelligence and Investigative Support Center (HIDTA) | Salem |
| Medford Area Drug and Gang Enforcement (HIDTA) | Medford |
| Oregon State Police Training Initiative (HIDTA) | Salem |
| Portland Area Metro Gang Task Force (HIDTA) | Milwaukie |
| Regional Organized Crime Narcotics Task Force (HIDTA) | Portland |
| Tactical Diversion Squad (DEA) | Portland |
| Westside Interagency Narcotics Team (HIDTA) | Beaverton |
| United States Marshals Service Fugitive Task Force (USMS) | Portland |

## TASK FORCE COORDINATION

All Oregon task forces receiving OCDETF, JAG/Byrne or HIDTA funding are encouraged to use the Oregon State Intelligence Network (OSIN), which is managed by the Oregon Department of Justice for subject and event deconfliction.

All drug task forces share information with the Oregon HIDTA IISC and NDIC field specialists. Many of the task forces work together on investigations and subsequently share information and resources. The Oregon HIDTA IISC publishes a weekly intelligence bulletin that is sent electronically to law enforcement agencies throughout the State. The Oregon HIDTA conducts quarterly information-sharing meetings with task force managers and supervisors. The Oregon Narcotics Association coordinates training conferences for narcotics officers annually. WSIN coordinators conduct information-sharing meetings on a regular basis with drug task force commanders throughout the State.

The Oregon HIDTA IISC is co-located with the State of Oregon Fusion Center, which shares information routinely and freely with the JTTF based in Portland.

## *HIDTA EVALUATION*

All of the Oregon HIDTA enforcement initiatives implement the HIDTA's Strategy by concentrating HIDTA resources for enforcement and investigative enhancements. These tools enable the HIDTA to target the members of high-value DTOs, which results in better cases, targeted prosecutions, reduced drug trafficking, reduced drug use and availability, improved community livability, and reduced drug-related crime and violence.

In 2009, the HIDTA disrupted or dismantled 49 DTOs, compared to 53 the prior year. International and multi-state DTOs are often larger organizations which require more investigative resources to disrupt or dismantle than local DTOs. Of the 49 DTOs disrupted or dismantled in 2009, 33 (67 percent) were international and multi-state in scope.

# Philadelphia/Camden HIDTA – Designated in 1995
## Executive Director – Jeremiah Daley

### PURPOSE AND GOALS

The mission of the Philadelphia/Camden HIDTA (PC HIDTA) is to reduce drug trafficking and related violent crime in the PC HIDTA region. To accomplish this, the PC HIDTA will:

- Facilitate interagency cooperation at the local, state, and Federal levels to strengthen law enforcement's ability to investigate DTOs and associated money laundering and violence;
- Improve intelligence gathering, analysis, and sharing capabilities to dismantle and/or disrupt drug gangs; and
- Provide mission-critical resources and services otherwise unavailable to regional law enforcement agencies.

### STRATEGY

In light of both the new and persistent challenges it faces, PC HIDTA focuses on the following strategic priorities:

- Systematic targeting, investigation, apprehension and prosecution of the region's violent drug traffickers and major DTOs, with particular emphasis on violent drug gangs;
- Continuous identification and removal from the marketplace of the products and proceeds of drug trafficking by intelligence-driven interdiction and money laundering investigation;
- Targeted pursuit and apprehension of drug offenders and violent fugitives, capitalizing on PC HIDTA-supported partnerships;
- Improved collection, analysis and dissemination of drug and related criminal intelligence in support of PC HIDTA initiatives and area law enforcement objectives;
- Maximized inter-agency information sharing by expanded electronic connectivity within and beyond the PC HIDTA, utilizing both proven and emergent technologies and systems; and
- Enhancement of participating agencies' personnel through accessible and cost-efficient training arranged and delivered by PC HIDTA and its professional development partners.

### LOCATION

The PC HIDTA operates out of Philadelphia, Pennsylvania. It includes the counties of:

- Pennsylvania (Philadelphia - City of Philadelphia), Chester and Delaware; and
- New Jersey (Camden - City of Camden).

## INITIATIVES

The PC HIDTA has 11 initiatives, which include 1 management, 1 training, 1 intelligence and 8 investigation/interdiction initiatives.

## SHORT-TERM OBJECTIVES

| YEAR | DTOs Expected to be Disrupted/ Dismantled | Target Return on Investment: Assets | Target Return on Investment: Drugs | Number of Deconflictions Expected to be Submitted | Number of Investigations Expected to be Provided Analytical Support | Number of Initiative Leads Expected to be Referred |
|------|------|------|------|------|------|------|
| 2010 | 70 | $3 | $10 | 8,000 | 137 | 114 |

## THREAT ASSESSMENT

The most significant trafficking and abuse threats to the PC HIDTA region include cocaine, crack cocaine, heroin, marijuana, methamphetamine, and diverted pharmaceutical drugs. Marijuana remains the most widely abused illicit drug in the Lower Delaware Valley. Recent investigations reveal high potency marijuana is readily available in the region; in addition, indoor marijuana grow operations have increasingly been encountered in both suburban and urban locations. Passage of the New Jersey Compassionate Use Medical Marijuana Act in January 2010, permitting the use of medical marijuana for qualifying patients, is expected to complicate law enforcement efforts regarding marijuana trafficking. The use, diversion, and distribution of licit pharmaceutical drugs are among the most serious threats facing law enforcement, treatment, and medical professionals in the Lower Delaware Valley. Law enforcement officials report that due to the effectiveness of prescription drug monitoring programs in the region, some pharmaceutical traffickers are traveling to areas without strict monitoring to purchase their product and bring back into the region for resale.

The PC HIDTA anticipates that street gangs will pose an expanding threat to the PC HIDTA region. Gangs, such as the Bloods in Camden, NJ, have been and continue migrating to suburban locations. This trend presents a new threat to communities previously untouched by drug-related violence.

## INTELLIGENCE INITIATIVES

The mission of the PC HIDTA IISC is to provide strategic and tactical intelligence and enforcement support to HIDTA Initiatives as well as HIDTA participating agencies. The vision of the IISC is to pursue coordination, cooperation, collaboration, and integration among regional law enforcement agencies. The IISC accomplishes this by facilitating cooperation among Federal, state, and local law enforcement agencies to share information and implement synchronized enforcement activities; enhancing intelligence sharing among Federal, state, and local law enforcement agencies; providing reliable intelligence to law enforcement agencies needed to design effective enforcement strategies and operations; and supporting coordinated law enforcement strategies to maximize use of available resources to reduce the supply of illegal drugs in the region and in the United States as a whole.

Through the use of traditional methods, innovative tools, and superior analytical techniques, the IISC provides near real-time and real-time investigative coordination (commonly described as event and target deconfliction); develops investigative leads and targeting information; provides analytical support to regional law enforcement initiatives; and provides operational and strategic intelligence related to drug distribution, money-laundering, and drug-related violence.

The IISC was the initial initiative of the PC HIDTA and has been funded since the HIDTA's establishment. At that time, the initiative focused primarily on officer safety through case/event/subject deconfliction and information sharing through electronically searchable databases. Facilitated by the PC HIDTA Watch Center, these functions continue to be priorities, with the emphasis on deconfliction and information-sharing connectivity throughout the Mid-Atlantic region to the Washington/Baltimore HIDTA and NY/NJ HIDTA, as well as Federal, state, and local law enforcement agencies.

In addition to close collaboration with the Delaware, New Jersey, and Pennsylvania State Criminal Intelligence Centers, the IISC coordinates with local intelligence nodes located with the Camden Co. Prosecutor's Office's Joint Camden Task Force (JCTF) and the Philadelphia Police Department's Criminal Intelligence Unit (PPD-CIU). The JCTF node operates as an independent entity providing direct support to the JCTF and southern New Jersey and is completely integrated into the HIDTA-funded JCTF. The PPD-CIU serves as an intelligence collection sub-system for both the Philadelphia Police Department and the PC HIDTA. The PPD-CIU and the IISC collaborate to identify collection requirements and synchronize human intelligence collection and reporting.

The IISC continues to grow its research and analysis capability to provide a full range of services from case support through strategic intelligence analysis and reporting. Analytical staff are professionally developed through training and collaboration with other offices to exploit information using emergent technologies and non-traditional sources. Furthering inter-regional information exchange between HIDTAs, the IISC will identify opportunities to collaborate on issues of mutual strategic interest.

In 2010, an agreement was reached with the Southwest Border HIDTA and Western Union that will allow for "near real time" access of Western Union, MoneyGram and future Sigue, Dolex, and Continental Exchange Systems transactions and records. The IISC analysts and other supporting agencies will have transaction records sent from anywhere in the world to the Southwest border within 200 miles of each border. We expect this initiative to be extremely successful in 2011 in identifying money laundering organizations and aiding in the seizure of assets.

## TASK FORCES OPERATING IN THE HIDTA REGION

The table below highlights the Federally-funded drug enforcement task forces operating in the HIDTA region. Multiple HIDTA task forces may make up an overarching HIDTA enforcement or investigative initiative.

| TASK FORCES | LOCATIONS |
| --- | --- |
| Camden County HIDTA Task Force (HIDTA) | Camden Co., NJ |
| Chester County HIDTA Task Force (HIDTA) | Chester Co., PA |
| Delaware County HIDTA Task Force (HIDTA) | Delaware Co., PA |
| USMS Fugitive Apprehension Initiative (HIDTA) | Eastern District of PA |
| Money Laundering & Drug Asset Forfeiture Task Force (HIDTA) | Metropolitan Philadelphia, PA area |
| Violent Drug Gang Task Force (HIDTA/DOJ-Safe Streets) | Metropolitan Philadelphia, PA area |
| Drug Trafficking Organization Task Force Initiative (HIDTA) | Philadelphia, PA |
| DEA Interdiction Initiative Task Force (HIDTA) | Metropolitan Philadelphia, PA |
| Suburban Camden County Drug Task Force (Byrne) | Camden County, NJ |
| Tactical Diversion Squad (DEA) | Philadelphia, PA |
| DEA-Phila. Task Force Group 4 (DEA) | Philadelphia, PA |
| DEA-Phila. Task Force Group 5 (DEA) | Philadelphia, PA |
| DEA-Task Force Group 6 (DEA) | Philadelphia, PA |
| DEA-Phila. Task Force Group 7 (DEA) | Philadelphia, PA |
| ICE-Seaport Contraband Smuggling Group (DHS-ICE) | Eastern District of Pennsylvania |
| ICE-Airport & Critical Infrastructure Protection Group (DHS-ICE) | Philadelphia, PA |
| ICE-Gang Enforcement & Public Safety Task Force (DHS-ICE) | Eastern & Middle Districts of Pennsylvania |
| DEA-Camden RO Task Force (DEA) | Camden, Burlington, Gloucester & Salem Cos., NJ |
| FBI-Violent Offender Gang Task Force (DOJ-Safe Streets/FBI) | Camden Co., NJ |

## TASK FORCE COORDINATION

The PC HIDTA designates and funds eight task force initiatives that support the HIDTA's overall strategy and addresses drug trafficking, money laundering and associated violent crime threats to the region. Five initiatives are directly engaged in drug law enforcement; the others address the collateral criminal behavior of money laundering, fugitives, and violent drug gangs that fester in conjunction with drug trafficking.

Through structured and unstructured communication channels, drug enforcement task forces in the PC HIDTA region continuously coordinate investigative activities with each other, the HIDTA, and OCDETF program administrators at managerial and operational levels. Law enforcement leaders in the PC HIDTA area set a mutually-supportive atmosphere through the Executive Board and its committees, and regularly confer with each other on strategic issues. Task force supervisors, agency managers, and prosecutors discuss case developments and intelligence developed by their investigators within and across agency lines, determining what resources need to be applied to bring about successful outcomes. At the operational level, supervisors and investigators from the various task forces regularly interact with each other, participating in OCDETF case review and coordination meetings, PC HIDTA initiative commanders meetings, and other structured settings, as well as informally.

All agencies' task forces participating in the PC HIDTA, by mutual agreement and program policy, as well as many non-HIDTA law enforcement agencies in the region, voluntarily and willingly contribute to and query the event and target deconfliction systems offered by the PC HIDTA IISC. Event deconfliction is provided 16 hours a day, 7 days a week via the IISC Watch Center, staffed by Philadelphia Police Department personnel, using an electronic system known as the "RISSafe Officer Safety Event Deconfliction System." This web-based platform, developed & operated by the RISS Program, permits agencies to enter information about pending law enforcement "events" – e.g. controlled purchases, "reverse stings," surveillance activities, warrant service, etc. – including date, time, and location. Such information is compared with other records previously entered to identify potential conflicts, at which time task force supervisors are simultaneously notified and contact information exchanged.

After PC HIDTA's normal operational hours, submissions are automatically forwarded to the Pennsylvania State Police Department Watch Center, which has partnered with PC HIDTA and the region's RISS Project – the Middle Atlantic-Great Lakes Organized Crime Law Enforcement Network (MAGLOCLEN) – in implementing this system. Because RISSafe is a nationwide system, to which a number of HIDTAs, RISS Projects, and their participant agencies contribute, events planned to occur outside of the PC HIDTA region can also be "deconflicted," thereby increasing officer/agent safety and coordination of action.

Target deconfliction is provided around the clock by way of electronic connectivity through the PC HIDTA Information Sharing Network to the "Case Explorer" system. Developed and maintained by the Washington-Baltimore HIDTA, Case Explorer permits investigators to enter records of cases they are investigating, to include target name(s), biographical information and physical description, address(es) of interest, associate(s), vehicles used, type of criminal activity the target is believed to engage in, and numerous other fields of data. With each record, contact information for investigators and their supervisors is recorded. Upon a subsequent entry with points of data matching the original record, parallel notifications are made to each investigator and their supervisors of a potential investigative overlap.

Investigators and their managers can communicate their interest, determine if independent or merged investigation should occur, and exchange investigative details heretofore unknown to each other, often accelerating the pace of enforcement action.

Beyond comparing targets in the immediate region, the Case Explorer system connects with the Washington-Baltimore HIDTA and New York/New Jersey HIDTA, as well, permitting comparison of target information throughout these regions. Furthermore, the Case Explorer system connects with the National Virtual Pointer System (NVPS), through which a number of other Federal and regional target Deconfliction systems are queried for targets in common. The Case Explorer system also aids analytical efforts, as the data is retrievable by analysts at the PC HIDTA IISC, permitting closed cases to be examined for relevant leads in current investigations and assessments.

The PC HIDTA and its IISC provide several platforms for information-sharing activities among task forces. In addition to the deconfliction measures, the PC HIDTA facilitates identification, targeting, and investigation of high-threat DTOs by its Joint Intelligence and Operations Coordination Group (JIOCG) meetings. Monthly meetings, attended by first-line task force supervisors, analysts, and prosecutors (from PC HIDTA participant agencies as well as non-HIDTA agencies in the region), permit face-to-face exchange of intelligence, in addition to electronically submitted target information. This group's discussions complement the OCDETF program by promoting new cases for OCDETF designation, by increasing investigator's attention to currently designated cases, and by providing intelligence leads that connect activities of strategic targets identified by the JIOCG and the RPOTs and CPOTs identified under the OCDETF program.

Investigative information contained in multiple databases maintained by agency participants is shared within the PC HIDTA community and other law enforcement agencies by way of the "Digital Information Gateway" (DIG) system acquired and managed by the PC HIDTA. This commercial software allows data from disparate systems, either in structured fields or unstructured text formats, to be queried and retrieved by analysts from the IISC and/or investigators at remote access points at agency/task force offices.

In addition to HIDTA-operated information-sharing systems, task forces exchange information with each other and with the larger law enforcement community through the State criminal intelligence centers operated by the Pennsylvania State Police (PaCIC) and New Jersey State Police (ROIC). The PC HIDTA maintains daily contact with these centers as well, and has collaborated with them on a number of drug trafficking, money laundering, and gang-related projects.

Along with case-specific analytical support, such as telephone toll and dialed number analysis, time and event charting, and background investigative workups, the PC HIDTA IISC also produces strategic analyses, threat assessments and intelligence bulletins, derived from requests for information to regional agencies that generate responses from task force participants, drug enforcement agencies and non-law enforcement agencies (such as public health departments) with valuable data, and information sources. Typically, such assessments and bulletins are electronically disseminated, resulting in up-to-date information exchanges with task forces and agency leadership.

The HIDTA also acts as an access point for state and local law enforcement to the EPIC National Seizure System, permitting entry to and query of nationwide data on drug and asset seizures from around the United States to be analyzed to formulate investigative leads. Furthermore, the PC HIDTA also acts as a liaison for its participant agencies with NDIC, working with NDIC field program specialists and Domestic Intelligence section analysts to acquire needed information for national drug threat assessments.

All counties in the PC HIDTA region are served by the FBI Philadelphia Field Office JTTF. A close relationship exists between the HIDTA IISC and the FBI Philadelphia Office Field Intelligence Group (FIG), and by extension, the JTTF. Designated liaison analysts provide a ready conduit between the PC HIDTA and the JTTF for any issues that may have bearing on homeland security threats. In addition, the FBI FIG supervisor sends the IISC manager unclassified "Intelligence Information Reports" (IIRs) pertaining to potential terrorist threats on a continuous basis. These reports, in turn, are disseminated to task forces and agency criminal intelligence centers for follow-up and reply to FBI offices with any additional information developed.

The PC HIDTA sends representation from its IISC to the region's "Anti-Terrorism Advisory Committee and Law Enforcement Sub-committee" meetings, jointly held by the U.S. Attorneys' Office, Eastern District of Pennsylvania (USAO-EDPA) and the FBI Philadelphia Field Office, where strategic and operational briefings on terror-related subjects are presented and discussed among law enforcement and public safety participants, and to the USAO-EDPA's "Money Laundering Work Group," where IRS "Suspicious Activity Reports" are reviewed for connection to terrorist financing as well as drug trafficking and tax evasion. FBI-JTTF members are part of both of these work groups.

## HIDTA EVALUATION

The PC HIDTA continues to promote ways to further multi-agency participation and cooperation within its area of responsibility. It remains the premier example of information and intelligence sharing in the region. In 2009, the PC HIDTA Performance Management Process (PMP) statistics reflected a downward trend in overall accomplishments as the result of a temporary shift of mission and operational focus. A marked increase in murder and violent crime in 2008 in the Philadelphia/Camden HIDTA area of responsibility made the shift necessary. Federal, state and local personnel resources usually dedicated to drug-related crime, and supporting HIDTA initiatives, were directed by their parent agencies to engage and decrease the violence. Although the short-term re-direction of focus of several HIDTA resources caused a decrease in operations directed against DTOs, the overall result was a reduction in violent crime. That reduction has ensured a better quality of life for citizens in the affected areas.

Of significant note is the "turnaround" in the city of Camden, NJ, which, in 2009 achieved its lowest rate of all major crimes since 1969. The leading and most notable statistic was the 38 percent drop in homicides, from 55 in 2008 to 34 in 2009. Law enforcement efforts, including the state-led Violence Reduction Initiative, the HIDTA-funded Joint Camden Task Force, and community-supported initiatives were instrumental in this noteworthy and encouraging turnaround.

Likewise, the city of Philadelphia has recorded fewer murders for the second year in a row. The 305 murders recorded in the city in 2009 reflect a drop of 8.4 percent from 2008, comparable to the 8.6 percent drop in all violent crime recorded for the year. PCHIDTA initiatives joined with Operation Pressure Point, a seasonal seven-month joint crime-fighting effort with 16 other law enforcement agencies successfully targeted a dozen violent areas of the city every weekend over the spring, summer, and fall. This initially followed a similar data-driven push that helped reduce murders by 15 percent in 2008. As we move forward in 2011, Operation Pressure Point resumes in the spring, and will help determine whether the city will be able to match these drops in violent crime.

While emphasizing operations directed against violent crime, the PCHIDTA continued to target the regional drug trafficking threat in 2009. PCHIDTA task forces dismantled or disrupted 40 DTOs, 20 of which were multi-state or international in scope, and 6 were designated as OCDETF cases. For every dollar spent on law enforcement and intelligence activities by the PCHIDTA, an ROI of $5.46 in drug seizures and $1.71 in cash and asset seizures was realized; for a total overall ROI of $7.17.

142

## Puerto Rico and U.S. Virgin Islands HIDTA
## Designated in 1994
## Executive Director – Jose Alvarez

### PURPOSE AND GOALS

The Puerto Rico/U. S. Virgin Islands (PR/USVI) HIDTA participating agencies create intelligence-driven task forces comprised of Federal, state, and local law enforcement agents to eliminate or reduce drug trafficking and its associated criminal activities. The PR/USVI HIDTA promotes the sharing of accurate and timely information and intelligence and continues to operate a major intelligence driven joint investigation system, using the latest technology and with full participation by all Federal, state, and local agencies. This seamless integration of land, sea, and air resources will continue to be dedicated to dismantling and disrupting major DTOs operating in the Caribbean Basin (i.e., RPOTS/CPOTS) and their related criminal activities, with a specific focus in the area of money laundering.

### STRATEGY

The PR/USVI HIDTA continues to foster cooperative and effective working relationships with the 26 Federal, state and local agencies that participate in the HIDTA. The strategic plan incorporates 13 law enforcement or support joint task forces positioned throughout the region to counter drug trafficking and its related criminal activity. Implementation of three new strategies this year is anticipated to further improve, or contribute to, intelligence driven operations:

- the Caribbean Corridor Strike Force, a major multi-agency marine interdiction initiative established with partial funding the previous year, and now a key initiative meeting a critical need;
- a merger between the Blue Lightning Strike Force and the DEA led St. Croix Major Organization Investigations Initiative, now renamed St. Croix Major Organization Investigations-Marine Interdiction; and
- the initiation of an intelligence unit within the largest HIDTA initiative, Fuerzas Unidas de Rapida Acción (FURA), the Air and Marine Interdiction Program.

### LOCATION

The PR/USVI HIDTA is headquartered in San Juan, PR. However, initiatives are strategically placed on St. Thomas and St. Croix, USVI as well as within the Commonwealth of PR.

### INITIATIVES

The 13 initiatives of the PR/USVI HIDTA include: 1 management, 1 training, 1 intelligence, 8 investigative and 2 marine interdiction initiatives.

## SHORT-TERM OBJECTIVES

| YEAR | DTOs Expected to be Disrupted/ Dismantled | Target Return on Investment: Assets | Target Return on Investment: Drugs | Number of Deconflictions Expected to be Submitted | Number of Investigations Expected to be Provided Analytical Support | Number of Initiative Leads Expected to be Referred |
|------|------|------|------|------|------|------|
| 2010 | 38* | $2 | $23 | 9,750 | 150 | 59 |

## THREAT ASSESSMENT

The primary drug threats in the PR/USVI HIDTA remain cocaine, crack cocaine, marijuana and, to a lesser extent, heroin. Marijuana originating in Mexico is transported to PR and the USVI from Texas, Arizona, and California via air courier services. As an emerging threat, the PR/USVI HIDTA has seen an increase in DTOs that are operating out of public housing projects selling prescription drugs. Maritime and air transportation remains the main method for cocaine, heroin, and marijuana trafficking in the Caribbean. Colombian-produced heroin is transported to PR and the USVI almost exclusively through air methods, both directly from South American departure points as well as through the Continental United States (CONUS), often through internal carriers (swallowers). Internal carriers or swallowers, known as "mulas," continue to be a smuggling trend and one of the most common methods used to smuggle small quantities of drugs. Drug money laundering has been, and continues to be, of significant concern. The High Intensity Financial Crime Area (HIFCA) reports that leaders of high profile money laundering organizations are usually located in Central or South American countries with cells and contacts operating in PR, the USVI, and the DR. Investigations have revealed that DTOs and MLOs continue to utilize bulk cash smuggling as one of the methods to move about their illegal proceeds from CONUS, via PR, into the DR, and on to South America. DTOs in PR are in constant competition for control of the drug market. In CY 2009, there were 894 murders in PR – a 9.7 percent increase from CY 2008. During the same period, there were 54 murders in the USVI – an increase of 24 percent from the previous year. A significant number of these murders are believed to be drug related.

## INTELLIGENCE INITIATIVES

The PR/USVI HIDTA IISC analyzes information and delivers accurate and timely strategic, organizational and tactical intelligence on cocaine, heroin, marijuana trafficking and distribution related criminal activity within PR and the USVI. This initiative is designed to improve the functioning of all law enforcement initiatives by providing them with critical, relevant and timely intelligence. The IISC facilitates efficient information sharing on drug trafficking/distribution; money laundering; and illegal firearms used in drug related crime activities among PR/USVI HIDTA participating agencies, non-participating agencies, and with law enforcement communities nationwide.

The HIDTA IISC shares information with all initiatives through the use of many commercial and criminal databases such as: ACS, DRUGX, TECS, CHOICEPOINT, PEN LINK, FOIMS TELEPHONE APPLICATION, Internet, ROCIC, LEXIS-NEXIS, and others. The IISC provides electronic connectivity with other HIDTA initiatives through the use of CNCMS. The IISC provides event and case deconfliction; Post Seizure Analysis; telephone toll analysis; active Pen-Registers; intelligence profiles; Title III support; charts, graphs, trend and pattern analysis; and financial analysis. The IISC provides coordination with EPIC, NDIC and JIATF-E.

The IISC offers 24/7 coverage via a Hotline Deconfliction Number. The Duty Analyst provides immediate assistance.

## TASK FORCES OPERATING IN THE HIDTA REGION

The table below highlights the Federally-funded drug enforcement task forces operating in the HIDTA region. Multiple HIDTA task forces may make up an overarching HIDTA enforcement or investigative initiative.

| TASK FORCES | LOCATIONS |
|---|---|
| Air & Marine Interdiction Program (HIDTA) | San Juan, PR |
| Caribbean Corridor OCDETF Strike Force (HIDTA) | San Juan, PR |
| Fajardo Major Organization Investigations (HIDTA) | Fajardo, PR |
| HIDTA Training Initiative (HIDTA) | San Juan, PR |
| Investigative Support Center (HIDTA) | San Juan, PR |
| Management & Coordination Support (HIDTA) | San Juan, PR |
| Money Laundering Initiative (HIDTA) | San Juan, PR |
| Ponce Major Organization Investigations / Mayaguez Satellite (HIDTA) | Ponce/Mayaguez, PR |
| Puerto Rico Fugitive Task Force (HIDTA) | San Juan, PR |
| Safe Neighborhoods (HIDTA) | San Juan, PR |
| San Juan Major Organization Investigations (HIDTA) | San Juan, PR |
| Tactical Diversion Squad (DEA) | Ponce, PR |
| Tactical Diversion Squad (DEA) | San Juan, PR |
| St. Croix Major Organization Investigations/Marine Interdiction (HIDTA) | St. Croix, USVI |
| St. Thomas Major Organization Investigations (HIDTA) | St. Thomas, USVI |
| FBI OCDETF Task Force (FBI) | San Juan, PR |
| FBI OCDETF Task Force (FBI) | St. Croix, USVI |
| Safe Streets Gang Task Force (FBI) | San Juan, PR |
| Safe Streets Gang Task Force (FBI) | Fajardo, PR |
| Safe Streets Gang Task Force (FBI) | Ponce, PR |
| Safe Streets Gang Task Force (FBI) | Aguadilla, PR |

## TASK FORCE COORDINATION

The PR/USVI HIDTA plays an important role in coordinating and sharing information with state and local law enforcement agencies. There are over 26 law enforcement agencies participating in the PR/USVI HIDTA. The HIDTA shares intelligence electronically, using U.S. Department of Justice information systems; Regional Information Sharing Systems (RISS);

Regional Organized Crime Information Center (ROCIC);SIPRNet; HIDTA IISCs; and other sources as well as other law enforcement and task forces outside the PR/USVI HIDTA.

PR/USVI HIDTA task forces coordinate activities and operations through subject and event deconfliction utilizing the Secure Automated Fast Event Tracking Network (SAFETNet) administered by the GC HIDTA. The initiatives share information through the IISC, which provides coverage to all PR/USVI HIDTA initiatives 24 hours/7 days a week. The PR/USVI HIDTA operates a hot line in its IISC. The hot line information is shared with all of the initiatives in the HIDTA. The IISC is made up of intelligence/criminal research specialists/analysts, task force officers, and special agents from: the DEA, ICE, FBI, CBP, ATF, PR Special Investigations Bureau (NIE), PR Department of Corrections and Rehabilitation, PR National Guard, and the USVI National Guard. The IISC is in the process of establishing a satellite investigative support office in St. Thomas to specialize in investigative support to the USVI. Implementation is projected within the year.

The OCDETF attorney and the PR/USVI HIDTA collaborate on both the OCDETF and HIDTA strategic plans and Threat Assessments through the U.S. Attorney's Office for the District of Puerto Rico. Over 42 percent of OCDETF active cases originate within PR/USVI HIDTA task forces.

The HIDTA's IISC works with the law enforcement community in efforts to support each other in the intelligence arena.

## HIDTA EVALUATION

The PR/USVI HIDTA has a strong management team and includes a very active training initiative and a translation support initiative. The PR National Guard staff a translation unit that is integral to the success of the HIDA in this bilingual environment. The HIDTA Strategy and all initiatives remain focused on the threats in the region. The Executive Board actively monitors all initiatives and their performance through their annual presentations to the Board; reviews of their performance at the time of budgetary considerations; and monitoring their PMP. The Executive Board also considers the annual Internal Reviews conducted by HIDTA Management Staff.

The PR/USVI HIDTA was initiated as an "interdiction" HIDTA when first established, and its objective was to interdict the drugs moving through the region. Its mission has since expanded to include investigations of major DTOs and regional threats. This HIDTA continues to target large complex DTOs and MLOs, which results in lengthy cases, many of which have an international nexus.

The USVI initiatives have aggressively targeted the on-island cultivation of marijuana. They have increased their eradication efforts from once per year to twice per year.

In 2009, HIDTA initiatives identified 232 DTOs operating in the PR/USVI area. Whereas it expected to dismantle or disrupt 45 DTOs/MLOs, however, the HIDTA disrupted or dismantled 53 DTOs/MLOs in 2009, compared to 29 in 2008. The PR/USVI HIDTA exceeded its projected outcomes by 17 percent.

**Rocky Mountain HIDTA – Designated in 1996**
**Executive Director – Thomas Gorman**

### *PURPOSE AND GOALS*

The mission of the Rocky Mountain (RM) HIDTA is to support the *National Drug Control Strategy* to reduce drug use. Specifically, the Rocky Mountain HIDTA seeks to facilitate cooperation and coordination among Federal, state, and local drug enforcement efforts. This mission is accomplished through intelligence-driven, joint multi-agency co-located drug task force initiatives sharing information and working cooperatively with other drug enforcement initiatives, including interdiction.

### *STRATEGY*

The Rocky Mountain HIDTA (RMHIDTA) has a strong management team that stresses cooperation and collaboration amongst the initiatives to address current drug threats at local, state, and national levels, while impacting the availability and abuse of all drugs throughout the country.

The Executive Board's ongoing efforts are dedicated to facilitating coordination and cooperation among the 10 Federal agencies and 103 state/local agencies that partner to 1) reduce drug availability by eliminating or disrupting DTOs, and 2) improve the efficiency and effectiveness of law enforcement efforts within the HIDTA. The Board's efforts help achieve common goals and respond to current drug threats effectively and efficiently by structuring the HIDTA initiatives that facilitate collaboration and coordination, and information sharing among all task forces and drug units, including those that are not in the HIDTA area and those that are not Federally funded.

The HIDTA's strategy is supported by an extensive training program, an intelligence initiative, aggressive enforcement initiatives, and a criminal interdiction program. Enforcement teams focus on methamphetamine, the number one threat to the RMHIDTA region. Additionally, highway enforcement initiatives were established in Colorado, Wyoming, Utah and Montana to address DTOs that transport illicit drugs into and through the region. A drug prevention initiative was also added to the RMHIDTA Strategy. Enforcement initiatives coupled with drug prevention gives the HIDTA multiple tools to combat drug trafficking and drug abuse.

### *LOCATION*

The RMHIDTA operates out of Denver, Colorado. It encompasses 34 designated counties in 4 states:

- Colorado: Adams, Arapahoe, Boulder, Denver, Douglas, Eagle, El Paso, Garfield, Grand, Jefferson, La Plata, Larimer, Mesa, Moffat, Pueblo, Routt, and Weld;
- Montana: Cascade, Flathead, Lewis and Clark, Missoula, and Yellowstone;
- Utah: Davis, Salt Lake, Summit, Utah, Washington, and Weber
- Wyoming: Albany, Campbell, Laramie, Natrona, Sweetwater, and Uinta

## INITIATIVES

The RMHIDTA has 33 initiatives, which include 1 management, 1 training, 1 intelligence, 4 interdiction and 26 investigative initiatives.

## SHORT-TERM OBJECTIVES

| YEAR | DTOs Expected to be Disrupted/ Dismantled | Target Return on Investment: Assets | Target Return on Investment: Drugs | Number of Deconflictions Expected to be Submitted | Number of Investigations Expected to be Provided Analytical Support | Number of Initiative Leads Expected to be Referred |
|---|---|---|---|---|---|---|
| 2010 | 122 | $2.24 | $33.73 | 12,500 | 435 | 637 |

## THREAT ASSESSMENT

Methamphetamine distribution and abuse pose the greatest overall drug threat to the Rocky Mountain HIDTA region, while marijuana is the most widely available and abused illicit drug in the region. Mexican DTOs are the principal suppliers of wholesale quantities of methamphetamine, marijuana, cocaine, and black tar heroin to the Rocky Mountain HIDTA region from locations along the Southwest border, while west coast Asian DTOs supply high-potency marijuana and MDMA (ecstasy) to the region from sources in Canada. These DTOs exploit the region's centralized location, and extensive transportation infrastructure to distribute wholesale quantities of ice, methamphetamine, cocaine, marijuana, and heroin. The region is transected by Interstate Highways I-15, I-25, I-70, I-80, I-90 and I-94. These major interstate routes are used by DTOs to transport illicit drugs from California, Arizona, and Texas to markets in Denver and major Midwest cities such as Omaha, Kansas City, and Chicago. Criminal groups also transport high grade marijuana ("B.C. bud") from Canada to and through Montana and Wyoming. Similar to other areas of the country, prescription drug abuse has increased significantly in the Salt Lake City area since 2002.

## INTELLIGENCE INITIATIVES

The IISC funded since 1997 is located in Denver, Colorado, and operates a cell with two analysts in Salt Lake City, Utah, and another cell with one analyst in Colorado Springs, Colorado. An intelligence unit in Wyoming also receives RMHIDTA funds to support the Wyoming Law Enforcement Information Network (subject deconfliction) connectivity to the Rocky Mountain Information Network (RMIN/RISS). The IISC provides a mechanism to integrate various agency intelligence systems into one centralized source for investigative inquiries by HIDTA agency personnel. The IISC utilizes database inquiries and alerts agencies of investigative conflicts. The IISC also provides tactical case analysis for investigative agencies and develops strategic intelligence to provide timely and accurate information for threat assessments.

## TASK FORCES OPERATING IN THE HIDTA REGION

The table below highlights the Federally-funded drug enforcement task forces operating in the HIDTA region. Multiple HIDTA task forces may make up an overarching HIDTA enforcement or investigative initiative.

| TASK FORCES | LOCATIONS |
|---|---|
| Colorado Criminal Interdiction (HIDTA) | Denver, CO |
| Colorado Springs Metro Drug Task Force (HIDTA) | Colorado Springs, CO |
| Front Range Drug Task Force (HIDTA) | Aurora, CO |
| Fugitive Location and Apprehension Group (HIDTA) | Aurora, CO |
| Metro Gang Drug Task Force (HIDTA) | Aurora, CO |
| North Metro Drug Task Force (HIDTA) | Broomfield, CO |
| Northern Colorado Drug Task Force (HIDTA) | Ft. Collins, CO |
| Southern Colorado Drug Task Force (HIDTA) | Colorado Springs, CO |
| Southwest Drug Task Force (HIDTA) | Durango, CO |
| Two Rivers Drug Enforcement Team (HIDTA) | Glenwood Springs, CO |
| Weld County Drug Task Force (HIDTA) | Greeley, CO |
| West Metro Drug Task Force (HIDTA) | Golden, CO |
| Western Colorado Drug Task Force (HIDTA) | Grand Junction, CO |
| Tactical Diversion Squad (DEA) | Denver, CO |
| Central Montana Drug Task Force (HIDTA) | Great Falls, MT |
| Eastern Montana Drug Task Force (HIDTA) | Billings, MT |
| Missoula County Drug Task Force (HIDTA) | Missoula, MT |
| Missouri River Drug Task Force (HIDTA) | Bozeman, MT |
| Montana Criminal Interdiction Program (HIDTA) | Great Falls, MT |
| Northwest Drug Task Force (HIDTA) | Kalispell, MT |
| Davis Metro Narcotics Strike Force (HIDTA) | Kaysville, UT |
| Salt Lake City Metro Narcotics Task Force (HIDTA) | Salt Lake City, UT |
| Utah County Major Crimes Task Force (HIDTA) | Orem, UT |
| Utah Criminal Interdiction Program (HIDTA) | Salt Lake City, UT |
| Tactical Diversion Squad (DEA) | Salt Lake City, UT |
| Washington County Drug Task Force (HIDTA) | St. George, UT |
| Weber Morgan Narcotics Strike Force (HIDTA) | Ogden, UT |
| Wyoming Central Enforcement Team (HIDTA) | Casper, WY |
| Wyoming Criminal Interdiction Program (HIDTA) | Cheyenne, WY |
| Wyoming Northeast Enforcement Team (HIDTA) | Sheridan, WY |
| Wyoming Southeast Enforcement Team (HIDTA) | Cheyenne, WY |
| Wyoming Southwest Enforcement Team (HIDTA) | Rock Springs, WY |
| Mountain Enforcement Team (Byrne/JAG) | Jackson, WY |

| TASK FORCES | LOCATIONS |
|---|---|
| Northwest Enforcement Team (Byrne/JAG) | Powell, WY |
| Central Utah Narcotic Task Force (Byrne/JAG) | Richfield, UT |
| Iron/Garfield County Narcotic Task Force (Byrne/JAG) | Cedar City, UT |
| Big Muddy River (Byrne/JAG) | Wolf Point, MT |
| Tri-Agency Drug Task Force (Byrne/JAG) | Havre, MT |

## *TASK FORCE COORDINATION*

All task force initiatives receiving HIDTA funding are required to utilize the subject deconfliction systems in the states where they are located. RMHIDTA task force initiatives that are located in metropolitan areas are required to use the HIDTA's RISSafe event deconfliction system. Task forces that are not HIDTA-funded voluntarily use RISSafe to enhance officer safety and event deconfliction. Task forces in the states that are not Federally funded also voluntarily use the State's law enforcement information network for subject deconfliction. Deconfliction 'hits' require interagency communication and coordination to prevent investigative overlap.

All drug task forces share information with the RMHIDTA IISC and National Drug Intelligence Center (NDIC) field specialists on a regular, informal basis and formally by a mandated report and threat assessment survey. The task force teams, particularly those that are located in the Denver Metropolitan area, often work together on overlapping investigations and/or resource sharing. The HIDTA coordinates either with the drug investigators association or those responsible for JAG/Byrne funding and conducts periodic drug unit commander meetings for all drug units and task forces throughout the HIDTA, regardless of the funding sources. The purpose of these meetings is to exchange information on drug trafficking threats and to address issues of mutual concern.

## *HIDTA EVALUATION*

The RMHIDTA has submitted data and information indicating the program is meeting its short-term goals and performance targets, and is achieving its stated mission and long-term goals. The Executive Board is closely monitoring the performance of the initiatives and task force initiatives and reassigns the weakest performing task forces to improve efficiency and effectiveness. ONDCP has previously encouraged the program's management to increase its interaction and collaboration with other HIDTA programs and agencies to destabilize national and transnational drug trafficking networks. The HIDTA has reported improvements in collaboration and information sharing in 2009, and has established performance targets for 2010 to further increase the number of intelligence and case referrals. As a result of this increased emphasis on collaboration by the RMHIDTA's management during 2009, the number of investigative leads provided to other HIDTAs and other agencies almost doubled, from 409 in 2008 to 769 in 2009. Prior to the RMHIDTA, there was only sporadic information sharing among agencies; however, through HIDTA-sponsored deconfliction systems, case referrals and meetings, this sharing has become routine. For example, the number of case referrals going outside the Rocky Mountain region to other areas of the country went from an average of less than 20 to over 400 referrals per year.

In 2009, RMHIDTA initiatives identified 266 DTOs and disrupted or dismantled 107. RMHIDTA initiatives seized $162 million (wholesale value) of drugs and $11.5 million in illegally-gained assets.

## South Florida HIDTA– Designated in 1990
## Executive Director – Timothy Wagner

### PURPOSE AND GOALS

The mission of the South Florida HIDTA (SFLHIDTA) is to disrupt the market for illegal drugs in the region by assisting Federal, state, local, and tribal law enforcement entities participating in the HIDTA to dismantle DTOs and MLOs, with particular emphasis on drug trafficking regions that have harmful effects on other parts of the United States.

### STRATEGY

SFLHIDTA continues to foster cooperative and effective working relationships among Federal, state, and local agencies, contributing over 677 full-time personnel co-located and united to achieve the common goals of disrupting and dismantling DTOs through long-term multiagency investigations and operations. The SFLHIDTA Strategy consists of 25 initiatives focused on the multiple regional drug threats identified in the SFLHIDTA Threat Assessment. The initiatives are designed to dismantle the major DTOs and simultaneously disrupt their flow of drugs and monetary assets. The initiatives are structured to apply the collective expertise of local, state, and Federal agencies.

Expansion of multi-HIDTA approaches to identifying, disrupting, and dismantling traditional threats and emerging ones such as pharmaceutical diversion and indoor marijuana grows is a critical feature of the HIDTA's short and long-term strategy. Significant progress has been achieved on these fronts in 2009/2010. SFLHIDTA intends to build on this progress in 2011 and 2012.

### LOCATION

The SFLHIDTA operates out of Miramar, Florida. It includes Broward, Miami-Dade, Monroe, and Palm Beach Counties.

### INITIATIVES

The SFL HIDTA has 25 initiatives, which include 1 management, 2 support, 1 intelligence, 1 prosecution, 1 prevention and 19 investigation/ interdiction initiatives.

### SHORT-TERM OBJECTIVES

| YEAR | DTOs Expected to be Disrupted/ Dismantled | Target Return on Investment: Assets | Target Return on Investment: Drugs | Number of Deconflictions Expected to be Submitted | Number of Investigations Expected to be Provided Analytical Support | Number of Initiative Leads Expected to be Referred |
|---|---|---|---|---|---|---|
| 2010 | 125 | $9 | $72 | 10,100 | 820 | 484 |

## THREAT ASSESSMENT

Major drug threats in the SFLHIDTA region include diverted pharmaceuticals, cocaine, crack cocaine, heroin, and hydroponic marijuana. Money laundering continues to be a major threat associated with all illicit drug trafficking. The scope of the money laundering threat in this region remains significant and of sufficient scope to warrant national level interest. South Florida remains a command and control center for South American and Caribbean drug trafficking and money laundering organizations. Street gangs reflected record growth in their membership over the last year, based on data reported in the SFLHIDTA Survey for 2009. Gangs have a nexus to illicit drug distribution across the entire metropolitan area from Key West to northern Palm Beach County, the latter reporting the largest increases. Hydroponic marijuana production in South Florida is a major illicit drug threat for the region. Production remains highly prevalent and continues to increase despite the numerous successful multi-agency interdiction operations focused on this threat. The indoor marijuana threat is characterized by increased violent crime in the form of home invasions, armed robberies, kidnappings, arsons, and homicides committed in furtherance of these criminal enterprises.

Diversion of pharmaceutical medications has become another major threat in South Florida. This drug market has expanded so rapidly that it warrants additional attention due to its impact on drug abuse and the general health of all age groups. This state, like the rest of the Nation, is facing an explosive epidemic involving the abuse of prescription drugs. In South Florida, hundreds of pain management clinics are operating and dispensing drugs in uncontrolled quantities. Due to the high concentration of pill mills and prescription drug availability in Florida, oxycodone products, Xanax (alprazolam), Diazepam (Valium), and others (steroids for example) are being made available in all drug markets, in large quantities, and at low prices, contributing to increases in prescription drug abuse.

While limited, Mexican DTO presence in the region appears to be increasing and may be related to the importation and distribution of commercial-grade marijuana, methamphetamine (powder and crystal), and cocaine. These illicit drugs arrive via land routes, airlines, and parcel services from all Southwest border states, including Texas, Arizona, New Mexico, and California.

## INTELLIGENCE INITIATIVES

The mission statement of the SFLHIDTA intelligence unit is to facilitate the timely, effective, and cooperative exchange of information from Federal, state, local, commercial, and HIDTA databases with HIDTA initiatives and participating agencies. Strategic and tactical intelligence is collected, analyzed, and disseminated in support of drug distribution, drug-related money laundering, firearms trafficking, and gang-related violence investigations. The Intelligence Center (SFLHIC) is a multi-agency coalition of Federal, state, and local agencies that co-locates agency representatives and their respective agencies and proprietary databases. The SFLHIC also maintains the HIDTA's pointer index and deconfliction systems. Information technology services are provided by employing state-of-the-art automation and communications technologies and developing total systems that provide efficient information. The SFLHIC was first funded by HIDTA and began operations in 1994.

## TASK FORCES OPERATING IN THE HIDTA REGION

The table below highlights the Federally-funded drug enforcement task forces operating in the HIDTA region. Multiple HIDTA task forces may make up an overarching HIDTA enforcement or investigative initiative.

| TASK FORCES | LOCATIONS |
|---|---|
| Southeast Florida Regional Task Force (HIDTA) | Weston |
| Metro Broward Drug Task Force (HIDTA) | Plantation |
| Russian/Eurasian Organized Crime Task Force (HIDTA) | Plantation |
| IRS Task Force (HIDTA) | Plantation |
| Operation Top Heavy (HIDTA) | Plantation |
| Blue Lightning Operations Center/Rapid Deployment Operations (HIDTA) | Miramar |
| Transportation Conspiracy Unit (HIDTA) | Plantation |
| South Florida Organized Fraud Task Force (HIDTA) | Plantation |
| Major Case Initiative (HIDTA) | Miami |
| Cobra 13 FBI Group (HIDTA) | Miami |
| Gang Strike Force (HIDTA) | Miami |
| Global Crime Task Force (HIDTA) | Miami |
| South Florida Money Laundering Strike Force (HIDTA) | Miami |
| Tactical Diversion Squad (DEA) | Miami |
| Key West Drug Trafficking Task Force (HIDTA) | Key West |
| Monroe HIDTA Task Force (HIDTA) | Marathon |
| Palm Beach County Narcotics Task Force (HIDTA) | West Palm Beach |
| Street Terror Offender Program (HIDTA) | Miami |
| Street Gang and Criminal Organization Task Force (HIDTA) | Miami |
| Violent Crime and Drug Trafficking Organizations (HIDTA) | Miami |

## TASK FORCE COORDINATION

All SFLHIDTA-funded task forces are required to coordinate with the SFLHIC regarding information and intelligence sharing, and are mandated to submit case, subject, and event information for deconfliction through the National Information Narcotics Joint Agencies System (NINJAS). Non-HIDTA agencies operating within the SFLHIDTA are encouraged to share their information and deconflict their case, subject, and event information with the SFLHIC. A total of 88 Federal, state, and local law enforcement agencies deconflict their investigations through the SFLHIC.

Strategic analysts from the SFLHIC solicit current drug trends and related information from regional law enforcement agencies for analysis that is incorporated into the HIDTA's annual drug Threat Assessment. This report, along with other intelligence products, is disseminated to the law enforcement community, NDIC, EPIC, other HIDTAs, and ONDCP.

South Florida law enforcement and intelligence resources operate under a mutually agreed upon "Information and Intelligence Sharing Plan" developed by the Southeast Region

Domestic Security Task Force. This plan is the architecture for a regional "fusion system" which directs the sharing of information in an organized manner.

## *HIDTA EVALUATION*

In 2009, the SFLHIDTA made progress toward achieving its performance objectives, and continues to target the regional drug trafficking threat. The focus of the HIDTA is high-level investigations. Of the 134 DTOs dismantled or disrupted, 41 percent were international in scope[14]. The program has the demonstrated ability to focus its investigative efforts at a high level, and yet operate below the national average cost per DTO and have a competitive ROI.

In addition to continuing its efforts effectively targeting the highest levels of South American- and Caribbean-based drug trafficking and money laundering organizations, SFLHIDTA has aggressively targeted the emergent threat of indoor marijuana cultivation and pharmaceutical diversion related to a local proliferation of pain clinics. SFLHIDTA initiatives, in conjunction with DEA Tactical Diversion Squads, are investigating several pain clinics engaged in illegal operations that result in diversion. The goal of the investigation is to bring Federal charges against the clinic operators and owners, as warranted. This multi-state investigation is coordinated with other HIDTAs to target the DTOs that illegally distribute drugs obtained via the Miami-area pain clinics throughout the east coast.

---

[14] An *International DTO/MLO is an* organization, or identifiable cell of an organization, that regularly conducts illegal drug trafficking or money laundering activities in more than one country or that is based in one country and conducts or coordinates illegal activities in another. To be considered an international organization, the group must have an established connection to an international DTO/MLO. Simply being a customer of such an organization is not sufficient. (PMP Definitions and Key Terms).

## SWB HIDTA - Arizona Region – Designated in 1990
## Director – Terence Azbill

### PURPOSE AND GOALS

The mission of the Southwest Border HIDTA/Arizona Region (SWB HIDTA/AZ Region) is to increase the safety of Arizona's citizens by substantially reducing drug trafficking and money laundering, thereby reducing drug-related crime and violence in the region.

### STRATEGY

The SWB HIDTA/AZ Region's Strategy includes multi-agency co-located task forces to counter identified drug-threats. Composed of Federal, state, local, and tribal agencies, the task forces target the threats in a geographical region or provide specialized expertise directed at a specific threat. Based on the task force's mission, participating agencies in the SWB HIDTA/AZ Region have specific strategies, policies, and procedures. The SWB HIDTA/AZ Region Executive Committee, consisting of seven local, three state, and ten Federal members, is the Arizona Region policy making committee. The Executive Committee synchronizes the strategy targeting the drug threat to reduce drug-related crime. As the coordination umbrella for all HIDTA initiatives and special projects in each jurisdiction, the Executive Committee empowers three subcommittees for specific objectives: intelligence, management, and finance.

A "centerpiece" co-located or collaborative multi-agency task force initiative in each county focuses on major drug case development and drug smuggling. These multi-dimensional task forces meet HIDTA program guidance criteria. Other initiatives augment the primary task forces by targeting money laundering, drug-related violence and corruption, fugitive apprehension, surveillance, training, and technical or intelligence support. Multi-state and international cases are encouraged and pursued as a priority. These include CPOT, RPOT, and OCDETF cases.

The Arizona Region facilitates the Domestic Highway Enforcement (DHE) concept/Region 1 program by coordinating planning sessions and operational plans, sharing information/intelligence, and providing GIS - situation mapping (Sit-Map) of seizures nationwide.

### LOCATION

The SWB HIDTA/AZ Region operates out of Tucson, Arizona. It encompasses nine counties: Cochise, La Paz, Maricopa, Mohave, Navajo, Pima, Pinal, Santa Cruz, and Yuma.

### INITIATIVES

The SWB HIDTA/AZ Region has 21 initiatives, which include 3 support (one utilizes discretionary funds), 2 intelligence, and 16 investigation/interdiction initiatives (one utilizes discretionary funds). The SWB HIDTA/AZ Region also participates with the other four SWB Regions in a prevention initiative using discretionary funds. This recently established initiative is in the early stages of development and is intended to create a border-wide demand reduction initiative employing a balanced approach between supply reduction and demand reduction.

Member agencies will participate in drug awareness, education, and community norm change through regional efforts.

## SHORT-TERM OBJECTIVES

| YEAR | DTOs Expected to be Disrupted/ Dismantled | Target Return on Investment: Assets | Target Return on Investment: Drugs | Number of Deconflictions Expected to be Submitted | Number of Investigations Expected to be Provided Analytical Support | Number of Initiative Leads Expected to be Referred |
|------|------|------|------|------|------|------|
| 2010 | 88 | $4 | $72 | 8,700 | 300 | 856 |

## THREAT ASSESSMENT

The SWB HIDTA/AZ Region faces multi-pronged threats of northbound smuggling of marijuana, methamphetamine, and illegal aliens, and southbound smuggling of currency and weapons. Both engender escalation of violence directed against law enforcement and the public south of the border.

To facilitate their smuggling, Mexican DTOs implement a variety of methodologies to exploit the porous Arizona/Mexico border and Arizona's vast public and tribal lands. From Arizona, their marijuana warehousing and distribution networks extend throughout the United States via the interstate highway system. Affiliations with Mexican illegal alien smugglers; east coast Jamaican DTOs; and United States-based prison, outlaw motorcycle, and street gangs enhance their capabilities to market their illegal drugs. These gang members are usually violent and unfamiliar with the territory. Active, identified, or admitted gang members involved in incidents recently reported by law enforcement are: Batos Locos; Calle13 Latinos Contes of Chicago; Sureños, some with gang affiliation in East Los Angeles; Sureño13; and MS-13.

Mexican criminal enterprises engage in a pervasive campaign of border violence. Mexican states bordering the southwestern United States are at the epicenter of violence in Mexico. Gun battles in the streets, brutal executions, and assassinations of law enforcement officers and public officials are at epidemic levels in northern Mexico. The possibility this gang-related violence will spill over into Arizona is a principal concern to the SWB HIDTA/AZ Region. One continuing threat in the Phoenix area is the large number of 'drop houses' used to facilitate the transfer of illegal aliens throughout the United States.

## INTELLIGENCE INITIATIVES

The Investigative/Intelligence Support Center (IISC) in the SWB HIDTA/AZ Region Intelligence System is the primary IISC with personnel located in Pima, Pinal, and Yuma Counties. The Arizona Drug Intelligence Task Force was merged with the Arizona Weapons and Drug Intelligence Group (AWDIG) and is located in Maricopa County. AWDIG is a node within the Arizona Region. Both provide strategic, operational, and tactical intelligence support to the Arizona Region Enforcement Initiatives.

The Intelligence Division is an AZ Department of Public Safety (DPS)-led Federal, state, and local initiative. It is the central initiative of the IISC and is comprised of Post-Seizure

Analysis Teams (PSAT) and an All Source Analysis Team (ASAT). Each group has a specific focus area, but interacts with the others in order to accomplish the mission of the IISC. PSAT focuses on identifying the connection between seizures of smuggled narcotics, narcotics-related asset seizures, narcotics-related violent crimes, and the arrested persons associated with those crimes. The team provides intelligence research assistance to the region's multi-agency task forces and agencies conducting narcotics investigations through telephone tolls, link analysis, trend and pattern analysis, and analytical case support. PSAT also provides participating agencies' databases on-site to conduct various searches on behalf of the task forces and other law enforcement agencies. All intelligence information from the task forces is processed through the PSAT for case deconfliction and initiation and intelligence coordination. ASAT is the SWB HIDTA/AZ Region's focal point for all sources of information and intelligence. It collects, evaluates, processes, and disseminates intelligence to the PSAT and SWB HIDTA/AZ Region task forces and other counter-narcotic agencies. It is responsible for the development of Geographic Information System (GIS) intelligence products and the technical and analytical support of GIS. The ASAT provides the tactical/operational intelligence for DHE operations and other counterdrug projects as requested, and maintains and operates the GIS-SitMap. Also, ASAT intake sections act as a Watch Center during normal duty hours for event deconfliction submissions and citizen call-ins. The SWB HIDTA/AZ Region provides deconfliction services to a total of 85 Federal, state, and local law enforcement agencies.

The Arizona Drug Intelligence Task Force (ADITF) merger with AWDIG enhances the Arizona Region capabilities to target trafficking organizations who smuggle weapons into Mexico. The AWDIG is a multi-agency task force comprised of an intelligence research specialist, investigators, and analysts from local, state, and Federal agencies. The node is managed by AZ DPS and DEA. The AWDIG Squad #1 utilizes advanced computer technology to assist in the collation, analysis, retrieval, and dissemination of all the collected data. The squad has a protocol for documenting major criminal drug conspiracies and money laundering investigations. This information supports historical conspiracy investigations; money laundering and bulk cash smuggling investigations; and agencies preparing prosecutions on significant Mexican DTOs and other criminal organizations operating in Arizona and throughout the southwest border region. The squad assists other law enforcement agencies and HIDTA initiatives by identifying connectivity to international, national, and multi-state on-going criminal drug conspiracy cases, money laundering cases and other associated cases. Furthermore, the squad collects, collates and analyzes criminal intelligence for dissemination on Colombian DTOs, methamphetamine manufacturers/distributors, Outlaw Motorcycle Gangs (OMG), Asian Criminal Enterprises (ACE), Russian Organized Crime Groups (ROC), and Violent Street Gangs (VSG) operating in Arizona and along the Southwest border.

The AWDIG Squad #2 focuses personnel and resources to interdict illegal weapon shipments to Mexico. The squad utilizes agency databases and commercial programs to assist in the collation, analysis, retrieval, and dissemination of all the collected data. The squad will use the ATF eTrace firearms tracing system, which is part of Project Gunrunner. By identifying source states with an Arizona recovery, further reductions in weapons trafficking into Mexico will reduce violence. The squad provides information for identifying possible weapons trafficking organizations, DTOs / MLOs involved with weapons smugglings, and connects those associated with border violence. By providing intelligence regarding potential suspects and deconflicting like investigations, coordination and prosecution of weapon cases is enhanced. The squad will work with law enforcement partners supporting Mexico's efforts to reduce the flow of drugs, money and weapons across the shared border and enhance border security by reducing the illicit methods and pathways.

The AWDIG works collaboratively with the HIDTA Investigative Center in Tucson, the Arizona Counter Terrorism Information Center (ACTIC), other HIDTA IISCs, EPIC, and agencies who have a need and right-to-know. AWDIG's priorities are set by the Executive Committee after review and recommendations by the Intelligence Subcommittee. Those priorities are coordinated with the Region's IISC priorities for efficiency and effectiveness within the Arizona Region.

## TASK FORCES OPERATING IN THE HIDTA REGION

The table below highlights the Federally-funded drug enforcement task forces operating in the HIDTA region. Multiple HIDTA task forces may make up an overarching HIDTA enforcement or investigative initiative.

| TASK FORCES | LOCATIONS |
| --- | --- |
| Intelligence and Investigative Support Center (HIDTA) | Pima, Pinal, and Yuma Counties |
| Tucson Financial Task Force (HIDTA) | Pima County |
| Domestic Highway Enforcement (HIDTA) | Arizona Region |
| Arizona Warrant Apprehension (HIDTA) | Maricopa, Pima, and Yuma Counties |
| Border Anti-Narcotics Network (HIDTA) | Pima County (Ajo / West Desert area) |
| Cochise County Border Alliance Group (HIDTA) | Cochise County |
| Counter Narcotics Alliance (HIDTA) | Pima County |
| Tactical Diversion Squad (DEA) | Tucson |
| La Paz County Narcotics Task Force (HIDTA) | La Paz County |
| Maricopa County Drug Suppression Task Force (HIDTA) | Maricopa County |
| Mohave Area General Narcotics Enforcement Team (HIDTA) | Mohave County |
| Metro Intelligence Support & Technical Investigative Center (HIDTA) | Maricopa County |
| Pinal County HIDTA Task Force (HIDTA) | Pinal County |
| Santa Cruz County Metro Task Force (HIDTA) | Santa Cruz County |
| Yuma County Narcotics Task Force (HIDTA) | Yuma County |
| Arizona Weapons and Drug Intelligence Group (HIDTA) | Maricopa County |
| Apache County Cooperative Enforcement Narcotics Team | Apache County |
| Northern Arizona Street Crimes Task Force | Coconino County |
| Gila County Narcotics Enforcement Task Force | Gila County |
| Southeastern Arizona Drug, Gang, and Violent Crime Task | Graham County |

| TASK FORCES | LOCATIONS |
|---|---|
| Force | |
| Greenlee County Narcotics Task Force | Greenlee County |
| Navajo County Major Crimes Apprehension Team (HIDTA) | Navajo County |
| Partners Against Narcotics Trafficking | Yavapai County |
| Maricopa County Neighborhood Narcotics Enforcement Team | Maricopa County |
| Pinal County Drug and Gang Enforcement Multi-Agency Task Force | Pinal County |
| Pima County HIDTA Investigative Task Force | Pima County |

## TASK FORCE COORDINATION

The SWB HIDTA/AZ Region provides a forum for sharing important trends in drug trafficking and issues relating to current events along the Southwest border, and specifically the Arizona/Mexico border. The SWB HIDTA/AZ Region coordinates the direct/indirect sharing of information among other SWB HIDTA regions and task forces through personal relationships, hosting intelligence meetings, and dissemination of information via electronic and hard copy formats at the Federal, state, local, and tribal levels. Initiatives located geographically in Phoenix and Tucson are co-located in the two metropolitan areas. The IISC and related nodes with Federal, state, and local agency personnel provide the agency databases for research and communication. Further dissemination of information occurs through the National Seizure System, EPIC, National Virtual Pointer System, and RISS for regional and national coordination.

The Coordinated Operational Planning System and Situational Map provide law enforcement agencies with information utilized to coordinate Region Domestic Highway Enforcement interdiction and enforcement activities. The SWB HIDTA/AZ Region works closely with EPIC and other HIDTAs to ensure the information is shared.

The various drug task forces in Arizona use RISSafe for both event and case deconfliction. Additional programs or software utilized within the Region enhance case or subject deconfliction. The systems provide for notification to enforcement groups conducting operations on the same target or area so a resolution can be arranged. There are regional intelligence meetings held around the State of Arizona where information and intelligence is shared and exchanged. Joint interdiction operations are coordinated through the DHE program.

The SWB HIDTA/AZ Region Director and the IISC Manager are members of the Southern Arizona JTTF Executive Committee. This allows collaboration, information sharing, and insight into information requirements of the JTTF. In addition, the Southwest border HIDTA Arizona Region houses the Southern Arizona Counter Terrorism Information Center (ACTIC) squad, which allows direct contact with the State intelligence fusion center. Electronic connectivity to fusion centers adds to the sharing of information. The ACTIC houses Federal, state, and local agency personnel having multi-crime and public safety responsibilities, to include terrorism.

The SWB HIDTA/AZ Region Director participates as a member of the Unified Command for the Alliance to Combat Transnational Threats (ACTT) and HIDTA personnel are part of the coordination efforts.

The National Drug Intelligence Center has assigned an analyst to the IISC to provide another avenue of coordination and dissemination of information to HIDTAs across the country.

### *HIDTA EVALUATION*

The SWB HIDTA/AZ Region has accomplished a significant portion of its performance goals and objectives in CY 2009, disrupting or dismantling 101 of the 110 targeted DTOs and MLOs, or 92 percent. Of the 101 DTOs/MLOs disrupted or dismantled, 33 were international in scope. The Arizona Region had a ROI of $77.92; had 17,471 deconflictions; provided analytical support to 2,698 cases; and provided 2,827 leads to other HIDTAs and agencies. The SWB HIDTA/AZ Region faces unique challenges associated with having within its region the Tohono O'Odham Native American reservation that straddles the United States/Mexico border. To address these challenges, HIDTA provides support to the Tohono O'Odham Nation through a Safe Trails initiative led by the FBI. SWB HIDTA/AZ Region is an active participant in the State's intelligence center and works with the Governor's office to monitor the violence occurring just south of the border with Mexico. Additionally, the Arizona Region has recently added Navajo County to the Region, providing funds for narcotics interdiction, investigations and quality of life issues on three reservations. The Tri-state HIDTA Southwest Meth and Pharmaceutical Initiative is also the Native American Project coordinator for the Arizona Region and provides coordination to the reservations in Arizona.

# SWB HIDTA - California Region
## Designated in 1990
## Director – Kean McAdam

### PURPOSE AND GOALS

The mission of the SWB HIDTA/California Region (SWB HIDTA/CA Region), more familiarly known as the California Border Alliance Group or CBAG, is to measurably reduce drug trafficking, thereby reducing the impact of illicit drugs in the region and in other areas of the country. To accomplish this mission, the SWB HIDTA/CA Region assists in the coordination of joint operational and supporting initiatives to deter, disrupt, dismantle, and ultimately destroy the most significant DTOs, and their supporting transportation and money laundering organizations.

### STRATEGY

The SWB HIDTA/CA Region assists in the coordination of joint operational and supporting initiatives to deter, disrupt, dismantle, and ultimately destroy the most significant DTOs and their supporting transportation and money laundering organizations. The SWB HIDTA/CA Region also emphasizes efforts against methamphetamine manufacturing, precursor supply, and abuse through innovative enforcement operations and demand reduction programs utilizing a multi-agency, joint concept of operations. The SWB HIDTA/CA Region continues to foster cooperative and effective working relationships among 700 Federal, state, and local full-time and part-time personnel from 50 agencies, who participate in initiatives to disrupt and dismantle DTOs and reduce the demand for drugs.

### LOCATION

The SWB HIDTA/CA Region operates out of San Diego, California. It is made up of two counties: Imperial and San Diego.

### INITIATIVES

The Region has 18 initiatives, which include 1 management and coordination, 4 support, 1 demand reduction, 1 prosecution, 1 intelligence, 9 investigation/interdiction initiatives, as well as the National Methamphetamine Pharmaceuticals Initiative (NMPI).

### SHORT-TERM OBJECTIVES

| YEAR | DTOs Expected to be Disrupted/ Dismantled | Target Return on Investment: Assets | Target Return on Investment: Drugs | Number of Deconflictions Expected to be Submitted | Number of Investigations Expected to be Provided Analytical Support | Number of Initiative Leads Expected to be Referred |
|------|------|------|------|------|------|------|
| 2010 | 43 | $1.38 | $167.56 | 124,000 | 100 | 120 |

## THREAT ASSESSMENT

San Diego and Imperial counties are national distribution centers for illicit drugs entering the United States from Mexico, and Central and South America, including heroin, cocaine, methamphetamine, and marijuana, and from major domestic marijuana production sites. In 2009, over 290,000 kilograms of drugs valued at over $2.3 billion were seized and permanently removed from the market, as well as over $27.25 million in proceeds and assets. As mandated by the HIDTA program, SWB HIDTA/CA Region initiatives focus on larger drug operations, resulting in 74 OCDETF cases, of which 34 were CPOTs or RPOTs. Investigations (including the 2009 OCDETF Case of the Year – Operation Imperial Emperor) indicate that traffickers operating within the region continue to supply major markets throughout the United States, including Las Vegas, Portland, Boston, Detroit, Miami, New Orleans, New York, Chicago, Tampa, and Charlotte.

## INTELLIGENCE INITIATIVES

The San Diego Law Enforcement Coordination Center (SD-LECC) provides coordination and information sharing among local, state, and Federal law enforcement agencies within the two-county region, nationally, and with all other HIDTAs, DHS Fusion Centers and RISS projects. The SD-LECC's goals are to: 1) conform to the General Counterdrug Intelligence Plan; 2) conform to the ONDCP/SWB/SWB HIDTA/CA Region program guidance; 3) conform to the RISS/WSIN guidelines; 4) Conform to DHS Fusion Center Guidelines and Baseline Capability requirements; and 5) support all law enforcement entities in reducing crime, drug trafficking, and drug use in America.

The SD-LECC functions as the all-crimes Intelligence and Investigative Support Center and Homeland Security Fusion Center for the SWB HIDTA/CA Region, and the principal intelligence coordination center for participating drug and all-crimes law enforcement agencies, prosecutors, and other local, state, and Federal agencies. The primary elements include: 1) a Watch Center for case deconfliction through the exchange of vital narcotic and criminal intelligence information, and the use of maps and a relational database to coordinate and deconflict crucial law enforcement activities, such as investigations, surveillances, searches, and arrests, in the interest of case and officer safety; 2) a surveillance/ technical equipment pool; 3) investigative support units (ISU) that provide tactical analytical case support and focus on targeting and strategic planning; 4) a gang team and a border and financial crimes team with analysts and agents who focus on strategic and operational intelligence and tactical case support in their respective crime areas; and 5) an information technology (IT) unit which provides support to the SWB HIDTA/CA Region and affiliated initiatives, the SD-LECC, and the Imperial Valley Law Enforcement Coordination Center - including the development and implementation of IT policy, network planning and implementation, and hardware/software support.

The SD-LECC prepares the SWB HIDTA/CA Region Annual Threat Assessment that is the baseline for area strategies - and subsequently for the Region's initiatives. The initiatives achieve the desired outcomes of the strategies, which are: improved intelligence support to the region and other HIDTAs, disruption/dismantlement of significant DTOs, fully coordinated counterdrug interdiction operations along the border and with the other Southwest border HIDTA Regions, and a decrease in drug use.

The FBI's JTTF and the Regional Terrorism Threat Assessment Center (RTTAC) are also located at the center. The SD-LECC has recently been reorganized with complete integration of HIDTA IISC and DHS Fusion Center components under a single command structure, organized only by subject- and/or functional area. It is truly an all-crimes fusion center. The FBI has agreed to fund the rent at the facility for the next 10 years, at approximately $1.5 million per year. The fusion center is designed to be a partnership consisting of local, state, and Federal agencies that act as an information-sharing gateway with the intent to assist law enforcement and other public safety entities to detect, prevent, and solve crimes and potential acts of terrorism, through the production of tactical, operational, and strategic intelligence.

Local, state, and Federal agencies, including the San Diego County Sheriff's Department, the San Diego Police Department, the Chula Vista Police Department, the California National Guard, the California Department of Justice, CBP, the FBI, the DEA, and ICE are combining their intelligence resources at the center, partially through contributed personnel from all of these agencies. Other participants in the San Diego center include a full-time Marijuana Initiative analyst, a representative from the NDIC, and a DHS analyst.

Information integration is being accomplished through deployment of a new LAN for use by all center participants. There are currently 165 integrated workstations. Capabilities of the LAN, called LECCnet, include an intelligence report depository on the portal that proactively notifies users of content based on alert subscriptions, and the ability for authorized users to securely access their LECCnet files and applications remotely. Additionally, seven different agency networks have been installed, further increasing the ability to share, correlate, and analyze intelligence information. Future objectives include the deployment of LECCnet at both the SWB HIDTA/CA Region and the Imperial Valley Law Enforcement Coordination Center.

In Imperial County, the Investigative Support Unit is co-located at the Imperial Valley Law Enforcement Coordination Center, along with the Street Interdiction Team and Border Interdiction Team, DEA's Major Mexican Traffickers Group, and the Imperial County Narcotic Task Force. The Imperial Valley LECC will undergo a major expansion in 2011, in order to accommodate additional co-located enforcement groups to include two BEST teams, the new FBI Safe Streets task force, and expanded US Marshal and US Attorney's Office presence in Imperial County. Additionally, the new LECC will include a regional dispatch and communications center for all local agencies in the county.

## TASK FORCES OPERATING IN THE HIDTA REGION

The table below highlights the Federally-funded drug enforcement task forces operating in the HIDTA region. Multiple HIDTA task forces may make up an overarching HIDTA enforcement or investigative initiative.

| TASK FORCES | LOCATIONS |
|---|---|
| Imperial Valley Drug Coalition (HIDTA) | Imperial |
| Marine Task Force (HIDTA) | San Diego |
| Major Mexican Traffickers Initiative (HIDTA) | San Diego and Imperial |

| TASK FORCES | LOCATIONS |
| --- | --- |
| San Diego Narcotics Task Force - Commercial Interdiction Unit (HIDTA) | San Diego |
| San Diego Violent Crime Task Force (HIDTA) | San Diego and San Marcos |
| Operation Alliance Joint Task Force (HIDTA) | San Diego |
| Combined Border Prosecutions Initiative (HIDTA) | San Diego and Imperial |
| Domestic Marijuana Initiative (HIDTA) | San Diego |
| San Diego Regional Pharmaceutical Narcotic Enforcement Team (HIDTA) | San Diego |
| Tactical Diversion Squad (DEA) | San Diego |
| San Diego/Imperial Counties Law Enforcement Coordination Center (HIDTA) | San Diego |
| National Methamphetamine and Pharmaceuticals Initiative (HIDTA) | San Diego |
| Regional Computer Forensics Laboratory (HIDTA) | San Diego |
| CBAG Marijuana Eradication and Investigation Initiative (HIDTA) | San Diego County |
| Border Crimes Suppression Team (SWB Recovery Act - DOJ) | San Diego |
| DHS-ICE Border Enforcement Security Teams (4 total) (DHS and HIDTA) | San Diego and Imperial Counties |
| DEA Narcotic Task Force (DEA and partial HIDTA) | San Diego |

## *TASK FORCE COORDINATION*

Each agency has its own strategies, requirements, and missions. The SWB HIDTA/CA Region Executive Committee coordinates the integration and synchronization of efforts to reduce drug trafficking, eliminate unnecessary duplication, and improve the direction, production, and systematic sharing of intelligence.

The Executive Committee provides a coordination umbrella over networked joint task forces, the intelligence center, task forces not funded by the SWB HIDTA/CA Region, and single agency task forces and narcotics units within the region's area of responsibility. The Committee is formed of 16 Members/Officers, eight Federal and eight state/local, with the chair and vice-chair rotating between Federal and state/local yearly. The Chair and Vice Chair of the SWB HIDTA/CA Region are also members of the Southwest Border HIDTA Executive Board.

The SD-LECC Executive Board, co-chaired by Federal and state/local representatives, provides guidance and oversight to the Intelligence and Investigative Support Center (the San Diego/Imperial Law Enforcement Coordination Center - SDLECC) and develops intelligence policies for the approval of the Executive Committee.

To accomplish its mission, the SWB HIDTA/CA Region coordinates intelligence-driven, joint, multi-agency coordinated initiatives, which are organized into five mutually supporting subsystems. The emphasis is on seamless mutual support between intelligence, interdictors, investigators, and prosecutors, with cross-attachment and co-location of enforcement groups responsible for differing operational methods, target regions, and target levels of investigation.

The flow of information, both intelligence and investigative/operational, is critical to comprehensive success against the widely varying drug threats in the region.

All task forces and member agencies utilize the subject and event deconfliction services of the SDLECC: over 100,000 subject inquiries and 11,000 critical enforcement events were handled by the SDLECC in 2009. The SDLECC is a node in the WSIN (which covers California, Oregon, Washington, Arkansas, and Hawaii). These inquiries and events are electronically shared on a real-time basis with all the participants in the WSIN system, and most significantly with the HIDTA IISCs in the western States. Further, the SDLECC is the co-location and combination of the HIDTA IISC and the regional Homeland Security Fusion Center. One facility with free access houses the joint intelligence analysis center, the Regional Terrorism Threat Analysis Center, JTTF. In this way, the agencies in the region have committed to full intelligence and information sharing and fusion.

The SWB HIDTA/CA Region Intelligence Subsystem links and integrates with the Intelligence Subsystems of the other SWB HIDTA Regions, utilizing border-wide IISC participation in Operation Cobija, DHE, IISC Managers meetings, the RISS, Anti-Drug Network- Unclassified (ADNET-U), and other sensitive but unclassified (SBU) networks. Additionally, the CBAG holds quarterly initiative meetings to exchange information and address issues of mutual concern.

## *HIDTA EVALUATION*

The SWB HIDTA/CA Region is meeting its performance objectives and goals in a cost-effective manner. The Region targets CPOTs, regional DTOs, and multi-state targets to disrupt and/or dismantle. It has been directly involved in investigating high-priority targets or providing intelligence to the agencies conducting those investigations. The California Region has a state-of-the-art Intelligence and Investigative Support Center in which all units are co-located and comingled, thereby ensuring immediate sharing of information. The region also participates with LA CLEAR for deconfliction. The SWB HIDTA/CA Region recently expanded its prevention efforts by joining with the other three HIDTAs within the State and establishing a prevention initiative.

During 2009, SWB HIDTA/CA Region initiatives identified 218 DTOs and targeted 200. By the end of year, 20 of targeted DTOs, and money-laundering organizations were disrupted or dismantled. In addition, 5 DTOs were totally dismantled; a significant achievement. The SWB HIDTA/CA Region strives to investigate larger, more complex DTOs where the greatest positive impact can be achieved. Disrupting or dismantling a large, complex DTO generally takes longer than stopping a street-level operation, but doing so can substantially reduce the illicit drug marketplace. SWB HIDTA/CA Region initiatives targeted more complex cases involving larger DTOs. They initiated 13 OCDETF cases, for a total of 74 OCDETF cases open during the year, of which 21 were Consolidated Priority Organization Targets (CPOTs.) There were 7 CPOT and 3 RPOT designations in 2009.

These investigations achieved highly significant milestones in 2009, with arrests, indictments, and extraditions of key Mexican cartel members.

# SWB HIDTA - New Mexico Region – Designated in 1990
## Director – Ernesto Ortiz

## PURPOSE AND GOALS

The mission of the SWB HIDTA/New Mexico Region (SWB HIDTA/NM Region) is to reduce drug availability by creating intelligence-driven drug task forces aimed at eliminating or reducing domestic drug trafficking and its harmful consequences. This is accomplished through initiatives that enhance and help to coordinate drug trafficking control efforts among Federal, state, and local law enforcement agencies. This mission will develop a synchronized system involving coordinated intelligence, interdiction, investigation, and prosecution efforts to measurably reduce drug trafficking, thereby reducing the impact of illicit drugs in the State and other areas of the country.

## STRATEGY

The SWB HIDTA/NM Region's integrated systems approach will use intelligence to synchronize the efforts of enforcement, prosecution, and support initiatives. There are 17 initiatives that include 16 multi-jurisdictional task forces with 1 Tribal, 41 local, 15 state and 10 Federal law enforcement participating agencies. These initiatives will focus on interdiction, investigation, prosecution, and intelligence sharing. SWB HIDTA/NM Region initiatives will continue to focus efforts to reduce the transshipment/distribution of illicit drugs and prescription controlled drugs into and through New Mexico, and the transshipment of money and weapons south across the Southwest border. The region emphasizes the development of Consolidated CPOTs, RPOTs, and OCDETF level cases initiated through interdiction and investigative efforts.

## LOCATION

The SWB HIDTA/NM Region operates out of Las Cruces, New Mexico. It is made up of 16 counties: Bernalillo, Chaves, Doña Ana, Eddy, Grant, Hidalgo, Lea, Lincoln, Luna, Otero, Rio Arriba, Sandoval, Santa Fe, San Juan, Torrance, and Valencia.

## INITIATIVES

The SWB HIDTA/NM Region has 17 initiatives, which include 1 management and coordination, 1 training, 1 support (Crime Lab), 1 prosecution, 1 intelligence, and 12 investigation/interdiction initiatives.

## SHORT-TERM OBJECTIVES

| YEAR | DTOs Expected to be Disrupted/ Dismantled | Target Return on Investment: Assets | Target Return on Investment: Drugs | Number of Deconflictions Expected to be Submitted | Number of Investigations Expected to be Provided Analytical Support | Number of Initiative Leads Expected to be Referred |
|------|------|------|------|------|------|------|
| 2010 | 79 | $1.69 | $12.91 | 2,600 | 270 | 996 |

## THREAT ASSESSMENT

Illicit drug smuggling and transshipments are the major drug threats in the state of New Mexico. The quantity of illegal drugs transported through New Mexico far outweighs the consumption rate within the state. However, the distribution and abuse of Mexican ice methamphetamine pose a serious threat to the SWB HIDTA/NM Region.

The State's proximity to Mexico, its geography along the 180 mile sparsely populated, shared border, the presence of well established DTOs with direct ties to Mexican cartels, and its transportation infrastructure make it a principal drug smuggling area and transshipment and distribution center for marijuana, cocaine, heroin, methamphetamine, and other illicit drugs, including prescription controlled drugs, in the region and many other domestic drug markets. The state's geography continues to be the most significant factor contributing to the drug threat in New Mexico. The open border areas between POEs, mostly a mixture of farmlands and mountainous terrain in the "Boot Heel" area of southwest New Mexico, coupled with a limited law enforcement presence and access to the State's transportation infrastructure, makes this area vulnerable for exploitation by DTOs. Criminal groups, street, prison, and outlaw motorcycle gangs, as well as local independent dealers exacerbate the drug problem in New Mexico as retail-level distributors.

## INTELLIGENCE INITIATIVES

The New Mexico Investigative Support Center (NMISC) is a full service IISC that supports all law enforcement and judicial initiatives in their efforts to address and target drug threats in New Mexico. The IISC is the intelligence and information sharing center for the HIDTA in the New Mexico Region. The IISC enhances the ability of HIDTA initiatives to disrupt and dismantle DTOs through collaboration, analysis, and information sharing. The IISC assists initiatives with intelligence-driven investigations through research, analysis, and coordination of information. The IISC provides tactical, investigative, and strategic intelligence to HIDTA initiatives and other law enforcement agencies. The IISC's core functions include: event and subject deconfliction, case support and post-seizure analysis, Pen-Register and Wire-Tap support, threat assessments, officer safety bulletins, and a multitude of other special projects. The IISC maintains a Wide Area Network that includes connectivity to commercial and law enforcement databases for the HIDTA in New Mexico. The mission-critical systems on the IISC network include the ORION intelligence database, a deconfliction system (SAFETNet), and wiretap/pen register equipment. Approximately 70 law enforcement agencies participate in the deconfliction system with ten of these being agencies that are not related to the HIDTA. The IISC provides training as needed, coordinates all intelligence matters, and acts as the interagency liaison on information sharing for the SWB HIDTA/NM. The IISC supports major drug investigations, including RPOT/CPOT and OCDETF cases. The IISC is the primary collection hub for all domestic highway enforcement operations in the State of New Mexico. Additionally, the strategic and tactical units of the IISC provide intelligence support to marijuana eradication efforts in the State of New Mexico. The IISC generates and disseminates intelligence regarding financial crimes and targets via direct access to the FinCEN Network and participation in the U.S. Attorney-sponsored SARs Review Team.

The SWB HIDTA/NM Region's primary Intelligence and Investigative Support Center is located in Albuquerque, New Mexico, and operates a node in Las Cruces, New Mexico. The Las

Cruces Node is managed by an ICE agent while the Albuquerque is co-managed by DEA, FBI, and Albuquerque PD. The FBI is the lead agency for this initiative, and DEA fully participates, as do other Federal, state, and local agencies. The Region includes a large Native American population and has added several initiatives that conduct operations in Indian Country.

## TASK FORCES OPERATING IN THE HIDTA REGION

The table below highlights the Federally-funded drug enforcement task forces operating in the HIDTA region. Multiple HIDTA task forces may make up an overarching HIDTA enforcement or investigative initiative.

| TASK FORCES | LOCATIONS |
|---|---|
| Region VII Border Drug Task Force (HIDTA) | Deming |
| NM DEA HIDTA Task Force (HIDTA) | Albuquerque and Las Cruces |
| FBI Safe Streets (HIDTA) | Albuquerque |
| Fugitive/Violent Offender Task Force (HIDTA) | Albuquerque |
| Middle Rio Grande Valley Task Force (HIDTA) | Albuquerque |
| NM Enhanced Linewatch Operations (HIDTA) | Southern New Mexico |
| NM DPS (HIDTA) | New Mexico |
| Region II HIDTA Narcotics Task Force (HIDTA) | Farmington |
| Region III Multi-Jurisdictional Drug Task Force (HIDTA) | Santa Fe |
| Region VI Drug Task Force– Lincoln County (HIDTA) | Lincoln County (Ruidoso) |
| Region VI Drug Task Force – Chaves County (HIDTA) | Chaves County (Roswell) |
| Region VI Drug Task Force – Lea County (HIDTA) | Lea County (Hobbs) |
| Region VI Drug Task Force – Otero County (HIDTA) | Otero County (Alamogordo) |
| Region VI Drug Task Force – Pecos Valley (HIDTA) | Carlsbad |
| Regional Interagency Drug Task Force (HIDTA) | Las Cruces |
| FBI Safe Streets Task Force (FBI) | Farmington and Las Cruces |
| Project Exile (ATF) | Albuquerque |
| BEST ( ICE) | New Mexico – Statewide (Based out of El Paso, Texas) |
| Methamphetamine Initiative Task Force – 2nd Judicial DA | Albuquerque |
| New Mexico DEA Tactical Diversion Squad (Pharmaceuticals) | Albuquerque, New Mexico |
| JTTF – FBI | Albuquerque, New Mexico |
| Public Corruption & Border Crimes Task Force (FBI) | Based out of Hartsville, Tennessee |
| Region IV Drug Task Force (JAG) | Las Cruces, New Mexico |
| Region V Drug Task Force (JAG) | Clovis, New Mexico |
| Safe Trails (FBI) | Farmington, New Mexico |
| NM Gang Task Force (JAG) | Albuquerque, New Mexico |
| OCDETF Strike Force (U.S. Attorneys' Office) | Las Cruces, NM |

## TASK FORCE COORDINATION

The SWB HIDTA/NM Region provides a coordination umbrella for Federal, state, local, and tribal drug enforcement efforts. The Executive Committee, which includes participation from 20 key law enforcement organizations throughout the state, provides leadership and fosters an attitude of teamwork and equality between its Federal, state, local, and tribal partners. It also ensures a strategy-driven, systemic approach to synchronize drug enforcement efforts and leverage resources, thereby increasing the efficiency and effectiveness of drug control strategies among participating agencies. Co-location of Federal, state, local, and tribal investigators is the key to success in this program. Its Executive Committee mandates information sharing by all participating agencies, thereby making collaboration more effective. Frequently, SWB HIDTA/NM Region cases receive OCDETF designation, which makes more resources available.

The region mandates its task forces, and encourages non-HIDTA law enforcement participants, to use event and case/subject deconfliction. This mitigates officer safety issues, minimizes duplication of efforts, and leverages resources. The SWB HIDTA/NM Region IISC (NM IISC) is the coordinating hub for deconfliction activities in New Mexico.

The NM IISC coordinates the sharing of information for all its initiatives. It also shares information with other law enforcement agencies and intelligence centers. The IISC facilitates the sharing of information concerning organizational structures of DTOs, transportation, and distribution modes of operation and other related intelligence. Drug task forces, groups, or units, not already part of or affiliated with a HIDTA task force, coordinate with HIDTA electronically or through daily contact. Non-HIDTA local police and sheriffs' offices are informed of investigations within their jurisdiction for coordination and deconfliction purposes and, if necessary, for local participation.

The SWB HIDTA/NM Region also sponsors a Narcotics Information Sharing Training Conference semiannually. The day-and-a-half conference serves as a venue for sharing information, ideas, and tactics among drug enforcement initiatives. The conference also includes participation from representatives from Mexico. The Region evaluates its initiatives annually in regards to sharing information. It conducts annual, onsite reviews and monitors each initiative through the use of the HIDTA PMP system.

## HIDTA EVALUATION

The SWB HIDTA/NM Region uses the PMP system to monitor the attainment of performance outputs/outcomes for all its initiatives. Additionally, it has incorporated an evaluation system that includes a midyear review and an in-depth annual onsite inspection. The focus of the annual inspection is to verify compliance with local policy and program guidance specifically related to performance, finances, and property/equipment. The inspection includes a physical audit of operational, financial, and property/equipment records.

In 2009, the SWB HIDTA/NM Region disrupted or dismantled 98 DTOs, compared to 120 the prior year. HIDTA initiatives had identified 224 DTOs operating in the Region, of which 120 DTOs were expected to be dismantled or disrupted.

## SWB HIDTA - South Texas Region – Designated in 1990
## Director – Antonio Garcia

### PURPOSE AND GOALS

The mission of the SWB HIDTA/South Texas Region (SWB HIDTA/STX Region) is to reduce drug availability by creating intelligence-driven drug task forces aimed at eliminating or reducing domestic drug trafficking and its harmful consequences through enhancing and helping to coordinate illicit drug trafficking control efforts among Federal, state, local, and tribal law enforcement agencies.

### STRATEGY

Federal, state, and local law enforcement agencies combine their efforts with multi-jurisdictional co-located /commingled drug task forces and initiatives. These intelligence-driven drug task forces pursue coordinated efforts to reduce the smuggling, transshipment, and distribution of drugs into and through the State of Texas. The SWB HIDTA/STX Region employs intelligence-driven investigations and interdiction activities targeted at drug transshipments, including extensive systematic follow-up investigations involving intelligence analysis and sharing of information, along with an aggressive prosecution structure that focus on the disruption and dismantlement of DTOs in accordance with the *National Southwest Border Counternarcotics Strategy*. SWB HIDTA/STX Region initiatives are organized seamlessly into four types: 1) Enforcement (Interdiction, Investigation and Prosecution), 2) Intelligence and Information Sharing, 3) Support and 4) Management and Coordination. Through an intensive initiative and task force review and inspection process, along with statistical information gathered through the HIDTA PMP system, the Executive Committee holds initiatives accountable for their productivity.

### LOCATION

The SWB HIDTA/STX Region operates out of San Antonio, Texas. It is made up of 15 counties: Bexar, Cameron, Dimmit, Hidalgo, Jim Hogg, Kinney, La Salle, Maverick, Starr, Travis (added in March 2010), Val Verde, Webb, Willacy, Zapata, and Zavala.

### INITIATIVES

The Region has 23 initiatives, which include 1 management, 1 training, 6 intelligence, and 15 investigation/ interdiction initiatives.

## SHORT-TERM OBJECTIVES

| YEAR | DTOs Expected to be Disrupted/ Dismantled | Target Return on Investment: Assets | Target Return on Investment: Drugs | Number of Deconflictions Expected to be Submitted | Number of Investigations Expected to be Provided Analytical Support | Number of Initiative Leads Expected to be Referred |
|---|---|---|---|---|---|---|
| 2010 | 67 | $4.86 | $38.70 | 13,650 | 745 | 82,047 |

## THREAT ASSESSMENT

The SWB HIDTA/STX Region is a principal high-transit smuggling corridor for illicit drugs and illegal aliens along the United States/Mexico border. It continues to be a major transshipment corridor for marijuana, cocaine, heroin, methamphetamine, and other illegal narcotics. The Region consists of 15 counties, with 13 situated along the United States/Mexico border. These counties represent 50 percent of the Texas/Mexico border. Seventeen of the 25 ports of entry along the Texas/Mexico border are within the South Texas Region. The POEs, coupled with the Region's interstate highways, make the Region one of the most strategically important drug smuggling corridors in use by both domestic and Mexican DTOs. Despite the low population in some areas, the Region greatly influences drug trafficking and availability at the national level. Gang activity continues to be a threat in the area, due to gang associations with the Gulf Cartel and other DTOs and cartels.

## INTELLIGENCE INITIATIVES

The STX HIDTA Intelligence Initiative consists of six investigative/intelligence support centers strategically located in key geographical areas[15]. Its principal investigative support center is the South Texas HIDTA Investigative Support Center (STHIC), located in San Antonio. The STHIC is a full-service IISC which also includes a subject and event Deconfliction Center. The STHIC provides near real-time interaction with intelligence elements across the region and Nation through HIDTA.net and other Federal, state, and local systems. The STHIC includes a Deconfliction Center; an operational and tactical analytical support team; and a strategic analysis unit. Each Intelligence center provides near real-time criminal and open source database query checks and case support; analytical case support including telephone toll, link, and event/flow analysis; charting and forecasting; drug trends reporting and assessing; events; and enforcement. With multi-agency, joint task force personnel, the Intelligence Centers strive to give near-real-time responses to LEA queries regarding information within their available databases. The centers furnish analytical support by collecting, analyzing, reporting, and processing information received into useable intelligence relevant to customer needs. Besides providing deconfliction services to the South Texas HIDTA Region, the STHIC has partnered with the North Texas HIDTA in providing deconfliction support to the NTX HIDTA region, including the State of Oklahoma. The Deconfliction Center responded to LEA in 81 counties across central and south Texas in CY 2009. The SWB STX HIDTA partnerships and LEA across the Nation may access the STHIC's numerous intelligence products via its website on HIDTA.net.

---

[15] These investigative/intelligence support centers are located in Austin, Brownsville, Del Rio, Laredo, McAllen, and San Antonio.

## TASK FORCES OPERATING IN THE HIDTA REGION

The table below highlights the Federally-funded drug enforcement task forces operating in the HIDTA region. Multiple HIDTA task forces may make up an overarching HIDTA enforcement or investigative initiative.

| TASK FORCES | LOCATIONS |
|---|---|
| Brownsville HIDTA Investigative Task Force (HIDTA) | Brownsville |
| Border Patrol Intelligence Center (HIDTA) | Del Rio |
| Eagle Pass Multi-Agency Investigative Task Force (HIDTA) | Eagle Pass |
| Hidalgo County Task Force (HIDTA) | Edinburg |
| Laredo Financial Narcotics Enforcement Task Force (HIDTA) | Laredo |
| Laredo Multi-agency Task Force (HIDTA) | Laredo |
| McAllen Intelligence Center (HIDTA) | McAllen |
| Multi-agency Drug Related Public Corruption Task Force (HIDTA) | McAllen |
| McAllen DEA Task Force (HIDTA) | McAllen |
| McAllen ICE Task Force (HIDTA) | McAllen |
| San Antonio DEA Task Force (HIDTA) | San Antonio |
| San Antonio Department of Public Safety Task Force (HIDTA) | San Antonio |
| San Antonio Police Department Task Force (HIDTA) | San Antonio |
| South Texas HIDTA Del Rio Task Force (HIDTA) | Del Rio |
| South Texas HIDTA Intelligence Center (HIDTA) | San Antonio |
| South Texas HIDTA McAllen Initiative (HIDTA) | McAllen |
| South Texas HIDTA San Antonio Initiative (HIDTA) | San Antonio |
| Starr County HIDTA Task Force (HIDTA) | Rio Grande City |
| Unified Narcotics Intelligence Task Force (HIDTA) | Brownsville |
| White Sands HIDTA Task Force (HIDTA) | Brownsville |
| OCDETF Strike Force (DOJ) | Laredo, Webb County; McAllen, Hidalgo County |
| DEA Funded Task Forces (DEA) | San Antonio, Bexar County |
| Tactical Diversion Squad (DEA) | Austin |
| BEST Task Forces, Immigration and Custom Enforcement (DHS) | Laredo, Webb County; Harlingen, Cameron County |
| Joint Terrorism Task Force (FBI) | San Antonio, Bexar County; McAllen, Hidalgo County; Brownsville, Cameron County; Laredo, Webb County |
| Safe Streets Task Force (FBI) | San Antonio, Bexar County; McAllen, Hidalgo County; Brownsville, Cameron County; Laredo, Webb County |

## TASK FORCE COORDINATION

Regularly scheduled Intelligence and Information Conferences are held across the SWB HIDTA/STX Region. Regular attendees include representatives from the North Texas (NTX) HIDTA, Houston HIDTA, other Southwest border HIDTA Regions, as well as NDIC and EPIC. Many of the attendees are from non-HIDTA participating agencies as well as the Texas National Guard, and military personnel from the Department of Defense's Joint Task Force North (JTFN). Personnel from Federal agencies participate in the South Texas HIDTA-sponsored information-sharing conferences, as well. From these conferences, numerous agencies acquire new knowledge and information on the South Texas HIDTA Investigative Support and Deconfliction Center. The Deconfliction Center provides deconfliction services to law enforcement agencies in 162 counties in south and north Texas, and Oklahoma. Some 359 Federal, state, and local agencies receive deconfliction support through the South Texas IISC. All task force personnel are mandated by the Executive Committee and their respective agency heads to participate in the deconfliction process, resulting in enhanced officer safety and the merging of investigations.

The SWB HIDTA/STX Region has implemented "Gateway/Destination" information-sharing meetings to bring together personnel from those HIDTAs that are directly impacted by drug trafficking activity originating in the South Texas area. These two-way exchanges of information have identified significant links between ongoing investigations in different jurisdictions, resulting in solving of one homicide investigation, a number of fugitive arrests, and several investigative conspiracy cases. These meetings also constitute an action item in the implementation of the *National Drug Control Strategy.*

The SWB HIDTA/STX Region does not routinely or directly participate with either the Southern or Western Judicial Districts JTTF. However, JTTF task forces frequently participate in the South Texas HIDTA Region intelligence and information-sharing conferences. The Region's IISC provides support as requested by the JTTF on a case-by-case or event-to-event basis. The SWB HIDTA/STX Region participates with the Texas Division of Emergency Management (DEM), Texas Border Support Operations Center (BSOC), and the State Fusion Center in the sharing of pertinent information.

## HIDTA EVALUATION

The SWB HIDTA/STX Region and its management staff are committed to meeting performance objectives and inputting that data into the HIDTA PMP database. The South Texas Region disrupted or dismantled 42 of the 82 DTOs expected to be disrupted or dismantled. Of those 42, 39 were either multi-state or international in scope. Often, these investigations require a longer period of time to develop. The Region has 73 open OCDETF cases, including 13 initiated within the last year. In CY 2009 South Texas had 43 active CPOT cases and 9 active RPOT cases. This Southwest Border HIDTA Region has established four intelligence nodes along the border with Mexico and has linked information with the Texas Narcotics Information System and the three other HIDTAs within the State. The South Texas management staff and Executive Committee remain dedicated to the accomplishment of the HIDTA's mission and goals.

# SWB HIDTA - West Texas Region
## Designated in 1990
## Director – Travis Kuykendall

## PURPOSE AND GOALS

The mission of the SWB HIDTA/West Texas Region (SWB HIDTA/WTX Region) is to dismantle the DTOs in the region and to stop the flow of illegal drugs into the United States, through cooperative efforts in intelligence, investigation, interdiction, forfeiture, and prosecution initiatives.

## STRATEGY

The SWB HIDTA/WTX Region continues to foster cooperative and effective working relationships among 1 U.S. Attorneys' Office, 10 Federal agencies, 7 state agencies, and 19 local agencies to achieve the common goals of disrupting and dismantling DTOs, and securing the West Texas 12-county region of the Southwest border, preventing multi-ton quantities of illicit drugs from ever reaching their intended market.

## LOCATION

The SWB HIDTA/WTX Region operates out of El Paso, Texas. The West Texas Region shares 520 miles of border with Mexico. It is made up of 12 counties: Brewster, Crockett, Culberson, Ector, El Paso, Hudspeth, Jeff Davis, Midland, Pecos, Presidio, Reeves, and Terrell.

## INITIATIVES

The Region has 16 initiatives, which include 1 management and coordination, 1 training, 1 prosecution, 1 intelligence, and 12 investigation/interdiction initiatives.

## SHORT-TERM OBJECTIVES

| YEAR | DTOs Expected to be Disrupted/ Dismantled | Target Return on Investment: Assets | Target Return on Investment: Drugs | Number of Deconflictions Expected to be Submitted | Number of Investigations Expected to be Provided Analytical Support | Number of Initiative Leads Expected to be Referred |
|------|-------------------------------------------|-------------------------------------|-------------------------------------|----------------------------------------------------|---------------------------------------------------------------------|-----------------------------------------------------|
| 2010 | 139 | $2 | $25 | 16,750 | 167 | 661 |

## THREAT ASSESSMENT

The West Texas Region continues to be a major smuggling and transshipment area, supplying illicit drugs of all kinds to most of the major cities in the Nation. Mexican DTOs are the primary organizational threat to the West Texas Region. They maintain sophisticated command-and-control centers in Mexico, where they exert nearly total control over drug smuggling operations in the region. Control of drug trafficking in the El Paso, Texas/Juarez, Mexico plaza is currently in flux. Multiple Mexican drug-trafficking cartels have been battling for control of drug trafficking in the region, leading to extreme levels of violence on the Mexican border state of Chihuahua (which includes Ciudad Juarez). This violence has spun out of control, and none of these organizations has yet been able to establish dominance. Seizures of cocaine, heroin, marijuana, and methamphetamine, while increasing slightly in 2009, were at significantly lower levels than in 2008, most likely the result of the ongoing violent conflict between cartels in the El Paso/Juarez plaza, and increased, coordinated law enforcement "surge" operations along the border. However, seizure levels still indicate the West Texas corridor is a major source for all illicit drugs trafficked throughout the Nation. In 2009, approximately 2,284 murders in Juarez were attributed to the drug violence that has gripped the city. In 2010, the number of drug-related murders in Juarez was approximately 3,203.

## *INTELLIGENCE INITIATIVES*

The West Texas Region Intelligence Initiative (WTRII) was created to provide a seamless intelligence support system for the narcotics and other law enforcement operational initiatives and units in the Region. This multi-agency system – led by the El Paso County Sheriff's Office, and co-managed with the FBI and DEA – is designed to provide timely, actionable information to the agent/officer. Deconfliction services provided by the WTRII help improve officer safety issues and maximize the efficient use of resources. As a central hub for law enforcement agency intelligence sharing and dissemination, the WTRII aims to directly improve the efficiency and effectiveness of law enforcement organizations and their efforts within the HIDTA.

The WTRII consists of three nodes, which provide operational units with a seamless intelligence support system. The structure and policies of the entire initiative comply with the General Counterdrug Intelligence Plan (GCIP).

The West Texas Region IISC is the hub of the WTRII and is located in the El Paso Federal Criminal Justice Building. The IISC is the initial point of contact on all service requests to the WTRII. It also sponsors yearly marketing presentations (on services provided by the WTRII), to all law enforcement personnel in the region. The Alpine/Marfa/Big Bend Intelligence Center (AMBBIC) provides limited intelligence support in the Alpine/Marfa/Big Bend areas of the SWB HIDTA/WTX Region. TNIS provides national database connectivity, a central information repository and limited analytical support. The IISC coordinates the efforts of the AMBBIC and TNIS components of the initiative so the narcotics agent/officer is serviced by a seamless intelligence support system. The El Paso Police Department, Customs and Border Protection, Immigration and Customs Enforcement, and the Texas Department of Public Safety Intelligence units in the El Paso area also support the IISC in its mission.

The IISC provides database query, deconfliction pointer index services, and a full range of tactical and strategic analytical support and reports. The IISC develops intelligence-driven investigations to provide to the operational units. It is the hub of communications between all of the agencies/initiatives, the West Texas Region administrative center, and the other SWB Regions through the development and operation of a secure intranet/e-mail system. The AMBBIC is located at the CBP/Border Patrol-Marfa station, which services law enforcement personnel in Presidio, Brewster, Jeff Davis and Pecos counties. The CBP/Border Patrol-Marfa Sector is the lead agency, and is electronically connected to the El Paso IISC via a WAN with e-mail capabilities. The AMBBIC provides limited query, tactical, and analytical support to the operational units in their area. Deconfliction, strategic analytical support, and communications issues are handled at the El Paso IISC. Collateral duty agents at each of the CBP/Border Patrol checkpoints along the border are also participating in this initiative by feeding intelligence information to the IISC through the AMBBIC.

The Texas Narcotics Information System (TNIS) is the data repository for the WTR-IISC. They assist with analytical and deconfliction support for operational units in the West Texas area. Texas DPS is the POC at the WTRII and provides 10 analysts to the various Texas HIDTAs, 2 of which are located at the El Paso IISC. The SWB HIDTA/WTX Region funds two records technicians who provide statewide deconfliction support at the Texas Department of Public Safety Headquarters in Austin. Due to the availability of information at the DPS Headquarters and the limited number of analysts, it is not feasible to co-locate analysts at all of the initiatives. The SWB HIDTA/WTX and STX Regions support TNIS, as do the North Texas HIDTA and the Houston HIDTA.

### TASK FORCES OPERATING IN THE HIDTA REGION

The table below highlights the Federally-funded drug enforcement task forces operating in the HIDTA region. Multiple HIDTA task forces may make up an overarching HIDTA enforcement or investigative initiative.

| TASK FORCES | LOCATIONS |
|---|---|
| Alpine Multi-Agency Task Force (HIDTA) | Alpine |
| Border Corruption Task Force (HIDTA) | El Paso |
| El Paso Multi-Agency Task Force (HIDTA) | El Paso |
| Enterprise Money Laundering Initiative (HIDTA) | El Paso |
| Operation Lone Star (HIDTA) | Marfa |
| Permian Basin Multi-Agency Task Force (HIDTA) | Midland |
| Southwest Trafficking Interdiction Narcotics Group (HIDTA) | El Paso |
| Stash House Task Force (HIDTA) | El Paso |
| Transportation Task Force (HIDTA) | El Paso |
| West Texas Smuggling Initiative (HIDTA) | El Paso |
| West Texas Fugitive/Violent Offender Task Force (HIDTA) | El Paso |
| Tactical Diversion Squad (DEA) | El Paso |
| El Paso Strike Force (OCDETF) | El Paso |
| BEST (ICE) | El Paso |

### TASK FORCE COORDINATION

All drug task forces receiving HIDTA funds are mandated to use the SWB HIDTA/WTX Region's RISSafe event and subject deconfliction services. All agencies receiving HIDTA funds are mandated to use RISSafe as well. Other task forces, whether Federally funded or not, utilize RISSafe to enhance officer safety and event deconfliction.

The SWB HIDTA/WTX IISC is the hub for all drug intelligence and investigation information in the West Texas area of responsibility. All agencies and task forces, whether HIDTA funded or not, share drug trafficking intelligence and case information through the IISC.

Through cooperation developed by the SWB HIDTA/WTX IISC, all information is available through the IISC to any law enforcement agency. All agencies in the West Texas HIDTA region, and many agencies outside of the Region's area of responsibility, participate in the services of the IISC. This participation ensures the full sharing of information to all law enforcement agencies in the region.

The SWB HIDTA/WTX Region has taken a leadership role among all agencies, task forces, and units in the region to facilitate coordination of operations, management of information and intelligence, and monitor events connected to the drug related violence in Juarez. This open, holistic approach is an effort to prevent and prepare for the spillover of violence into this region of the United States. All joint operations, task forces, and intelligence units, whether Federally funded or not, are involved in these processes.

The IISC is a member of, and is commingled with, the JTTF in El Paso, Texas.

## HIDTA EVALUATION

The SWB HIDTA/WTX Region is meeting its performance objectives in a cost-effective manner. The return on investment of $26 for each dollar invested represents a modest increase compared with 2008. The West Texas IISC continues to gather and share information with participating task force members and other Regions of the SWB HIDTA. The West Texas Region, along with the other SWB HIDTA Regions, is responding to a growing level of violence that impacts the United States side of the border with Mexico. The five SWB HIDTA Regions are increasingly interacting with each other to ensure critical trends, and intelligence information is shared. The West Texas IISC is within the Federal Building in El Paso with all Federal, state, and local partners. Information gathered here is shared with the other Regions of the SWB and with EPIC. West Texas continues to monitor the violence occurring south of the border, and has been effective in assisting its participating state and local partners.

In 2009, the SWB HIDTA/WTX Region identified 169 DTOs operating in its area of responsibility. 118 DOTs were targeted, and 91 (77 percent) were disrupted or dismantled. Disrupting or dismantling a large complex DTO generally takes longer than stopping a street level operation, but can substantially reduce the illicit drug trade.

# Washington/Baltimore HIDTA – Designated in 1994
## Executive Director – Thomas Carr

### PURPOSE AND GOALS

The mission of the Washington/Baltimore (W/B) HIDTA is to improve interagency collaboration, promote the sharing of accurate and timely information and intelligence, and provide specialized training and other resources to W/B HIDTA participating law enforcement and treatment/criminal justice agencies. This will enhance their ability to provide superior services and meet their performance targets. Through its state-of-the-art IISC, its highly trained and skilled professional staff will utilize the HIDTA Performance Management Process to improve the efficiency and effectiveness of HIDTA initiatives throughout the W/B HIDTA region and, when practical, in other areas of the country. The aim of the initiatives is to disrupt and dismantle DTOs and money laundering operations, prosecute traffickers, and seize their drugs and profits.

### STRATEGY

The W/B HIDTA will continue to foster cooperation and effective working relationships with the 107 Federal, state, and local agencies that participate in the HIDTA program. Information and intelligence sharing are becoming a routine practice due to the efforts of the W/B HIDTA participating agencies. The implementation of the HIDTA Gang Intelligence System, used to track criminal gangs, and the use of Case Explorer, HIDTA's case management system, will continue to facilitate information and intelligence sharing. These systems will aid W/B HIDTA's intelligence-driven initiatives to dismantle and disrupt DTOs, while W/B HIDTA's treatment and prevention initiatives will continue to reduce the demand for drugs in the region.

### LOCATION

The W/B HIDTA operates out of Greenbelt, Maryland. The 14 counties and 5 cities that comprise the HIDTA region include:

- The District of Columbia;
- Maryland: Anne Arundel, Baltimore, Charles, Howard, Montgomery, Prince George's, (City of Baltimore); and
- Virginia: Arlington, Chesterfield, Fairfax, Loudoun, Hanover, Henrico, Prince George, Prince William, (City of Alexandria, City of Petersburg, and City of Richmond)

### INITIATIVES

The W/B HIDTA has 48 initiatives, which include 1 management, 1 resource, 1 network support, 1 training, 1 intelligence, 3 prevention, 11 treatment, 3 prosecution, and 26 investigation initiatives.

## SHORT-TERM OBJECTIVES

| YEAR | DTOs Expected to be Disrupted/ Dismantled | Target Return on Investment: Assets | Target Return on Investment: Drugs | Number of Deconflictions Expected to be Submitted | Number of Investigations Expected to be Provided Analytical Support | Number of Initiative Leads Expected to be Referred |
|------|------|------|------|------|------|------|
| 2010 | 131 | $6 | $6 | 15,500 | 150 | 646 |

## THREAT ASSESSMENT

The primary drug threats to the W/B HIDTA region remain crack cocaine, cocaine, heroin, and marijuana, and pharmaceutical diversion and abuse. Methamphetamine is readily available in the region; however, the level of production in the HIDTA region has never been significant. The W/B HIDTA region has historically been primarily a consumer market, and drugs entering the area have typically been routed through another area, especially New York. Evidence suggests this pattern is changing. Mexican trafficking groups are becoming an increasing threat with more cases indicating drugs are coming into the region through hubs in North Carolina, Georgia, and directly from the Southwest border. Drug money laundering has been, and continues to be, of significant concern, and there are indicators that terrorist activities are linked to money laundering operations in the region. In addition, criminal street gangs, many of which are involved in the drug trade, have quickly multiplied. The W/B HIDTA has documented a large number of gangs and gang members operating throughout the region.

## INTELLIGENCE INITIATIVES

Formed in 1995, the Investigative Intelligence Unit (IIU) is designed to improve the ability of HIDTA enforcement initiatives to counter drug trafficking in the Washington/ Baltimore region by collecting, analyzing, and disseminating investigative intelligence that is accurate, detailed, and timely. This initiative facilitates the sharing of investigative intelligence among Federal, state, and local members of HIDTA initiatives and/or agencies. Intelligence Analysts use automated Federal and state law enforcement indices, PenLink, and i2 Analyst Notebook to assist in case support. The principal nature of investigative support involves communication analysis. The initiative provides operational intelligence support to investigations conducted by the HIDTA enforcement initiatives or their agencies. This includes time-sensitive analysis of Dialed Number Recorders, subpoenaed telephone calling data, targeted email addresses, nominee identification, seized documents, and financial data for all HIDTA initiative requesters. The IIU is part of the IISC and routinely interacts with the Watch Center Initiative.

The IISC was reorganized for 2010 by merging the Investigative Support Center Initiative with the Investigative Intelligence Initiative. The IISC is composed of two units: the Watch Center Unit and the Investigative Intelligence Unit. This initiative is designed to improve the ability of HIDTA enforcement, treatment/criminal justice and prevention initiatives to counter drug trafficking and use in the Washington/Baltimore region by collecting, analyzing, and disseminating information and intelligence that is accurate, detailed, and timely. This initiative facilitates the sharing of information and investigative intelligence among Federal, state, and local members of HIDTA initiatives, and their participating agencies. Analysts from both units, as well as those housed in other initiatives, meet monthly to exchange information, discuss best practices, and support each others' tactical, operational, and strategic efforts.

The Watch Unit (WU) at the W/B HIDTA has been funded since 1995 and has evolved through time to meet the ever-changing needs of law enforcement, treatment providers, and prevention agencies within the region. The mission of the WU is to provide strategic, operational, and tactical intelligence that HIDTA initiatives and HIDTA-participating agencies can use to identify the regional drug threat, set priority enforcement targets, facilitate the disruption of the market for illegal drugs, and help measure the performance of all HIDTA initiatives. This is accomplished by developing and maintaining a cadre of skilled analysts, allocating analytical resources in the most effective and efficient manner among the units within the WU, and working in close coordination with all applicable HIDTA initiatives and participating agencies.

In an effort to support the overall HIDTA goals, the specific goal of the W/B HIDTA WU is to improve the efficiency and effectiveness of the W/B HIDTA initiatives by assisting in the identification of DTOs and MLOs for the purpose of dismantlement and disruption.

## *TASK FORCES OPERATING IN THE HIDTA REGION*

The table below highlights the Federally-funded drug enforcement task forces operating in the HIDTA region. Multiple HIDTA task forces may make up an overarching HIDTA enforcement or investigative initiative.

| TASK FORCES | LOCATIONS |
|---|---|
| Baltimore DEA Heroin Initiative (HIDTA) | Baltimore, MD |
| Baltimore Seaport Initiative (HIDTA) | Baltimore, MD |
| Baltimore Special Investigation Group (HIDTA) | Baltimore, MD |
| Capital Area Regional Fugitive Task Force (HIDTA) | Greenbelt, MD |
| DEA Cross Border Initiative (HIDTA) | Washington, D.C. |
| Drug Money Laundering Initiative (HIDTA) | Baltimore, MD |
| Delivery Systems Parcel Interdiction Initiative (HIDTA) | Baltimore, MD |
| Major Drug Traffickers Initiative (HIDTA) | Baltimore, MD |
| Major Offenders Initiative (HIDTA) | Washington, D.C. |
| Mass Transportation Initiative (HIDTA) | Baltimore, MD |
| Northern Virginia Drug Initiative (HIDTA) | Annandale, VA |
| Northern Virginia Drug Money Laundering Initiative (HIDTA) | Annandale, VA |
| Northern Virginia Gang Initiative (HIDTA) | Manassas, VA |
| Northern Virginia Mass Transportation Initiative (HIDTA) | Washington, D.C. |
| Northern Virginia Regional Drug Initiative (HIDTA) | Annandale, VA |
| Northern Virginia SAR Initiative (HIDTA) | Annandale, VA |
| Prince George's Safe Streets Initiative (HIDTA) | Beltsville, MD |
| Metropolitan Area Drug Task Force (HIDTA) | Beltsville, MD |

| TASK FORCES | LOCATIONS |
|---|---|
| Richmond Metropolitan Drug Initiative (HIDTA) | Richmond, VA |
| Southern Maryland Drug Initiative (HIDTA) | Greenbelt, MD |
| Southern Maryland Interdiction Initiative (HIDTA) | Southern MD |
| Southern Maryland Major Conspiracy Initiative (HIDTA) | Greenbelt, MD |
| Strategic Task Force of Narcotics and Guns Initiative (HIDTA) | Washington, D.C. |
| Tactical Diversion Squad (DEA) | Washington, D.C. |
| Tactical Diversion Squad (DEA) | Baltimore, MD |
| Violent Crime Safe Street Initiative (HIDTA) | Baltimore, MD |
| Violent Traffickers Initiative (HIDTA) | Baltimore, MD |
| Washington Area Gang Initiative (HIDTA) | Washington, D.C. |
| Weapons Enforcement Initiative (HIDTA) | Baltimore, Maryland |

## TASK FORCE COORDINATION

Almost all Federally funded drug enforcement task forces in the HIDTA region that specifically target illegal drugs are funded by the HIDTA program. The W/B HIDTA has taken a leadership role in ensuring coordination and cooperation, as well as information sharing among all task forces and drug units operating throughout the HIDTA region. Intelligence products are routinely distributed to all task forces and drug units through the W/B HIDTA IISC. The W/B HIDTA is electronically linked to the Maryland Coordination and Analysis Center (MCAC), which is focused on the terrorist threat to the region. Any information related to the terrorist threat is immediately forwarded electronically to the MCAC or to the fusion centers in Virginia and Washington, DC. MCAC forwards drug related information to the IISC. The W/B HIDTA also signed an agreement to become a member of the Organized Crime Drug Enforcement Task Forces (OCDETF) Fusion Center. This agreement enhances the ability to share information for use in disrupting and dismantling drug trafficking organizations and/or money laundering organizations in the region and across the Nation.

All task forces and agencies are eligible to use the HIDTA event and case deconfliction services. Those receiving HIDTA funding are mandated to use W/B HIDTA's Case Explorer software for case and event deconfliction.

All drug task forces are eligible to share information through the W/B HIDTA IISC and NDIC Field Specialists. Agencies within the HIDTA region are formally solicited annually to provide information about the drug threat to the region in the HIDTA's Threat Assessment Survey. Additionally, W/B HIDTA's Gang Intelligence System is available to all agencies in Maryland, the District of Columbia, and Virginia. This system allows participating agencies to share gang data.

## HIDTA EVALUATION

In 2009, HIDTA initiatives identified 422 DTOs operating in the W/B HIDTA area. Whereas it expected to dismantle or disrupt 141 DTOs, the HIDTA disrupted or dismantled 150 DTOs and seized cash totaling $36,792,798 and other assets valued at $8,606,111.